Bookkeeping

FOR

DUMMIES

A Wiley Brand

2nd Edition

Bookkeeping

FOR

DUMMIES

A Wiley Brand

2nd Edition

by Lita Epstein, MBA

Bookkeeping For Dummies®, 2nd Edition

Published by: **John Wiley & Sons, Inc.,** 111 River Street, Hoboken, NJ 07030-5774, www.wiley.com

Copyright © 2015 by John Wiley & Sons, Inc., Hoboken, New Jersey

Published simultaneously in Canada

For general information on our other products and services, please contact our Customer Care Department within the U.S. at 877-762-2974, outside the U.S. at 317-572-3993, or fax 317-572-4002. For technical support, please visit www.wiley.com/techsupport.

Wiley publishes in a variety of print and electronic formats and by print-on-demand. Some material included with standard print versions of this book may not be included in e-books or in print-on-demand. If this book refers to media such as a CD or DVD that is not included in the version you purchased, you may download this material at http://booksupport.wiley.com. For more information about Wiley products, visit www.wiley.com.

Library of Congress Control Number: 2014945057

ISBN 978-1-118-95036-4; ISBN 978-1-118-95037-1 (ePub); ISBN 978-1-118-95038-8 (ePDF)

Manufactured in the United States of America

V10008229_021519

Contents at a Glance

Table of Contents

Introduction

● ●

*B*ookkeepers manage all the financial data for small companies. If you subscribe to the idea that information is power (which I do), you'll agree that the bookkeeper has a tremendous amount of power within a company. Information tracked in the books helps business owners make key decisions involving sales planning and product offerings and manage many other financial aspects of their business.

If it weren't for the hard work of bookkeepers, companies wouldn't have any clue about what happens with their financial transactions. Without accurate financial bookkeeping, a company owner wouldn't know how many sales were made, how much cash was collected, or how much cash was paid for the products sold to customers during the year. He also wouldn't know how much cash was paid to employees or how much cash was spent on other business needs throughout the year.

Accurate and complete financial bookkeeping is crucial to any business owner, but it's also important to those who work with the business, such as investors, financial institutions, and employees. People both inside (managers, owners, and employees) and outside the business (investors, lenders, and government agencies) all depend on the bookkeeper's accurate recording of financial transactions.

Yes, the bookkeeper's job is crucial and requires certain skills and talents. Bookkeepers must be detailed-oriented, enjoy working with numbers, and be meticulous about accurately entering those numbers in the books. They must be vigilant about keeping a paper trail and filing all needed backup information about the financial transactions entered into the books.

Whether you're a business owner keeping the books yourself or an employee keeping the books for a small business owner, your job is critical for the smooth financial operation of the company.

About This Book

In this book, I introduce you to the key aspects of bookkeeping and how to set up and use your financial books. I walk you through the basics of bookkeeping, starting with the process of setting up your company's books and developing

- ✔ A list of your company's accounts, called the Chart of Accounts.
- ✔ Your company's General Ledger, which summarizes all the activity in a company's accounts.
- ✔ Your company's journals, which give details about all your financial transactions.

Then I take you through the process of recording all your transactions — sales, purchases, and other financial activity. I also talk about how to manage payroll, governmental reporting, and external financial reporting.

Finally, I show you how to start the yearly cycle all over again by closing out the necessary accounts for the current year and opening up any new ones for the next year.

Yes, bookkeeping is a continuous cycle starting with financial transactions, recording those transactions in journals, posting those transactions to the General Ledger, testing your books to be sure that they're in balance, making any necessary adjustments or corrections to the books to keep them in balance, preparing financial reports to understand how well the business did during the year, and finally getting ready to start the process all over again for the next year.

You find out all about this cycle, starting with Chapter 2 and following the bookkeeping journey through closing out the year and getting ready for the next year in Chapter 22.

I've included a number of examples of how to apply the basics of bookkeeping to real-life situations. If you're primarily reading this book to gain a general knowledge of the subject and don't need to delve into all the nitty-gritty, day-to-day aspects of bookkeeping, you may want to skip over the paragraphs marked with the Example icon (see the section "Icons Used in This Book" later in this Introduction). Skipping the examples shouldn't interfere with your grasp of the key aspects of how to keep the books.

I use QuickBooks Pro throughout this book, so I show you some of its advanced features where appropriate. I also point out when I use a feature only available in QuickBooks Pro or a more advanced version.

Foolish Assumptions

While writing this book, I made some key assumptions about who you are and why you've picked up this book to get a better understanding of bookkeeping. I assume that you are

- ✔ A business owner who wants to know how to do your own books. You have a good understanding of business and its terminology but have little or no knowledge of bookkeeping and accounting.

✔ A person who does bookkeeping or plans to do bookkeeping for a small business and needs to know more about how to set up and keep the books. You have some basic knowledge of business terminology but don't know much about bookkeeping or accounting.

✔ A staff person in a small business who's just been asked to take over the company's bookkeeping duties. You need to know more about how transactions are entered into the books, how to prove out transactions to be sure that you're making entries correctly and accurately, and how to prepare financial reports using the data you collect.

Icons Used in This Book

For Dummies books use little pictures called *icons* to flag certain chunks of text that either you don't want to miss or you're free to skip. Here are the icons in *Bookkeeping For Dummies*, 2nd Edition:

Look to this icon for ideas on how to improve your bookkeeping processes and use the information in the book to manage your business.

This icon marks anything I want you to recall about bookkeeping after you're finished reading this book.

This icon points out any aspect of bookkeeping that comes with dangers or perils that may hurt the accuracy of your entries or the way in which you use your financial information in the future. I also use this icon to mark certain things that can get you into trouble with the government, your lenders, your vendors, your employees, or your investors.

This icon points to real-life specifics of how to do a particular bookkeeping function.

Beyond the Book

In addition to the material in the print or e-book you're reading right now, this book also comes with some access-anywhere goodies on the Web. Check out the free Cheat Sheet at www.dummies.com/cheatsheet/bookkeeping to see the building blocks for a successful bookkeeping system, key steps for keeping the books, tips on controlling your business cash, and calculating and testing cash flow.

This book includes some more in-depth companion articles, packed with late-breaking stuff that just wouldn't quite fit between the covers. Check out www.dummies.com/extras/bookkeeping to read articles on trends in electronic bookkeeping, point of service systems and how they impact tracking sales, using tablets and other devices and how they impact tracking cash, and the globalization of financial reporting. There's even an extra Part of Tens chapter on the top ten mobile apps for bookkeepers.

Where to Go From Here

Can you feel the excitement? You're now ready to enter the world of book-keeping! Because of the way *Bookkeeping For Dummies*, 2nd Edition is set up, you can start anywhere you like.

If you need the basics or if you're a little rusty and want to refresh your knowledge of bookkeeping, start with Part I. However, if you already know bookkeeping basics, are familiar with the key terminology, and know how to set up a Chart of Accounts, consider diving into Part II.

If you've set up your books already and feel comfortable with the basics of bookkeeping, you may want to start with Part III on how to enter various transactions. On the other hand, if your priority is using the financial information you've already collected, check out the financial reporting options in Part V.

Part I

Basic Bookkeeping: Why You Need It

getting started with

Bookkeeping

In this part . . .

- ✔ Introducing you to the world of bookkeeping
- ✔ Exploring bookkeeping basics
- ✔ Developing your financial roadmap

Chapter 1

So You Want to Do the Books

*F*ew small business owners actually hire accountants to work full time for them. For a small business, that expense is probably too great, so instead the owner hires a *bookkeeper* who serves as the company accountant's eyes and ears. In return, the accountant helps the bookkeeper develop good bookkeeping practices and reviews his or her work periodically (usually monthly).

In this chapter, I provide an overview of a bookkeeper's work. If you're just starting a business, you may be your own bookkeeper for a while until you can afford to hire one, so think of this chapter as your to-do list.

Delving into Bookkeeping Basics

Like most business people, you probably have great ideas for running your own business and just want to get started. You don't want to sweat the small stuff, like keeping detailed records of every penny spent; you just want to quickly build a business in which you can make lots of money.

Well slow down there — this isn't a race! If you don't carefully plan your bookkeeping operation and figure out exactly how and what financial detail you want to track, you'll have absolutely no way to measure the success (or failure, unfortunately) of your business efforts.

Bookkeeping, when done properly, gives you an excellent gauge of how well you're doing. It also provides you with lots of information throughout the year so you can test the financial success of your business strategies and make course corrections early in the year, if necessary, to ensure that you reach your year-end profit goals.

Bookkeeping can become your best friend for managing your financial assets and testing your business strategies, so don't shortchange it. Take the time to develop your bookkeeping system with your accountant before you even open your business's doors and make your first sale.

Picking your accounting method

You can't keep books unless you know how you want to go about doing so. The two basic accounting methods you have to choose from are *cash-basis accounting* and *accrual accounting*. The key difference between these two accounting methods is the point at which you record sales and purchases in your books. If you choose cash-basis accounting, you only record transactions when cash changes hands. If you use accrual accounting, you record a transaction when it's completed, even if cash doesn't change hands.

For example, suppose your company buys products to sell from a vendor but doesn't actually pay for those products for 30 days. If you're using cash-basis accounting, you don't record the purchase until you actually lay out the cash to the vendor. If you're using accrual accounting, you record the purchase when you receive the products, and you also record the future debt in an account called Accounts Payable.

I talk about the pros and cons of each type of accounting method in Chapter 2.

Understanding assets, liabilities, and equity

Every business has three key financial parts that must be kept in balance: assets, liabilities, and equity. *Assets* include everything the company owns, such as cash, inventory, buildings, equipment, and vehicles. *Liabilities* include everything the company owes to others, such as vendor bills, credit-card balances, and bank loans. *Equity* includes the claims owners have on the assets based on their portion of ownership in the company.

The formula for keeping your books in balance involves these three elements:

Assets = Liabilities + Equity

Because it's so important, I talk a lot about how to keep your books in balance throughout this book. You can find an initial introduction to this concept in Chapter 2.

Introducing debits and credits

To keep the books, you need to revise your thinking about two common financial terms: debits and credits. Most nonbookkeepers and nonaccountants think of debits as subtractions from their bank accounts. The opposite is true with credits — people usually see these as additions to their accounts, in most cases in the form of refunds or corrections in favor of the account holders.

Well, forget all you thought you knew about debits and credits. Debits and credits are totally different animals in the world of bookkeeping. Because keeping the books involves a method called *double-entry bookkeeping,* you have to make a least two entries — a debit and a credit — into your bookkeeping system for every transaction. Whether that debit or credit adds or subtracts from an account depends solely upon the type of account.

I know all this debit, credit, and double-entry stuff sounds confusing, but I promise it will become much clearer as you work through this book. I start explaining this critical yet somewhat confusing concept in Chapter 2.

Charting your bookkeeping course

You can't just enter transactions in the books willy-nilly. You need to know where exactly those transactions fit into the larger bookkeeping system. That's where your Chart of Accounts comes in; it's essentially a list of all the accounts your business has and what types of transactions go into each one.

I talk more about the Chart of Accounts in Chapter 3.

Recognizing the Importance of an Accurate Paper Trail

Keeping the books is all about creating an accurate paper trail. You want to track all of your company's financial transactions so if a question comes up at a later date, you can turn to the books to figure out what went wrong.

An accurate paper trail is the only way to track your financial successes and review your financial failures, a task that's vitally important in order to grow your business. You need to know what works successfully so you can repeat it in the future and build on your success. On the other hand, you need to know what failed so you can correct it and avoid making the same mistake again.

All your business's financial transactions are summarized in the General Ledger, and journals keep track of the tiniest details of each transaction. You can make your information gathering more effective by using a computerized accounting system, which gives you access to your financial information in many different formats. Controlling who enters this financial information into your books and who can access it afterwards is smart business and involves critical planning on your part. I address all these concepts in the following sections.

Maintaining a ledger

The granddaddy of your bookkeeping system is the General Ledger. In this ledger, you keep a summary of all your accounts and the financial activities that took place involving those accounts throughout the year.

You draw upon the General Ledger's account summaries to develop your financial reports on a monthly, quarterly, or annual basis. You can also use these account summaries to develop internal reports that help you make key business decisions. I talk more about developing and maintaining the General Ledger in Chapter 4.

Keeping journals

Small companies conduct hundreds, if not thousands, of transactions each year. If every transaction were kept in the General Ledger, that record would become unwieldy and difficult to use. Instead, most companies keep a series of journals that detail activity in their most active accounts.

For example, almost every company has a Cash Receipts Journal in which to keep the detail for all incoming cash and a Cash Disbursements Journal in which to keep the detail for all outgoing cash. Other journals can detail sales, purchases, customer accounts, vendor accounts, and any other key accounts that see significant activity.

You decide which accounts you want to create journals for based on your business operation and your need for information about key financial transactions. I talk more about the importance of journals, the accounts commonly journalized, and the process of maintaining journals in Chapter 5.

Computerizing

Most companies today use computerized accounting systems to keep their books. You should consider using one of these systems rather than trying to keep your books on paper. You'll find your bookkeeping takes less time and is probably more accurate with a computerized system.

In addition to increasing accuracy and cutting the time it takes to do your bookkeeping, computerized accounting also makes designing reports easier. These reports can then be used to help make business decisions. Your computerized accounting system stores detailed information about every transaction, so you can group that detail in any way that may assist your decision-making. I talk more about computerized accounting systems in Chapter 6.

Instituting internal controls

Every business owner needs to be concerned with keeping tight controls on company cash and how it's used. One way to institute this control is by placing internal restrictions on who has access to enter information into your books and who has access necessary to use that information.

You also need to carefully control who has the ability to accept cash receipts and who has the ability to disburse your business's cash. Separating duties appropriately helps you protect your business's assets from error, theft, and fraud. I talk more about controlling your cash and protecting your financial records in Chapter 7.

Using Bookkeeping's Tools to Manage Daily Finances

After you set up your business's books and put in place your internal controls, you're ready to use the systems you established to manage the day-to-day operations of your business. You'll quickly see how a well-designed bookkeeping system can make your job of managing your business's finances much easier.

Maintaining inventory

If your company keeps inventory on hand or in warehouses, tracking the costs of the products you plan to sell is critical for managing your profit potential. If you see inventory costs trending upward, you may need to adjust your own prices in order to maintain your profit margin. You certainly don't want to wait until the end of the year to find out how much your inventory cost you.

You also must keep careful watch on how much inventory you have on hand and how much was sold. Inventory can get damaged, discarded, or stolen, meaning that your physical inventory counts may differ from the counts you have in your books. Do a physical count periodically — at least monthly for most businesses and possibly daily for active retail stores.

In addition to watching for signs of theft or poor handling of inventory, make sure you have enough inventory on hand to satisfy your customers' needs. I talk more about how to use your bookkeeping system to manage inventory in Chapter 8.

Tracking sales

Everyone wants to know how well their sales are doing. If you keep your books up-to-date and accurate, you can get those numbers very easily on a daily basis. You can also watch sales trends as often as you think necessary, whether that's daily, weekly, or monthly.

Use the information collected by your bookkeeping system to monitor sales, review discounts offered to customers, and track the return of products. All three elements are critical to gauging the success of the sales of your products.

If you find you need to offer discounts more frequently in order to encourage sales, you may need to review your pricing, and you definitely need to research market conditions to determine the cause of this sales weakness. The cause may be new activities by an aggressive competitor or simply a slow market period. Either way, you need to understand the weakness and figure out how to maintain your profit goals in spite of any obstacles.

While sales tracking reveals an increase in the number of your products being returned, you need to research the issue and find the reason for the increase. Perhaps the quality of the product you're selling is declining, and you need to find a new supplier. Whatever the reason, an increased number of product returns is usually a sign of a problem that needs to be researched and corrected.

I talk more about how to use the bookkeeping system for tracking sales, discounts, and returns in Chapter 9.

Handling payroll

Payroll can be a huge nightmare for many companies. Payroll requires you to comply with a lot of government regulation and fill out a lot of government paperwork. You also have to worry about collecting payroll taxes and paying employer taxes. And if you pay employee benefits, you have yet another layer of record keeping to deal with.

I talk more about managing payroll and government requirements in Chapters 10 and 11. I also talk about year-end payroll obligations in Chapter 20.

Running Tests for Accuracy

All the time it takes to track your transactions isn't worth it if you don't periodically test to be sure you've entered those transactions accurately. The old adage "Garbage in, garbage out" holds very true for bookkeeping: If the numbers you put into your bookkeeping system are garbage, the reports you develop from those numbers will be garbage as well.

Proving out your cash

The first step in testing out your books includes proving that your cash transactions are accurately recorded. This process involves checking a number of different transactions and elements, including the cash taken in on a daily basis by your cashiers and the accuracy of your checking account. I talk about all the steps necessary to take to prove out your cash in Chapter 14.

Testing your balance

After you prove out your cash (see Chapter 14), you can check that you've recorded everything else in your books just as precisely. Review the accounts for any glaring errors and then test whether or not they're in balance by doing a trial balance. You find out more about trial balances in Chapter 16.

Doing bookkeeping corrections

You may not find your books in balance the first time you do a trial balance, but don't worry. It's rare to find your books in balance on the first try. In Chapter 17, I explain common adjustments that may be needed as you prove out your books at the end of an accounting period, and I also explain how to make the necessary corrections.

Finally Showing Off Your Financial Success

Proving out your books and ensuring their balance means you finally get to show what your company has accomplished financially by developing reports to present to others. It's almost like putting your business on a stage and taking a bow — well . . . at least you hope you've done well enough to take a bow.

If you've taken advantage of your bookkeeping information and reviewed and consulted it throughout the year, you should have a good idea of how well your business is doing. You also should have taken any course corrections to ensure that your end-of-the-year reports look great.

Preparing financial reports

Most businesses prepare at least two key financial reports, the balance sheet and the income statement, which they can show to company outsiders, including the financial institutions from which the company borrows money and the company's investors.

The balance sheet is a snapshot of your business's financial health as of a particular date. The balance sheet should show that your company's assets are equal to the value of your liabilities and your equity. It's called a *balance sheet* because it's based on a balanced formula:

Assets = Liabilities + Equity

The income statement summarizes your company's financial transactions for a particular time period, such as a month, quarter, or year. This financial statement starts with your revenues, subtracts the costs of goods sold, and then subtracts any expenses incurred in operating the business. The bottom line of the income statement shows how much profit your company made during the accounting period. If you haven't done well, the income statement shows how much you've lost.

I explain how to prepare a balance sheet in Chapter 18, and I talk more about developing an income statement in Chapter 19.

Paying taxes

Most small businesses don't have to pay taxes. Instead, their profits are reported on the personal tax returns of the company owners, whether that's one person (a *sole proprietorship*) or two or more people (a *partnership*). Only companies that have incorporated — become a separate legal entity in which investors buy stock (which I explain further in Chapter 21) — must file and pay taxes. (Partnerships and LLCs do not pay taxes unless they filed a special form to be taxed as a corporation, but they do have to file information returns, which detail how much the company made and how much profit each owner earned plus any costs and expenses incurred.)

I talk more about business structures and how they're taxed in Chapter 21.

Chapter 2

Getting Down to Bookkeeping Basics

In This Chapter

▶ Keeping business records

▶ Navigating the accounting cycle

▶ Choosing between cash-basis and accrual accounting

▶ Deciphering double-entry bookkeeping

*A*ll businesses need to keep track of their financial transactions — that's why bookkeeping and bookkeepers are so important. Without accurate records, how can you tell whether your business is making a profit or taking a loss?

In this chapter, I cover the key parts of bookkeeping by introducing you to the language of bookkeeping, familiarizing you with how bookkeepers manage the accounting cycle, and showing you how to understand the most difficult type of bookkeeping — double-entry bookkeeping.

Bookkeepers: The Record Keepers of the Business World

Bookkeeping, the methodical way in which businesses track their financial transactions, is rooted in accounting. *Accounting* is the total structure of records and procedures used to record, classify, and report information about a business's financial transactions. Bookkeeping involves the recording of that financial information into the accounting system while maintaining adherence to solid accounting principles.

Bookkeepers are the ones who toil day in and day out to ensure that transactions are accurately recorded. Bookkeepers need to be very detail oriented and love to work with numbers because numbers and the accounts they go into are just about all these people see all day. A bookkeeper is not required to be a certified public accountant (CPA).

Many small business people who are just starting up their businesses initially serve as their own bookkeepers until the business is large enough to hire someone dedicated to keeping the books. Few small businesses have accountants on staff to check the books and prepare official financial reports; instead, they have bookkeepers on staff who serve as the outside accountants' eyes and ears. Most businesses do seek an accountant with a CPA certification.

In many small businesses today, a bookkeeper enters the business transactions on a daily basis while working inside the company. At the end of each month or quarter, the bookkeeper sends summary reports to the accountant who then checks the transactions for accuracy and prepares financial statements.

In most cases, the accounting system is initially set up with the help of an accountant in order to be sure it uses solid accounting principles. That accountant periodically stops by the office and reviews the system to be sure transactions are being handled properly.

Accurate financial reports are the only way you can know how your business is doing. These reports are developed using the information you, as the bookkeeper, enter into your accounting system. If that information isn't accurate, your financial reports are meaningless. As the old adage goes, "Garbage in, garbage out."

Wading through Basic Bookkeeping Lingo

Before you can take on bookkeeping and start keeping the books, the first things you must get a handle on are key accounting terms. The following is a list of terms that all bookkeepers use on a daily basis.

Note: This isn't an exhaustive list of all the unique terms you need to know as a bookkeeper. For full coverage of bookkeeping terminology, turn to the Glossary at the back of the book.

Accounts for the balance sheet

Here are a few terms you'll want to know:

- ✔ **Balance sheet:** The financial statement that presents a snapshot of the company's financial position (assets, liabilities, and equity) as of a particular date in time. It's called a balance sheet because the things owned by the company (assets) must equal the claims against those assets (liabilities and equity).

On an ideal balance sheet, the total assets should equal the total liabilities plus the total equity. If your numbers fit this formula, the company's books are in balance. (I discuss the balance sheet in greater detail in Chapter 18.)

✔ **Assets:** All the things a company owns in order to successfully run its business, such as cash, buildings, land, tools, equipment, vehicles, and furniture.

✔ **Liabilities:** All the debts the company owes, such as bonds, loans, and unpaid bills.

✔ **Equity:** All the money invested in the company by its owners. In a small business owned by one person or a group of people, the owner's equity is shown in a Capital account. In a larger business that's incorporated, owner's equity is shown in shares of stock. Another key Equity account is *Retained Earnings,* which tracks all company profits that have been reinvested in the company rather than paid out to the company's owners. Small, unincorporated businesses track money paid out to owners in a Drawing account, whereas incorporated businesses dole out money to owners by paying *dividends* (a portion of the company's profits paid by share of common stock for the quarter or year).

Accounts for the income statement

Here are a few terms related to the income statement that you'll want to know:

✔ **Income statement:** The financial statement that presents a summary of the company's financial activity over a certain period of time, such as a month, quarter, or year. The statement starts with Revenue earned, subtracts out the Costs of Goods Sold and the Expenses, and ends with the bottom line — Net Profit or Loss. (I show you how to develop an income statement in Chapter 19.)

✔ **Revenue:** All money collected in the process of selling the company's goods and services. Some companies also collect revenue through other means, such as selling assets the business no longer needs or earning interest by offering short-term loans to employees or other businesses. (I discuss how to track revenue in Chapter 9.)

✔ **Costs of goods sold:** All money spent to purchase or make the products or services a company plans to sell to its customers. (I talk about purchasing goods for sale to customers in Chapter 8.)

✔ **Expenses:** All money spent to operate the company that's not directly related to the sale of individual goods or services. (I review common types of expenses in Chapter 3.)

Other common terms

Some other common terms include the following:

- **Accounting period:** The time for which financial information is being tracked. Most businesses track their financial results on a monthly basis, so each accounting period equals one month. Some businesses choose to do financial reports on a quarterly basis, so the accounting periods are three months. Other businesses only look at their results on a yearly basis, so their accounting periods are 12 months. Businesses that track their financial activities monthly usually also create quarterly and *annual reports* (a year-end summary of the company's activities and financial results) based on the information they gather.

- **Accounts Receivable:** The account used to track all customer sales that are made by store credit. *Store credit* refers not to credit-card sales but rather to sales for which the customer is given credit directly by the store and the store needs to collect payment from the customer at a later date. (I discuss how to monitor Accounts Receivable in Chapter 9.)

- **Accounts Payable:** The account used to track all outstanding bills from vendors, contractors, consultants, and any other companies or individuals from whom the company buys goods or services. (I talk about managing Accounts Payable in Chapter 8.)

- **Depreciation:** An accounting method used to track the aging and use of assets. For example, if you own a car, you know that each year you use the car its value is reduced (unless you own one of those classic cars that goes up in value). Every major asset a business owns ages and eventually needs replacement, including buildings, factories, equipment, and other key assets. (I discuss how you monitor depreciation in Chapter 12.)

- **General Ledger:** Where all the company's accounts are summarized. The General Ledger is the granddaddy of the bookkeeping system. (I discuss posting to the General Ledger in Chapter 4.)

- **Interest:** The money a company needs to pay if it borrows money from a bank or other company. For example, when you buy a car using a car loan, you must pay not only the amount you borrowed but also additional money, or interest, based on a percentage of the amount you borrowed. (I discuss how to track interest expenses in a business's books in Chapter 13.)

- **Inventory:** The account that tracks all products that will be sold to customers. (I review inventory valuation and control in Chapter 8.)

- **Journals:** Where bookkeepers keep records (in chronological order) of daily company transactions. Each of the most active accounts, including cash, Accounts Payable, Accounts Receivable, has its own journal. (I discuss entering information into journals in Chapter 5.)

✔ **Payroll:** The way a company pays its employees. Managing payroll is a key function of the bookkeeper and involves reporting many aspects of payroll to the government, including taxes to be paid on behalf of the employee, unemployment taxes, and workers' compensation. (I discuss employee payroll in Chapter 10 and the government side of payroll reporting in Chapter 11.)

✔ **Trial balance:** How you test to be sure the books are in balance before pulling together information for the financial reports and closing the books for the accounting period. (I discuss how to do a trial balance in Chapter 16.)

Pedaling through the Accounting Cycle

As a bookkeeper, you complete your work by completing the tasks of the accounting cycle. It's called a cycle because the workflow is circular: entering transactions, manipulating the transactions through the accounting cycle, closing the books at the end of the accounting period, and then starting the entire cycle again for the next accounting period.

The accounting cycle has eight basic steps, which you can see in Figure 2-1.

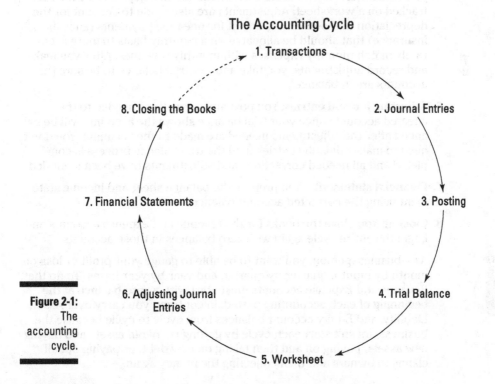

Figure 2-1:
The accounting cycle.

1. **Transactions:** Financial transactions start the process. Transactions can include the sale or return of a product, the purchase of supplies for business activities, or any other financial activity that involves the exchange of the company's assets, the establishment or payoff of a debt, or the deposit from or payout of money to the company's owners. All sales and expenses are transactions that must be recorded. I cover transactions in greater detail throughout the book as I discuss the basics of documenting business activities — recording sales, purchases, and assets, taking on new debt, or paying off debt.

2. **Journal entries:** The transaction is listed in the appropriate journal, maintaining the journal's chronological order of transactions. (The journal is also known as the "book of original entry" and is the first place a transaction is listed.) I talk more about journal entries in Chapter 5.

3. **Posting:** The transactions are posted to the account that it impacts. These accounts are part of the General Ledger, where you can find a summary of all the business's accounts. I discuss posting in Chapters 4 and 5.

4. **Trial balance:** At the end of the accounting period (which may be a month, quarter, or year depending on your business's practices), you calculate a trial balance.

5. **Worksheet:** Unfortunately, many times your first calculation of the trial balance shows that the books aren't in balance. If that's the case, you look for errors and make corrections called *adjustments,* which are tracked on a worksheet. Adjustments are also made to account for the depreciation of assets and to adjust for one-time payments (such as insurance) that should be allocated on a monthly basis to more accurately match monthly expenses with monthly revenues. After you make and record adjustments, you take another trial balance to be sure the accounts are in balance.

6. **Adjusting journal entries:** You post any corrections needed to the affected accounts once your trial balance shows the accounts will be balanced after the adjustments needed are made to the accounts. You don't need to make adjusting entries until the trial balance process is completed and all needed corrections and adjustments have been identified.

7. **Financial statements:** You prepare the balance sheet and income statement using the corrected account balances.

8. **Closing:** You close the books for the revenue and expense accounts and begin the entire cycle again with zero balances in those accounts.

As a businessperson, you want to be able to gauge your profit or loss on month by month, quarter by quarter, and year by year bases. To do that, Revenue and Expense accounts must start with a zero balance at the beginning of each accounting period. In contrast, you carry over Asset, Liability, and Equity account balances from cycle to cycle because the business doesn't start each cycle by getting rid of old assets and buying new assets, paying off and then taking on new debt, or paying out all claims to owners and then collecting the money again.

Tackling the Big Decision: Cash-basis or Accrual Accounting

Before starting to record transactions, you must decide whether to use cash-basis or accrual accounting. The crucial difference between these two processes is in how you record your cash transactions.

Waiting for funds with cash-basis accounting

With *cash-basis accounting*, you record all transactions in the books when cash actually changes hands, meaning when cash payment is received by the company from customers or paid out by the company for purchases or other services. Cash receipt or payment can be in the form of cash, check, credit card, electronic transfer, or other means used to pay for an item.

Cash-basis accounting can't be used if a store sells products on store credit and bills the customer at a later date. There is no provision to record and track money due from customers at some time in the future in the cash-basis accounting method. That's also true for purchases. With the cash-basis accounting method, the owner only records the purchase of supplies or goods that will later be sold when he actually pays cash. If he buys goods on credit to be paid later, he doesn't record the transaction until the cash is actually paid out.

Making the switch to accrual accounting

Changing between the cash-basis and accrual basis of accounting may not be simple, and you should check with your accountant to be sure you do it right. You may even need to get permission from the IRS, which tests whether you're seeking an unfair tax advantage when making the switch. You must even complete the IRS form Change in Accounting Method (Form 3115) within 180 days before the end of the year for which you make this change. You don't need to fill out Form 3115 if your business activity is changing fundamentally. For example, if you started as a service business and shifted to a business that carries inventory, you probably won't need permission for the accounting method change.

Businesses that should never use cash-basis accounting include

✔ Businesses that carry an inventory

✔ Businesses that incorporated as a C corporation (more on incorporation in Chapter 21)

✔ Businesses with gross annual sales that exceed $5 million

Depending on the size of your business, you may want to start out with cash-basis accounting. Many small businesses run by a sole proprietor or a small group of partners use cash-basis accounting because it's easy. But as the business grows, the business owners find it necessary to switch to accrual accounting in order to more accurately track revenues and expenses.

Cash-basis accounting does a good job of tracking cash flow, but it does a poor job of matching revenues earned with money laid out for expenses. This deficiency is a problem particularly when, as it often happens, a company buys products in one month and sells those products in the next month. For example, you buy products in June with the intent to sell, and pay $1,000 cash. You don't sell the products until July, and that's when you receive cash for the sales. When you close the books at the end of June, you have to show the $1,000 expense with no revenue to offset it, meaning you have a loss that month. When you sell the products for $1,500 in July, you have a $1,500 profit. So, your monthly report for June shows a $1,000 loss, and your monthly report for July shows a $1,500 profit, when in actuality you had revenues of $500 over the two months.

In this book, I concentrate on the accrual accounting method. If you choose to use cash-basis accounting, don't panic: You'll still find most of the bookkeeping information here useful, but you don't need to maintain some of the accounts I list, such as Accounts Receivable and Accounts Payable, because you aren't recording transactions until cash actually changes hands. If you're using a cash-basis accounting system and sell things on credit, though, you better have a way to track what people owe you.

Recording right away with accrual accounting

With *accrual accounting*, you record all transactions in the books when they occur, even if no cash changes hands. For example, if you sell on store credit, you record the transaction immediately and enter it into an Accounts Receivable account until you receive payment. If you buy goods on credit, you immediately enter the transaction into an Accounts Payable account until you pay out cash.

Like cash-basis accounting, accrual accounting has its drawbacks. It does a good job of matching revenues and expenses, but it does a poor job of tracking cash. Because you record revenue when the transaction occurs and not when you collect the cash, your income statement can look great even if you don't have cash in the bank. For example, suppose you're running a contracting company and completing jobs on a daily basis. You can record the revenue upon completion of the job even if you haven't yet collected the cash. If your customers are slow to pay, you may end up with lots of revenue but little cash. But don't worry. Chapter 9 covers managing Accounts Receivable so that you don't run out of cash because of slow-paying customers.

Many companies that use the accrual accounting method also monitor cash flow on a weekly basis to be sure they have enough cash on hand to operate the business. If your business is seasonal, such as a landscaping business with little to do during the winter months, you can establish short-term lines of credit through your bank to maintain cash flow through the lean times.

Seeing Double with Double-Entry Bookkeeping

All businesses, whether they use the cash-basis accounting method or the accrual accounting method (see the earlier section "Tackling the Big Decision: Cash-basis or Accrual Accounting" for details), use *double-entry bookkeeping* to keep their books. A practice that helps minimize errors and increase the chance that your books balance, double-entry bookkeeping gets its name because you enter all transactions twice.

When it comes to double-entry bookkeeping, the key formula for the balance sheet (Assets = Liabilities + Equity) plays a major role.

In order to adjust the balance of accounts in the bookkeeping world, you use a combination of *debits* and *credits*. You may think of a debit as a subtraction because you've found that debits usually mean a decrease in your bank balance. On the other hand, you've probably been excited to find unexpected credits in your bank or credit card that mean more money has been added to the account in your favor. Now, forget all that you ever learned about debits or credits. In the world of bookkeeping, their meanings aren't so simple.

The only definite thing when it comes to debits and credits in the bookkeeping world is that a debit is on the left side of a transaction and a credit is on the right side of a transaction. Everything beyond that can get very muddled. I show you the basics of debits and credits in this chapter, but don't worry if you're finding this concept very difficult to grasp. You get plenty of practice using these concepts throughout this book.

Before I get into all the technical mumbo jumbo of double-entry bookkeeping, here's an example of the practice in action. Suppose you purchase a new desk that costs $1,500 for your office. This transaction actually has two parts: You spend an asset — cash — to buy another asset — furniture. So, you must adjust two accounts in your company's books: the Cash account and the

Furniture account. Here's what the transaction looks like in a bookkeeping entry (I talk more about how to do initial bookkeeping entries in Chapter 4):

Account	Debit	Credit
Furniture	$1,500	
Cash		$1,500

To purchase a new desk for the office.

In this transaction, you record the accounts impacted by the transaction. The debit increases the value of the Furniture account, and the credit decreases the value of the Cash account. For this transaction, both accounts impacted are asset accounts, so, looking at how the balance sheet is affected, you can see that the only changes are to the asset side of the balance sheet equation:

Assets = Liabilities + Equity

Furniture increase = No change to this side of the equation

Cash decrease

In this case, the books stay in balance because the exact dollar amount that increases the value of your Furniture account decreases the value of your Cash account. At the bottom of any journal entry, you should include a brief explanation that explains the purpose for the entry. In the first example, I indicate this entry was "To purchase a new desk for the office."

To show you how you record a transaction if it impacts both sides of the balance sheet equation, here's an example that shows how to record the purchase of inventory. Suppose you purchase $5,000 worth of widgets on credit. (Haven't you always wondered what widgets were? Can't help you. They're just commonly used in accounting examples to represent something that's purchased.) These new widgets add value to your Inventory Asset account and also add value to your Accounts Payable account. (Remember, the Accounts Payable account is a Liability account where you track bills that need to be paid at some point in the future.) Here's how the bookkeeping transaction for your widget purchase looks:

Account	Debit	Credit
Inventory	$5,000	
Accounts Payable		$5,000

To purchase widgets for sale to customers.

Here's how this transaction affects the balance sheet equation:

Assets = Liabilities + Equity

Inventory increases = Accounts Payable increases = No change

In this case, the books stay in balance because both sides of the equation increase by $5,000.

Double-entry bookkeeping goes way back

No one's really sure who invented double-entry bookkeeping. The first person to put the practice on paper was Benedetto Cotrugli in 1458, but mathematician and Franciscan monk Luca Pacioli is most often credited with developing double-entry bookkeeping. Although Pacioli's called the "father of accounting," accounting actually occupies only one of five sections of his book, *Everything About Arithmetic, Geometry and Proportions,* which was published in 1494. Pacioli didn't actually *invent* double-entry bookkeeping; he just described the method used by merchants in Venice during the Italian Renaissance period. He's most famous for his warning to bookkeepers: "A person should not go to sleep at night until the debits equal the credits!"

You can see from the two example transactions how double-entry bookkeeping helps to keep your books in balance — as long as you make sure each entry into the books is balanced. Balancing your entries may look simple here, but sometimes bookkeeping entries can get very complex when more than two accounts are impacted by the transaction. Don't worry, you don't have to understand it totally now. I show you how to enter transactions throughout the book, depending on the type of transaction being recorded. I'm just giving you a quick overview to introduce the subject right now.

Differentiating Debits and Credits

Because bookkeeping's debits and credits are different from the ones you're used to encountering, you're probably wondering how you're supposed to know whether a debit or credit will increase or decrease an account. Believe it or not, identifying the difference will become second nature as you start making regular bookkeeping entries. But to make things easier, Table 2-1 is a chart that's commonly used by all bookkeepers and accountants.

Table 2-1	How Credits and Debits Impact Your Accounts	
Account Type	*Debits*	*Credits*
Assets	Increase	Decrease
Liabilities	Decrease	Increase
Income	Decrease	Increase
Expenses	Increase	Decrease

Copy Table 2-1 and post it at your desk when you start keeping your own books. I guarantee it will help you keep your debits and credits straight.

Chapter 3

Outlining Your Financial Road Map with a Chart of Accounts

In This Chapter

▶ Introducing the Chart of Accounts

▶ Reviewing the types of accounts that make up the chart

▶ Creating your own Chart of Accounts

Can you imagine the mess your checkbook would be if you didn't record each check you wrote? Like me, you've probably forgotten to record a check or two on occasion, but you certainly learn your lesson when you realize that an important payment bounces as a result. Yikes!

Keeping the books of a business can be a lot more difficult than maintaining a personal checkbook. Each business transaction must be carefully recorded to make sure it goes into the right account. This careful bookkeeping gives you an effective tool for figuring out how well the business is doing financially.

As a bookkeeper, you need a road map to help you determine where to record all those transactions. This road map is called the Chart of Accounts. In this chapter, I tell you how to set up the Chart of Accounts, which includes many different accounts. I also review the types of transactions you enter into each type of account in order to track the key parts of any business — assets, liabilities, equity, revenue, and expenses.

Getting to Know the Chart of Accounts

The *Chart of Accounts* is the road map that a business creates to organize its financial transactions. After all, you can't record a transaction until you know where to put it! Essentially, this chart is a list of all the accounts a business has, organized in a specific order; each account has a description that includes the type of account and the types of transactions that should be entered into that account. Every business creates its own Chart of Accounts based on how the business is operated, so you're unlikely to find two businesses with the exact same Charts of Accounts.

However, some basic organizational and structural characteristics are common to all Charts of Accounts. The organization and structure are designed around two key financial reports: the *balance sheet,* which shows what your business owns and what it owes, and the *income statement,* which shows how much money your business took in from sales and how much money it spent to generate those sales. (You can find out more about balance sheets in Chapter 18 and income statements in Chapter 19.)

The Chart of Accounts starts with the balance sheet accounts, which include

- ✔ **Current Assets:** Includes all accounts that track things the company owns and expects to use in the next 12 months, such as cash, accounts receivable (money collected from customers), and inventory

- ✔ **Long-term Assets:** Includes all accounts that track things the company owns that have a lifespan of more than 12 months, such as buildings, furniture, and equipment

- ✔ **Current Liabilities:** Includes all accounts that track debts the company must pay over the next 12 months, such as accounts payable (bills from vendors, contractors, and consultants), interest payable, and credit cards payable

- ✔ **Long-term Liabilities:** Includes all accounts that track debts the company must pay over a period of time longer than the next 12 months, such as mortgages payable and bonds payable

- ✔ **Equity:** Includes all accounts that track the owners of the company and their claims against the company's assets, which include any money invested in the company, any money taken out of the company, and any earnings that have been reinvested in the company

The rest of the chart is filled with income statement accounts, which include

- ✔ **Revenue:** Includes all accounts that track sales of goods and services as well as revenue generated for the company by other means

- ✔ **Cost of Goods Sold:** Includes all accounts that track the direct costs involved in selling the company's goods or services

- ✔ **Expenses:** Includes all accounts that track expenses related to running the business that aren't directly tied to the sale of individual products or services

When developing the Chart of Accounts, you start by listing all the Asset accounts, the Liability accounts, the Equity accounts, the Revenue accounts, and finally, the Expense accounts. All these accounts come from two places: the balance sheet and the income statement.

In this chapter, I review the key account types found in most businesses, but this list isn't cast in stone. You should develop an account list that makes the most sense for how you operate your business and the financial information you want to track. As I explore the accounts that make up the Chart of Accounts, I point out how the structure may differ for different businesses.

The Chart of Accounts is a money management tool that helps you track your business transactions, so set it up in a way that provides you with the financial information you need to make smart business decisions. You'll probably tweak the accounts in your chart annually and, if necessary, you may add accounts during the year if you find something for which you want more detailed tracking. You can add accounts during the year, but it's best not to delete accounts until the end of a 12-month reporting period. I discuss adding and deleting accounts from your books in Chapter 17.

Starting with the Balance Sheet Accounts

The first part of the Chart of Accounts is made up of balance sheet accounts, which break down into the following three categories:

- **Asset:** These accounts are used to track what the business owns. Assets include cash on hand, furniture, buildings, vehicles, and so on.

- **Liability:** These accounts track what the business owes, or, more specifically, claims that lenders have against the business's assets. For example, mortgages on buildings and lines of credit are two common types of liabilities.

- **Equity:** These accounts track what the owners put into the business and the claims owners have against assets. For example, stockholders are company owners that have claims against the business's assets.

The balance sheet accounts, and the financial report they make up, are so-called because they have to *balance* out. The value of the assets must be equal to the claims made against those assets. (Remember, these claims are liabilities made by lenders and equity made by owners.)

I discuss the balance sheet in greater detail in Chapter 18, including how it's prepared and used. This section, however, examines the basic components of the balance sheet, as reflected in the Chart of Accounts.

Tackling assets

First on the chart are always the accounts that track what the company owns — its assets: current assets and long-term assets.

Current assets

Current assets are the key assets that your business uses up during a 12-month period and will likely not be there the next year. The accounts that reflect current assets on the Chart of Accounts are as follows:

- ✔ **Cash in Checking:** Any company's primary account is the checking account used for operating activities. This is the account used to deposit revenues and pay expenses. Some companies have more than one operating account in this category; for example, a company with many divisions may have an operating account for each division.

- ✔ **Cash in Savings:** This account is used for surplus cash. Any cash for which there is no immediate plan is deposited in an interest-earning savings account so that it can at least earn interest while the company decides what to do with it.

- ✔ **Cash on Hand:** This account is used to track any cash kept at retail stores or in the office. In retail stores, cash must be kept in registers in order to provide change to customers. In the office, petty cash is often kept around for immediate cash needs that pop up from time to time. This account helps you keep track of the cash held outside a financial institution.

- ✔ **Accounts Receivable:** If you offer your products or services to customers on store credit (meaning *your* store credit system), then you need this account to track the customers who buy on your dime.

  Accounts Receivable isn't used to track purchases made on other types of credit cards because your business gets paid directly by banks, not customers, when other credit cards are used. Head to Chapter 9 to read more about this scenario and the corresponding type of account.

- ✔ **Inventory:** This account tracks the products on hand to sell to your customers. The value of the assets in this account varies depending on how you decide to track the flow of inventory in and out of the business. I discuss inventory valuation and tracking in greater detail in Chapter 8.

- ✔ **Prepaid Insurance:** This account tracks insurance you pay in advance that's credited as it's used up each month. For example, if you own a building and prepay one year in advance, each month you reduce the amount that you prepaid by 1/12 as the prepayment is used up.

Depending upon the type of business you're setting up, you may have other current asset accounts that you decide to track. For example, if you're starting a service business in consulting, you're likely to have a Consulting account for tracking cash collected for those services. If you run a business in which you barter assets (such as trading your services for paper goods), you may add a Barter account for business-to-business barter.

Long-term assets

Long-term assets are assets that you anticipate your business will use for more than 12 months. This section lists some of the most common long-term assets, starting with the key accounts related to buildings and factories owned by the company:

- **Land:** This account tracks the land owned by the company. The value of the land is based on the cost of purchasing it. Land value is tracked separately from the value of any buildings standing on that land because land isn't depreciated in value, but buildings must be depreciated. *Depreciation* is an accounting method that shows an asset is being used up. I talk more about depreciation in Chapter 12.

- **Buildings:** This account tracks the value of any buildings a business owns. As with land, the value of the building is based on the cost of purchasing it. The key difference between buildings and land is that the building's value is depreciated, as discussed in the previous bullet.

- **Accumulated Depreciation – Buildings:** This account tracks the cumulative amount a building is depreciated over its useful lifespan. I talk more about how to calculate depreciation in Chapter 12.

- **Leasehold Improvements:** This account tracks the value of improvements to buildings or other facilities that a business leases rather than purchases. Frequently when a business leases a property, it must pay for any improvements necessary in order to use that property the way it's needed. For example, if a business leases a store in a strip mall, it's likely that the space leased is an empty shell or filled with shelving and other items that may not match the particular needs of the business. As with buildings, leasehold improvements are depreciated as the value of the asset ages.

- **Accumulated Depreciation – Leasehold Improvements:** This account tracks the cumulative amount depreciated for leasehold improvements.

The following are the types of accounts for smaller long-term assets, such as vehicles and furniture:

- **Vehicles:** This account tracks any cars, trucks, or other vehicles owned by the business. The initial value of any vehicle is listed in this account based on the total cost paid to put the vehicle in service. Sometimes this value is more than the purchase price if additions were needed to make the vehicle usable for the particular type of business. For example, if a business provides transportation for the handicapped and must add additional equipment to a vehicle in order to serve the needs of its customers, that additional equipment is added to the value of the vehicle. Vehicles also depreciate through their useful lifespan.

- ✔ **Accumulated Depreciation – Vehicles:** This account tracks the depreciation of all vehicles owned by the company.

- ✔ **Furniture and Fixtures:** This account tracks any furniture or fixtures purchased for use in the business. The account includes the value of all chairs, desks, store fixtures, and shelving needed to operate the business. The value of the furniture and fixtures in this account is based on the cost of purchasing these items. These items are depreciated during their useful lifespan.

- ✔ **Accumulated Depreciation – Furniture and Fixtures:** This account tracks the accumulated depreciation of all furniture and fixtures.

- ✔ **Equipment:** This account tracks equipment that was purchased for use for more than one year, such as computers, copiers, tools, and cash registers. The value of the equipment is based on the cost to purchase these items. Equipment is also depreciated to show that over time it gets used up and must be replaced.

- ✔ **Accumulated Depreciation – Equipment:** This account tracks the accumulated depreciation of all the equipment.

The following accounts track the long-term assets that you can't touch but that still represent things of value owned by the company, such as organization costs, patents, and copyrights. These are called *intangible assets,* and the accounts that track them include

- ✔ **Organization Costs:** This account tracks initial start-up expenses to get the business off the ground. Many such expenses can't be written off in the first year. For example, special licenses and legal fees must be written off over a number of years using a method similar to depreciation, called *amortization,* which is also tracked. I discuss amortization in greater detail in Chapter 12.

- ✔ **Amortization – Organization Costs:** This account tracks the accumulated amortization of organization costs during the period in which they're being written-off.

- ✔ **Patents:** This account tracks the costs associated with *patents,* grants made by governments that guarantee to the inventor of a product or service the exclusive right to make, use, and sell that product or service over a set period of time. Like organization costs, patent costs are amortized. The value of this asset is based on the expenses the company incurs to get the right to patent the product.

- ✔ **Amortization – Patents:** This account tracks the accumulated amortization of a business's patents.

- ✔ **Copyrights:** This account tracks the costs incurred to establish copyrights, the legal rights given to an author, playwright, publisher, or any other distributor of a publication or production for a unique work of literature, music, drama, or art. This legal right expires after a set number of years, so its value is amortized as the copyright gets used up.

✔ **Goodwill:** This account is only needed if a company buys another company for more than the actual value of its tangible assets. Goodwill reflects the intangible value of this purchase for things like company reputation, store locations, customer base, and other items that increase the value of the business bought.

If you hold a lot of assets that aren't of great value, you can also set up an "Other Assets" account to track them. Any asset you track in the Other Assets account that you later want to track individually can be shifted to its own account. I discuss adjusting the Chart of Accounts in Chapter 17.

Laying out your liabilities

After you cover assets, the next stop on the bookkeeping highway is the accounts that track what your business owes to others. These "others" can include vendors from which you buy products or supplies, financial institutions from which you borrow money, and anyone else who lends money to your business. Like assets, liabilities are lumped into two types: current liabilities and long-term liabilities.

Current liabilities

Current liabilities are debts due in the next 12 months. Some of the most common types of current liabilities accounts that appear on the Chart of Accounts are

✔ **Accounts Payable:** Tracks money the company owes to vendors, contractors, suppliers, and consultants that must be paid in less than a year. Most of these liabilities must be paid 30 to 90 days from billing.

✔ **Sales Tax Collected:** You may not think of sales tax as a liability, but because the business collects the tax from the customer and doesn't pay it immediately to the government entity, the taxes collected become a liability tracked in this account. A business usually collects sales tax throughout the month and then pays it to the local, state, or federal government on a monthly basis. I discuss paying sales taxes in greater detail in Chapter 21.

✔ **Accrued Payroll Taxes:** This account tracks payroll taxes collected from employees to pay state, local, or federal income taxes as well as Social Security and Medicare taxes. Companies don't have to pay these taxes to the government entities immediately, so depending on the size of the payroll, companies may pay payroll taxes on a monthly or quarterly basis. I discuss how to handle payroll taxes in Chapter 10.

✔ **Credit Cards Payable:** This account tracks all credit-card accounts to which the business is liable. Most companies use credit cards as short-term debt and pay them off completely at the end of each month, but some smaller companies carry credit-card balances over a longer period of time. Because credit cards often have a much higher interest rate than most lines of credits, most companies transfer any credit-card debt they can't pay entirely at the end of a month to a line of credit at a bank. When it comes to your Chart of Accounts, you can set up one Credit Card Payable account, but you may want to set up a separate account for each card your company holds to improve tracking credit-card usage.

How you set up your current liabilities and how many individual accounts you establish depends on how detailed you want to track each type of liability. For example, you can set up separate current liability accounts for major vendors if you find that approach provides you with a better money management tool. For example, suppose that a small hardware retail store buys most of the tools it sells from Snap-on. To keep better control of its spending with Snap-on, the bookkeeper sets up a specific account called Accounts Payable – Snap-on, which is used only for tracking invoices and payments to that vendor. In this example, all other invoices and payments to other vendors and suppliers are tracked in the general Accounts Payable account.

Long-term liabilities

Long-term liabilities are debts due in more than 12 months. The number of long-term liability accounts you maintain on your Chart of Accounts depends on your debt structure. The two most common types are

- ✔ **Loans Payable:** This account tracks any long-term loans, such as a mortgage on your business building. Most businesses have separate loans payable accounts for each of their long-term loans. For example, you could have Loans Payable – Mortgage Bank for your building and Loans Payable – Car Bank for your vehicle loan.

- ✔ **Notes Payable:** Some businesses borrow money from other businesses using *notes*, a method of borrowing that doesn't require the company to put up an asset, such as a mortgage on a building or a car loan, as collateral. This account tracks any notes due.

In addition to any separate long-term debt you may want to track in its own account, you may also want to set up an account called "Other Liabilities" that you can use to track types of debt that are so insignificant to the business that you don't think they need their own accounts.

Eyeing the equity

Every business is owned by somebody. *Equity accounts* track owners' contributions to the business as well as their share of ownership. For a corporation, ownership is tracked by the sale of individual shares of stock because each stockholder owns a portion of the business. In smaller companies that are owned by one person or a group of people, equity is tracked using Capital and Drawing accounts. Here are the basic equity accounts that appear in the Chart of Accounts:

- ✔ **Common Stock:** This account reflects the value of outstanding shares of stock sold to investors. A company calculates this value by multiplying the number of shares issued by the value of each share of stock. Only corporations need to establish this account.

- ✔ **Retained Earnings:** This account tracks the profits or losses accumulated since a business was opened. At the end of each year, the profit or loss calculated on the income statement is used to adjust the value of this account. For example, if a company made a $100,000 profit in the past year, the Retained Earnings account would be increased by that amount; if the company lost $100,000, then that amount would be subtracted from this account.

- ✔ **Capital:** This account is only necessary for small, unincorporated businesses. The Capital account reflects the amount of initial money the business owner contributed to the company as well as owner contributions made after the initial start-up. The value of this account is based on cash contributions and other assets contributed by the business owner, such as equipment, vehicles, or buildings. If a small company has several different partners, then each partner gets his or her own Capital account to track his or her contributions.

- ✔ **Drawing:** This account is only necessary for businesses that aren't incorporated. It tracks any money that a business owner takes out of the business. If the business has several partners, each partner gets his or her own Drawing account to track what he or she takes out of the business.

Tracking the Income Statement Accounts

The income statement is made up of two types of accounts:

- ✔ **Revenue:** These accounts track all money coming into the business, including sales, interest earned on savings, and any other methods used to generate income.

- ✔ **Expenses:** These accounts track all money that a business spends in order to keep itself afloat.

The bottom line of the income statement shows whether your business made a profit or a loss for a specified period of time. I discuss how to prepare and use an income statement in Chapter 19. This section examines the various accounts that make up the income statement portion of the Chart of Accounts.

Recording the money you make

First up in the income statement portion of the Chart of Accounts are accounts that track revenue coming into the business. If you choose to offer discounts or accept returns, that activity also falls within the revenue grouping. The most common income accounts are

- **Sales of Goods or Services:** This account, which appears at the top of every income statement, tracks all the money that the company earns selling its products, services, or both.

- **Sales Discounts:** Because most businesses offer discounts to encourage sales, this account tracks any reductions to the full price of merchandise.

- **Sales Returns:** This account tracks transactions related to returns, when a customer returns a product because he or she is unhappy with it for some reason.

When you examine an income statement from a company other than the one you own or are working for, you usually see the following accounts summarized as one line item called Revenue or Net Revenue. Because not all income is generated by sales of products or services, other income accounts that may appear on a Chart of Accounts include

- **Other Income:** If a company takes in income from a source other than its primary business activity, that income is recorded in this account. For example, a company that encourages recycling and earns income from the items recycled records that income in this account.

- **Interest Income:** This account tracks any income earned by collecting interest on a company's savings accounts. If the company loans money to employees or to another company and earns interest on that money, that interest is recorded in this account as well.

- **Sale of Fixed Assets:** Any time a company sells a fixed asset, such as a car or furniture, any revenue from the sale is recorded in this account. A company should only record revenue remaining after subtracting the accumulated depreciation from the original cost of the asset.

Tracking the Cost of Sales

Before you can sell a product, you must spend some money to either buy or make that product. The type of account used to track the money spent is called a Cost of Goods Sold account. The most common are

- ✔ **Purchases:** Tracks the purchases of all items you plan to sell.

- ✔ **Purchase Discount:** Tracks the discounts you may receive from vendors if you pay for your purchase quickly. For example, a company may give you a 2 percent discount on your purchase if you pay the bill in 10 days rather than wait until the end of the 30-day payment allotment.

- ✔ **Purchase Returns:** If you're unhappy with a product you've bought, record the value of any returns in this account.

- ✔ **Freight Charges:** Charges related to shipping items you purchase for later sale. You may or may not want to keep track of this detail.

- ✔ **Other Sales Costs:** This is a catchall account for anything that doesn't fit into one of the other Cost of Goods Sold accounts.

Acknowledging the money you spend

Expense accounts take the cake for the longest list of individual accounts. Any money you spend on the business that can't be tied directly to the sale of an individual product falls under the expense account category. For example, advertising a storewide sale isn't directly tied to the sale of any one product, so the costs associated with advertising fall under this category.

The Chart of Accounts mirrors your business operations, so it's up to you to decide how much detail you want to keep in your expense accounts. Most businesses have expenses that are unique to their operations, so your list will probably be longer than the one I present here. However, you also may find that you don't need some of these accounts.

On your Chart of Accounts, the expense accounts don't have to appear in any specific order, so I list them here alphabetically. The most common are

- ✔ **Advertising:** Tracks expenses involved in promoting a business or its products. Money spent on newspaper, television, magazine, and radio advertising is recorded here as well as any money spent to print flyers and mailings to customers. For community events such as cancer walks or crafts fairs, associated costs are tracked in this account as well.

- ✔ **Bank Service Charges:** This account tracks any charges made by a bank to service a company's bank accounts.

- ✔ **Dues and Subscriptions:** This account tracks expenses related to business club membership or subscriptions to magazines.

- ✔ **Equipment Rental:** This account tracks expenses related to renting equipment for a short-term project. For example, a business that needs to rent a truck to pick up some new fixtures for its store records that truck rental in this account.

✔ **Insurance:** Tracks any money paid to buy insurance. Many businesses break this down into several accounts, such as Insurance – Employees Group, which tracks any expenses paid for employee insurance, or Insurance – Officers' Life, which tracks money spent to buy insurance to protect the life of a key owner or officer of the company. Companies often insure their key owners and executives because an unexpected death, especially for a small company, may mean facing many unexpected expenses in order to keep the company's doors open. In such a case, insurance proceeds can be used to cover those expenses.

✔ **Legal and Accounting:** This account tracks any money that's paid for legal or accounting advice.

✔ **Miscellaneous Expenses:** This is a catchall account for expenses that don't fit into one of a company's established accounts. If certain miscellaneous expenses occur frequently, a company may choose to add an account to the Chart of Accounts and move related expenses into that new account by subtracting all related transactions from the Miscellaneous Expenses account and adding them to the new account. With this shuffle, it's important to carefully balance out the adjusting transaction to avoid any errors or double counting.

✔ **Office Expense:** This account tracks any items purchased in order to run an office. For example, office supplies such as paper and pens or business cards fit in this account. As with miscellaneous expenses, a company may choose to track some office expense items in their own accounts. For example, if you find your office is using a lot of copy paper and you want to track that separately, you set up a Copy Paper expense account. Just be sure you really need the detail because the number of accounts can get unwieldy.

✔ **Payroll Taxes:** This account tracks any taxes paid related to employee payroll, such as the employer's share of Social Security and Medicare, unemployment compensation, and workers' compensation.

✔ **Postage:** Tracks money spent on stamps and shipping. If a company does a large amount of shipping through vendors such as UPS or Federal Express, it may want to track that spending in separate accounts for each vendor. This option is particularly helpful for small companies that sell over the Internet or through catalog sales.

✔ **Rent Expense:** Tracks rental costs for a business's office or retail space.

✔ **Salaries and Wages:** This account tracks any money paid to employees as salary or wages.

✔ **Supplies:** This account tracks any business supplies that don't fit into the category of office supplies. For example, supplies needed for the operation of retail stores are tracked using this account.

- ✔ **Travel and Entertainment:** This account tracks money spent for business purposes on travel or entertainment. Some business separate these expenses into several accounts, such as Travel and Entertainment – Meals, Travel and Entertainment – Travel, and Travel and Entertainment – Entertainment, to keep a close watch.

- ✔ **Telephone:** This account tracks all business expenses related to the telephone and telephone calls.

- ✔ **Utilities:** Tracks money paid for utilities (electricity, gas, and water).

- ✔ **Vehicles:** Tracks expenses related to the operation of company vehicles.

Setting Up Your Chart of Accounts

You can use the lists of accounts provided in this chapter to get started setting up your business's own Chart of Accounts. There's really no secret — just make a list of the accounts that apply to your business.

Don't panic if you can't think of every type of account you may need for your business. It's very easy to add to the Chart of Accounts at any time. Just add the account to the list and distribute the revised list to any employees that use it. (Even employees not involved in bookkeeping need a copy of your Chart of Accounts if they code invoices or other transactions and indicate to which account those transactions should be recorded.)

The Chart of Accounts usually includes at least three columns:

- ✔ **Account:** Lists the account names

- ✔ **Type:** Lists the type of account — asset, liability, equity, income, cost of goods sold, or expense

- ✔ **Description:** Contains a description of the type of transaction that should be recorded in the account

Many companies also assign numbers to the accounts, to be used for coding charges. If your company is using a computerized system, the computer automatically assigns the account number. Otherwise, you need to plan out your own numbering system. The most common number system is as follows:

- ✔ Asset accounts: 1,000 to 1,999

- ✔ Liability accounts: 2,000 to 2,999

- ✔ Equity accounts: 3,000 to 3,999

- ✔ Sales and Cost of Goods Sold accounts: 4,000 to 4,999

- ✔ Expense accounts: 5,000 to 6,999

This numbering system matches the one used by computerized accounting systems, making it easy at some future time to automate the books using a computerized accounting system. A number of different Charts of Accounts have been developed. When you get your computerized system, whichever accounting software you use, all you need to do is review the chart options for the type of business you run included with that software, delete any accounts you don't want, and add any new accounts that fit your business plan.

If you're setting up your Chart of Accounts manually, be sure to leave a lot of room between accounts to add new accounts. For example, number your Cash in Checking account 1,000 and your Accounts Receivable account 1,100. That leaves you plenty of room to add other accounts to track cash.

Figure 3-1 is a Chart of Accounts from QuickBooks 2014. Asset accounts are first, followed by liability, equity, income, and expense accounts.

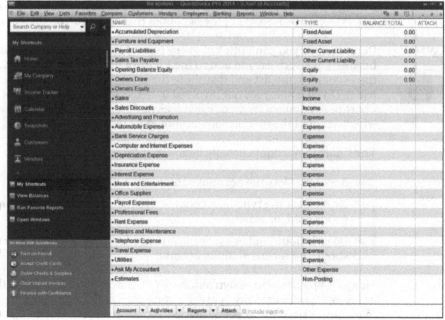

Figure 3-1:
The top portion of a sample Chart of Accounts.

NAME	TYPE	BALANCE TOTAL	ATTACH
Accumulated Depreciation	Fixed Asset	0.00	
Furniture and Equipment	Fixed Asset	0.00	
Payroll Liabilities	Other Current Liability	0.00	
Sales Tax Payable	Other Current Liability	0.00	
Opening Balance Equity	Equity	0.00	
Owners Draw	Equity	0.00	
Owners Equity	Equity		
Sales	Income		
Sales Discounts	Income		
Advertising and Promotion	Expense		
Automobile Expense	Expense		
Bank Service Charges	Expense		
Computer and Internet Expenses	Expense		
Depreciation Expense	Expense		
Insurance Expense	Expense		
Interest Expense	Expense		
Meals and Entertainment	Expense		
Office Supplies	Expense		
Payroll Expenses	Expense		
Professional Fees	Expense		
Rent Expense	Expense		
Repairs and Maintenance	Expense		
Telephone Expense	Expense		
Travel Expense	Expense		
Utilities	Expense		
Ask My Accountant	Other Expense		
Estimates	Non-Posting		

Part II
Keeping a Paper Trail

Find out how to use mobile apps and do some bookkeeping on the go in a free online article at www.dummies.com/extras/bookkeeping.

In this part . . .

- Filling out your ledgers.
- Keeping up your journals.
- Discovering how to computerize your books.
- Putting some controls on your books and your money.

Chapter 4

Ledgers: A One-Stop Summary of Your Business Transactions

In This Chapter
▶ Understanding the value of the General Ledger
▶ Developing ledger entries
▶ Posting entries to the ledger accounts
▶ Adjusting ledger entries
▶ Creating ledgers in computerized accounting software

As a bookkeeper, you may be dreaming of having one source that you can turn to when you need to review all entries that impact your business's accounts. (Okay, so maybe that's not exactly what you're dreaming about. Just work with me here.) The General Ledger is your dream come true. It's where you find a summary of transactions and a record of the accounts that those transactions impact.

In this chapter, you discover the purpose of the General Ledger. I tell you how to not only develop entries for the Ledger but also enter (or post) them. In addition, I explain how you can change already posted information or correct entries in the Ledger and how this entire process is streamlined when you use a computerized accounting system.

The Eyes and Ears of a Business

I'm not using eyes and ears literally here because, of course, the book known as the General Ledger isn't alive, so it can't see or speak. But wouldn't it be nice if the ledger could just tell you all its secrets about what happens with your money? That would certainly make it a lot easier to track down any bookkeeping problems or errors.

Instead, the General Ledger serves as the figurative eyes and ears of book-keepers and accountants who want to know what financial transactions have taken place historically in a business. By reading the General Ledger — not exactly interesting reading unless you love numbers — you can see, account by account, every transaction that has taken place in the business. (And to uncover more details about those transactions, you can turn to your business's journals, where transactions are kept on a daily basis. See Chapter 5 for the lowdown on journals.)

The General Ledger is the granddaddy of your business. You can find all the transactions that ever occurred in the history of the business in the General Ledger account. It's the one place you need to go to find transactions that impact Cash, Inventory, Accounts Receivable, Accounts Payable, and any other account included in your business's Chart of Accounts. (See Chapter 3 for more information about setting up the Chart of Accounts and the kinds of transactions you can find in each.)

Developing Entries for the Ledger

Because your business's transactions are first entered into journals, you develop many of the entries for the General Ledger based on information pulled from the appropriate journal. For example, cash receipts and the accounts that are impacted by those receipts are listed in the Cash Receipts journal. Cash disbursements and the accounts impacted by those disbursements are listed in the Cash Disbursements journal. The same is true for transactions found in the Sales journal, Purchases journal, General journal, and any other special journals you may be using in your business.

At the end of each month, you summarize each journal by adding up the columns and then use that summary to develop an entry for the General Ledger. Believe me, that takes a lot less time than entering every transaction in the General Ledger.

I introduce you to the process of entering transactions and summarizing journals in Chapter 5. Near the end of that chapter, I even summarize one journal and develop this entry for the General Ledger:

Account	Debit	Credit
Cash	$2,900	
Accounts Receivable		$500
Sales		$900
Capital		$1,500

Note that the Debits and Credits are in balance — $2,900 each. Remember all entries to the General Ledger must be balanced entries. That's the cardinal rule of double-entry bookkeeping. For more details about double-entry bookkeeping, read Chapter 2.

In this entry, the Cash account is increased by $2,900 to show that cash was received. The Accounts Receivable account is decreased by $500 to show customers paid their bills, and the money is no longer due. The Sales account is increased by $900, because additional revenue was collected. The Capital account is increased by $1,500 because the owner put more cash into the business.

Figures 4-1 to 4-4 summarize the remaining journal pages that I prepared in Chapter 5. Reviewing those summaries, I developed the following entries for the General Ledger:

Figure 4-1 — Summarized Cash Disbursements Journal
Figure 4-2 — Summarized Sales Journal
Figure 4-3 — Summarized Purchases Journal
Figure 4-4 — Summarized General Journal

Figure 4-1 shows a summary of the Cash Disbursements journal for a business.

Figure 4-1:
Summarizing cash transactions so they can be posted to the General Ledger.

Cheesecake Shop
Cash Disbursements Journal
March 2014

Date	Account Debited	Check #	PR	General Debit	Account Payble Debit	Salaries Debit	Cash Credit
3/1	Rent	1065		$800			$800
3/3	Accounts Payable - Henry's	1066			$500		$500
3/3	Accounts Payable - Helen's	1067			$250		$250
3/4	Salaries	1068				$350	$350
3/10	Credit Card Payable - AmBank	1069		$150			$150
	March General Ledger Summary				$750	$350	$2,050

The following General Ledger entry is based on the transactions that appear in Figure 4-1:

Account	Debit	Credit
Rent	$800	
Accounts Payable	$750	
Salaries	$350	
Credit Card Payable	$150	
Cash		$2,050

This General Ledger summary balances out at $2,050 each for the debits and credits. The Cash account is decreased to show the cash outlay, the Rent and Salaries expense accounts are increased to show the additional expenses, and the Accounts Payable and Credit Card Payable accounts are decreased to show that bills were paid and are no longer due.

Figure 4-2 shows the Sales journal for a sample business.

Figure 4-2:
Summa-
rizing sales
transactions
so they can
be posted to
the General
Ledger.

				Cheesecake Shop Sales Journal March 2014		
Date	Customer Account Debited	PR	Invoice Number	Accounts Receivable Debit	Sales Credit	
3/1	S. Smith		243	$200	$200	
3/1	Charlie's Garage		244	$300	$300	
3/3	P. Perry		245	$100	$100	
3/5	J. Jones		246	$200	$200	
	March General Ledger Summary			$800	$800	

The following General Ledger entry is based on the transactions that appear in Figure 4-2:

Account	Debit	Credit
Accounts Receivable	$800	
Sales		$800

Note that this entry is balanced. The Accounts Receivable account is increased to show that customers owe the business money because they bought items on store credit. The Sales account is increased to show that even though no cash changed hands, the business in Figure 4-2 took in revenue. Cash will be collected when the customers pay their bills.

Figure 4-3 shows the business's Purchases journal for one month. The following General Ledger entry is based on the transactions that appear in Figure 4-3:

Account	Debit	Credit
Purchases	$925	
Accounts Payable		$925

Like the entry for the Sales account, this entry is balanced. The Accounts Payable account is increased to show that money is due to vendors, and the Purchases expense account is also increased to show that more supplies were purchased.

Figure 4-4 shows the General journal for a sample business. The following General Ledger entry is based on the transactions that appear in Figure 4-4:

Account	Debit	Credit
Sales Return	$60	
Accounts Payable	$200	
Vehicles	$10,000	
Accounts Receivable		$60
Purchase Return		$200
Capital		$10,000

Checking for balance — Debits and Credits both total to $10,260.

In this entry, the Sales Return and Purchase Return accounts are increased to show additional returns. The Accounts Payable and Accounts Receivable accounts are both decreased to show that money is no longer owed. The Vehicles account is increased to show new company assets, and the Capital account, which is where the owner's deposits into the business are tracked, is increased accordingly.

Figure 4-3:
Summa-
rizing goods
to be sold
transactions
so they can
be posted to
the General
Ledger.

			Cheesecake Shop Purchases Journal March 2014			
Date	Vendor Account Credited	PR	Invoice Number	Purchases Debit	Accounts Payable Credit	
	3/1 Supplies from Henry's		1575	$750	$750	
	3/3 Packaging Boxes from Barry's		1235	$100	$100	
	3/5 Paper Goods from Helen's		1745	$75	$75	
	March General Ledger Summary			$925	$925	

					Accounts Payable	Accounts Receivable
Date	Account	PR	General Debit	General Credit	Debit	Credit
3/3	Sales Return		$60			
	S. Smith					$60
	Credit Memo 124					
3/5	Henry's Bakery Supplies				$200	
	Purchase Return			$200		
	Debit Memo 346					
3/5	Vehicles		$10,000			
	Owner Capital			$10,000		
	Transfer of Owner's Vehicle to Business					
	March General Ledger Summary				$200	$60

Cheesecake Shop
General Journal
March 2014

Figure 4-4:
Summarizing miscellaneous transactions so they can be posted to the General Ledger.

Posting Entries to the Ledger

After you summarize your journals and develop all the entries you need for the General Ledger (see the previous section), you post your entries into the General Ledger accounts.

When posting to the General Ledger, include transaction dollar amounts as well as references to where material was originally entered into the books so you can track a transaction back if a question arises later. For example, you may wonder what a number means, your boss or the owner may wonder why certain money was spent, or an auditor (an outside accountant who checks your work for accuracy) could raise a question.

Whatever the reason someone is questioning an entry in the General Ledger, you definitely want to be able to find the point of original entry for every transaction in every account. Use the reference information that guides you to where the original detail about the transaction is located in the journals to answer any question that arises.

For this particular business, three of the accounts — Cash, Accounts Receivable, and Accounts Payable — are carried over month to month, so each has an opening balance. Just to keep things simple, in this example I start each account with a $2,000 balance. One of the accounts, Sales, is closed at the end of each accounting period, so it starts with a zero balance.

Most businesses close their books at the end of each month and do financial reports. Others close them at the end of a quarter or end of a year. (I talk more about which accounts are closed at the end of each accounting period and which accounts remain open, as well as why that is the case, in Chapter 22.) For the purposes of this example, I assume that this business closes its books monthly. And in the figures that follow, I only give examples for the first five days of the month to keep things simple.

As you review the figures for the various accounts in this example, take notice that the balance of some accounts increases when a debit is recorded and decreases when a credit is recorded. Others increase when a credit is recorded and decrease when a debit is recorded. That's the mystery of debits, credits, and double-entry accounting. For more, flip to Chapter 2.

The Cash account (see Figure 4-5) increases with debits and decreases with credits. Ideally, the Cash account always ends with a debit balance, which means there's still money in the account. A credit balance in the cash account indicates that the business is overdrawn, and you know what that means — checks are returned for nonpayment.

Figure 4-5:
Cash
account in
the General
Ledger.

	Cheesecake Shop				
	Cash				
	March 2014				
Date	Description	Ref. #	Debit	Credit	Balance
	Opening Balance				$2,000
3/31	From Cash Receipts Journal	Journal P2	$2,900		
3/31	From Cash Disbursements Journal	Journal P3		$2,050	
	March Closing Balance				$2,850

The Accounts Receivable account (see Figure 4-6) increases with debits and decreases with credits. Ideally, this account also has a debit balance that indicates the amount still due from customer purchases. If no money is due from customers, the account balance is zero. A zero balance isn't necessarily a bad thing if all customers have paid their bills. However, a zero balance may be a sign that your sales have slumped, which could be bad news.

The Accounts Payable account (see Figure 4-7) increases with credits and decreases with debits. Usually, this account has a credit balance because money is still due to vendors, contractors, and others. A zero balance here equals no outstanding bills.

Cheesecake Shop Accounts Receivable March 2014					
Date	Description	Ref. #	Debit	Credit	Balance
	Opening Balance				$2,000
3/31	From Cash Receipts Journal	Journal P2		$500	
3/31	From Sales Journal	Journal P3	$800		
3/31	Credit Memo 124 (General Journal)	Journal P3		$60	
	March Closing Balance				$2,240

Figure 4-6: Accounts Receivable account in the General Ledger.

Cheesecake Shop Accounts Payable March 2014					
Date	Description	Ref. #	Debit	Credit	Balance
	Opening Balance				$2,000
3/31	From Accounts Payable	Journal P2	$750		
3/31	From Purchases Journal	Journal P3		$925	
3/31	Debit Memo 346 (General Journal)	Journal P5	$200		
	March Closing Balance				$1,975

Figure 4-7: Accounts Payable account in the General Ledger.

These three accounts — Cash, Accounts Receivable, and Accounts Payable — are part of the balance sheet, which I explain fully in Chapter 18. Asset accounts on the balance sheet usually carry debit balances because they reflect assets (in this case, cash) owned by the business. Cash and Accounts Receivable are asset accounts. Liability and Equity accounts usually carry credit balances because Liability accounts show claims made by creditors (in other words, money owed by the company to financial institutions, vendors, or others), and Equity accounts show claims made by owners (in other words, how much money the owners have put into the business). Accounts Payable is a liability account.

Here's how these accounts impact the balance of the company:

Assets = Liabilities + Equity

Cash Accounts Payable

(Usually debit balance) (Usually credit balance)

Accounts Receivable

(Usually debit balance)

The Sales account (see Figure 4-8) isn't a balance sheet account. Instead, it's used in developing the income statement, which shows whether or not a company made money in the period being examined. (For the lowdown on income statements, see Chapter 19.) Credits and debits are pretty straightforward when it comes to the Sales account: Credits increase the account, and debits decrease it. The Sales account usually carries a credit balance, which is a good thing because it means the company had income.

What's that, you say? The Sales account should carry a credit balance? That may sound strange, so let me explain the relationship between the Sales account and the balance sheet. The Sales account is one of the accounts that feeds the bottom line of the income statement, which shows whether your business made a profit or suffered a loss. A profit means that you earned more through sales than you paid out in costs or expenses. Expense and cost accounts usually carry a debit balance.

The income statement's bottom line figure shows whether or not the company made a profit. If Sales account credits exceed expense and cost account debits, then the company made a profit. That profit would be in the form of a credit, which then gets added to the Equity account called Retained Earnings, which tracks how much of your company's profits were reinvested into the company to grow it. If the company lost money, and the bottom line of the income statement showed that cost and expenses exceeded sales, then the number would be a debit. That debit would be subtracted from the balance in Retained Earnings to show the reduction to profits reinvested in the company.

Figure 4-8:
Sales account in the General Ledger.

Cheesecake Shop
Sales
March 2014

Date	Description	Ref. #	Debit	Credit	Balance
	Opening Balance				$0
3/31	From Cash Receipts Journal	Journal P2		$900	
3/31	From Sales Journal	Journal P3		$800	
	March Closing Balance				$1,700

If your company earns a profit at the end of the accounting period, the Retained Earnings account increases thanks to a credit from the Sales account. If you lose money, your Retained Earnings account decreases.

Because the Retained Earnings account is an Equity account and Equity accounts usually carry credit balances, Retained Earnings usually carries a credit balance as well.

After you post all the Ledger entries, you need to record details about where you posted the transactions on the journal pages (see Chapter 5 for more).

Adjusting for Ledger Errors

Your entries in the General Ledger aren't cast in stone. If necessary, you can always change or correct an entry with what's called an *adjusting entry*. Four of the most common reasons for General Ledger adjustments are

✔ **Depreciation:** A business shows the aging of its assets through depreciation. Each year, a portion of the original cost of an asset is written off as an expense, and that change is noted as an adjusting entry. Determining how much should be written off is a complicated process that I explain in greater detail in Chapter 12.

✔ **Prepaid expenses:** Expenses that are paid up front, such as a year's worth of insurance, are allocated by the month using an adjusting entry. This type of adjusting entry is usually done as part of the closing process at the end of an accounting period. I show you how to develop entries related to prepaid expenses in Chapter 17.

✔ **Adding an account:** Accounts can be added by way of adjusting entries at any time during the year. If the new account is being created to track transactions separately that once appeared in another account, you must move all transactions already in the books to the new account. You do this transfer with an adjusting entry to reflect the change.

✔ **Deleting an account:** Accounts should only be deleted at the end of an accounting period. I show you the type of entries you need to make in the General Ledger below.

I talk more about adjusting entries and how you can use them in Chapter 17.

Using Computerized Transactions to Post and Adjust in the General Ledger

If you keep your books using a computerized accounting system, posting to the General Ledger is actually done behind the scenes by your accounting software. You can view your transactions right on the screen. I show you how using two simple steps in QuickBooks, without ever having to make a General Ledger entry. Other computerized accounting programs let you view transactions on the screen too. I'm using QuickBooks for examples throughout the book, because it's the most popular system:

1. **In My Shortcuts, scroll down to "Accnt" to pull up the Chart of Accounts (see Figure 4-9).**

2. **Click on the account for which you want more detail. In Figure 4-10, I look into Accounts Payable and see the transactions when bills were recorded or paid.**

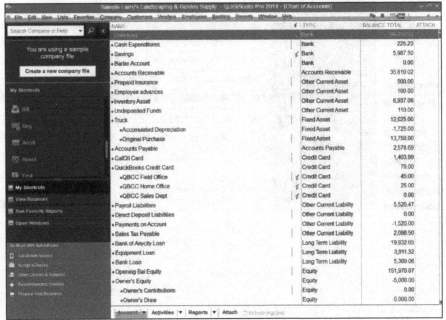

Figure 4-9:
A Chart of
Accounts as
it appears in
QuickBooks.

If you need to make an adjustment to a payment that appears in your computerized system, highlight the transaction, click Edit Transaction in the line below the account name, and make the necessary changes.

WARNING!

As you navigate the General Ledger created by your computerized bookkeeping system, you can see how easy it would be for someone to make changes that alter your financial transactions and possibly cause serious harm to your business. For example, someone could reduce or alter your bills to customers or change the amount due to a vendor. Be sure that you can trust whoever has access to your computerized system and that you have set up secure password access. Also, establish a series of checks and balances for managing your business's cash and accounts. Chapter 7 covers safety and security measures in greater detail.

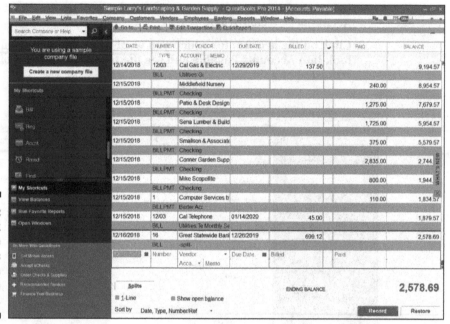

Figure 4-10:
A peek inside the Accounts Payable account in QuickBooks.

Chapter 5

Keeping Journals

• •

In This Chapter

▶ Starting things off with point of original entry

▶ Tracking cash, sales, and purchases

▶ Posting to the appropriate accounts

▶ Simplifying the journals process with computers

• •

*W*hen it comes to doing your books, you must start somewhere. You could take a shortcut and just list every transaction in the affected accounts, but after recording hundreds and maybe thousands of transactions in just one month, imagine what a nightmare you'd face if your books didn't balance and you had to find the error. It would be like looking for a needle in a haystack — a haystack of numbers!

Because you enter every transaction in two places — that is, as a debit in one account and a credit in another account — in a double-entry bookkeeping system, you need to have a place where you can easily match those debits and credits. (For more on the double-entry system, flip to Chapter 2.)

Long ago, bookkeepers developed a system of *journals* to give businesses a starting point for each transaction. In this chapter, I introduce you to the process of journalizing your transactions; I tell you how to set up and use journals, how to post the transactions to accounts impacted, and how to simplify this entire process by using a computerized bookkeeping program.

Establishing a Transaction's Point of Entry

In most companies that don't use computerized bookkeeping programs, a transaction's original point of entry into the bookkeeping system is through a system of journals.

Each transaction goes in the appropriate journal in chronological order. The entry should include information about the date of the transaction, the accounts to which the transaction was posted, and the source material used for developing the transaction.

If, at some point in the future, you need to track how a credit or debit ended up in a particular account, you can find the necessary detail in the journal where you first posted the transaction. (Before it's posted to various accounts in the bookkeeping system, each transaction gets a reference number to help you backtrack to the original entry point.) For example, suppose a customer calls you and wants to know why his account has a $500 charge. To find the answer, you go to the posting in the customer's account, track the charge back to its original point of entry in the Sales journal, use that information to locate the source for the charge, make a copy of the source (most likely a sales invoice or receipt), and mail the evidence to the customer.

If you've filed everything properly, you should have no trouble finding the original source material and settling any issue that arises regarding any transaction. For more on what papers you need to keep and how to file them, see Chapter 7.

It's perfectly acceptable to keep one general journal for all your transactions, but one big journal can be very hard to manage because you'll likely have thousands of entries in that journal by the end of the year. Instead, most businesses employ a system of journals that includes a Cash Receipts journal for incoming cash and a Cash Disbursements journal for outgoing cash. Not all transactions involve cash, however, so the two most common noncash journals are the Sales journal and the Purchases journal. I show you how to set up and use each of these journals in the sections that follow.

When Cash Changes Hands

Businesses deal with cash transactions every day, and as a business owner, you definitely want to know where every penny is going. The best way to get a quick daily summary of cash transactions is by reviewing the entries in your Cash Receipts journal and Cash Disbursements journal.

Keeping track of incoming cash

The Cash Receipts journal is the first place you record cash received by your business. The majority of cash received each day comes from daily sales; other possible sources of cash include deposits of capital from the company's owner, customer bill payments, new loan proceeds, and interest from savings accounts.

Each entry in the Cash Receipts journal must not only indicate how the cash was received but also designate the account into which the cash will be deposited. Remember, in double-entry bookkeeping, every transaction is entered twice — once as a debit and once as a credit. For example, cash taken in for sales is credited to the Sales account and debited to the Cash account. In this case, both accounts increase in value. (For more about debits and credits, flip to Chapter 2.)

In the Cash Receipts journal, the Cash account is always the debit because it's where you initially deposit your money. The credits vary depending upon the source of the funds. Figure 5-1 shows you what a series of transactions look like when they're entered into a Cash Receipts journal.

Figure 5-1: The first point of entry for incoming cash is the Cash Receipts journal.

	Cheesecake Shop Cash Receipts Journal March 2014			Prepared by:_____ Date _____ Approved by: _____ Date_____		
Date	Account Credited	PR	General Credit	Accounts Receivable Credit	Sales Credit	Cash Debit
3/1	Sales				$300	$300
3/2	Sales				$250	$250
3/3	Ck. 121 from S. Smith			$200		$200
3/3	Sales				$150	$150
3/4	Owner Capital		$1,500			$1,500
3/5	Ck 125 from J. Jones			$100		$100
3/5	Ck 567 from P. Perry			$200		$200
3/5	Sales				$200	$200

You record most of your incoming cash daily because it's cash received by the cashier, called *cash register sales* or simply *sales* in the journal. When you record checks received from customers, you list the customer's check number and name as well as the amount. In Figure 5-1, the only other cash received is a cash deposit from H.G. (the owner) to cover a cash shortfall.

The Cash Receipts journal in Figure 5-1 has seven columns of information:

- ✔ **Date:** The date of the transaction.
- ✔ **Account Credited:** The name of the account credited.
- ✔ **PR (post reference):** Where the transaction will be posted at the end of the month. This information is filled in at the end of the month when you do the posting to the General Ledger accounts. If the entry to be posted to the accounts is summarized and totaled at the bottom of the page, you can just put a check mark next to the entry in the PR column. For transactions listed in the General Credit or General Debit column, you should indicate an account number for the account into which the transaction is posted.

✔ **General Credit:** Transactions that don't have their own columns; these transactions are entered individually into the accounts impacted.

For example, according to Figure 5-1, H.G. deposited $1,500 of his own money into the Capital account on March 4th in order to pay bills. The credit shown there will be posted to the Capital account at the end of the month because the Capital account tracks all information about assets H.G. pays into the business.

✔ **Accounts Receivable Credit:** Any transactions that are posted to the Accounts Receivable account (which tracks information about customers who buy products on store credit).

✔ **Sales Credit:** Credits for the Sales account.

✔ **Cash Debit:** Anything that will be added to the Cash account.

You can set up your Cash Receipts journal with more columns if you have accounts with frequent cash receipts. The big advantage to having individual columns for active accounts is that, when you total the columns at the end of the month, the total for the active accounts is the only thing you have to add to the General Ledger accounts, which is a lot less work then entering every Sales transaction individually in the General Ledger account. This approach saves a lot of time posting to accounts that involve multiple transactions every month. Individual transactions listed in the General Credits column each need to be entered into the affected accounts separately, which takes a lot more time that just entering a column total.

As you can see in Figure 5-1, the top right-hand corner of the journal page has a place for the person who prepared the journal to sign and date and for someone who approves the entries to sign and date as well. If your business deals with cash, it's always a good idea to have a number of checks and balances to ensure that cash is properly handled and recorded. For more safety measures, see Chapter 7.

Following outgoing cash

Cash going out of the business to pay bills, salaries, rents, and other necessities has its own journal, the Cash Disbursements journal. This journal is the point of original entry for all business cash paid out to others.

No business person likes to see money go out the door, but imagine what creditors, vendors, and others would think if they didn't get the money they were due. Put yourself in their shoes: Would you be able to buy needed supplies if other companies didn't pay what they owed you? Not a chance.

You need to track your outgoing cash just as carefully as you track incoming cash (see the preceding section). Each entry in the Cash Disbursements journal must not only indicate how much cash was paid out but also designate which account will be decreased in value because of the cash disbursal. For example, cash disbursed to pay bills is credited to the Cash account (which goes down in value) and is debited to the account from which the bill or loan is paid, such as Accounts Payable. The debit decreases the amount still owed in the Accounts Payable account.

In the Cash Disbursements journal, the Cash account is always the credit, and the debits vary depending upon the outstanding debts to be paid. Figure 5-2 shows you what a series of transactions look like when they're entered in a Cash Disbursements journal.

Figure 5-2: The first point of entry for outgoing cash is the Cash Disbursements journal.

Cheesecake Shop
Cash Disbursements Journal
March 2014

Date	Account Debited	Check #	PR	General Debit	Account Payable Debit	Salaries Debit	Cash Credit
3/1	Rent	1065		$800			$800
3/3	Accounts Payable - Henry's	1066			$500		$500
3/3	Accounts Payable - Helen's	1067			$250		$250
3/4	Salaries	1068				$350	$350
3/10	Credit Card Payable - AmBank	1069		$150			$150

The Cash Disbursements journal in Figure 5-2 has eight columns of information:

✔ **Date:** The date of the transaction.

✔ **Account Debited:** The name of the account debited as well as any detail about the reason for the debit.

✔ **Check #:** The number of the check used to pay the debt.

✔ **PR (post reference):** Where the transaction will be posted at the end of the month. This information is filled in at the end of the month when you do the posting to the General Ledger accounts. If the entry to be posted to the accounts is summarized and totaled at the bottom of the page, you can just put a check mark next to the entry in the PR column. For transactions listed in the General Credit or General Debit columns, you should indicate an account number for the account into which the transaction is posted.

✔ **General Debit:** Any transactions that don't have their own columns; these transactions are entered individually into the accounts they impact.

For example, according to Figure 5-2, rent was paid on March 1st and will be indicated by a debit in the Rent Expense.

✔ **Accounts Payable Debit:** Any transactions that are posted to the Accounts Payable account (which tracks bills due).

✔ **Salaries Debit:** Debits to the Salaries expense account, which increase the amount of salaries expenses paid in a particular month.

✔ **Cash Credit:** Anything that's deducted from the Cash account.

You can set up your Cash Disbursements journal with more columns if you have accounts with frequent cash disbursals. For example, in Figure 5-2, the bookkeeper for this fictional company added one column each for Accounts Payable and Salaries because cash for both accounts is disbursed multiple times during the month. Rather than having to list each disbursement in the Accounts Payable and Salaries accounts, she can just total each journal column at the end of the month and add totals to the appropriate accounts. This approach sure saves a lot of time when you're working with your most active accounts.

Managing Sales Like a Pro

Not all sales involve the collection of cash; many stores allow customers to buy products on store credit using a store credit card. (I'm not talking about buying with a bank-issued credit card here; in that case, the bank, not the store or company making the sale, is the one who has to worry about collecting from the customer.)

Instead, store credit comes into play when a customer is allowed to take a store's products without paying immediately because he has an account that's billed monthly. This can be done by using a credit card issued by the store or some other method the company uses to track credit purchases by customers, such as having the customer sign a sales receipt indicating that the amount should be charged to the customer's account.

Sales made on store credit don't involve cash until the customer pays his bill. (In contrast, with credit-card sales, the store gets a cash payment from the card-issuing bank before the customer even pays the credit-card bill.) If your company sells on store credit, the total value of the products bought on any particular day becomes an item for the Accounts Receivable account, which tracks all money due from customers. I talk more about managing accounts receivable in Chapter 9.

Before allowing customers to buy on credit, your company should require customers to apply for credit in advance so that you can check their credit references.

When something's sold on store credit, usually the cashier drafts an invoice for the customer to sign when picking up the product. The invoice lists the items purchased and the total amount due. After getting the customer's signature, the invoice is tracked in both the Accounts Payable account and the customer's individual account.

Transactions for sales made by store credit first enter your books in the Sales journal. Each entry in the Sales journal must indicate the customer's name, the invoice number, and the amount charged.

In the Sales journal, the Accounts Receivable account is debited, which increases in value. The bookkeeper must also remember to make an entry to the customer's account records because the customer has not yet paid for the item and will have to be billed for it. The transaction also increases the value of the Sales account, which is credited.

Figure 5-3 shows a few days' worth of transactions related to store credit.

Figure 5-3:
The first point of entry for sales made on store credit is the Sales journal.

	Cheesecake Shop Sales Journal March 2014				
Date	Customer Account Debited	PR	Invoice Number	Accounts Receivable Debit	Sales Credit
3/1 S. Smith			243	$200	$200
3/1 Charlie's Garage			244	$300	$300
3/3 P. Perry			245	$100	$100
3/3 J. Jones			246	$200	$200

The Sales journal in Figure 5-3 has six columns of information:

- ✔ **Date:** The date of the transaction.

- ✔ **Customer Account Debited:** The name of the customer whose account should be debited.

- ✔ **PR (post reference):** Where the transaction will be posted at the end of the month. This information is filled in at the end of the month when you do the posting to the General Ledger accounts. If the entry to be posted to the accounts is summarized and totaled at the bottom of the page, you can just put a check mark next to the entry in the PR column. For transactions listed in the General Credit or General Debit columns, you should indicate an account number for the account into which the transaction is posted.

- ✔ **Invoice Number:** The invoice number for the purchase.

- ✔ **Accounts Receivable Debit:** Increases to the Accounts Receivable account.

- ✔ **Sales Credit:** Increases to the Sales account.

At the end of the month, the bookkeeper can just total the Accounts Receivable and Sales columns shown in Figure 5-3 and post the totals to those General Ledger accounts. She doesn't need to post all the details because she can always refer back to the Sales journal. However, each invoice noted in the Sales journal must be carefully recorded in each customer's account. Otherwise, the bookkeeper doesn't know who and how much to bill.

Keeping Track of Purchases

Purchases of products to be sold to customers at a later date are a key type of noncash transaction. All businesses must have something to sell, whether they manufacture it themselves or buy a finished product from some other company. Businesses usually make these purchases on credit from the company that makes the product. In this case, the business becomes the customer of another business.

Transactions for purchases bought on credit first enter your books in the Purchases journal. Each entry in the Purchases journal must indicate the vendor from whom the purchase was made, the vendor's invoice number, and the amount charged.

In the Purchases journal, the Accounts Payable account is credited, and the Purchases account is debited, meaning both accounts increase in value. The Accounts Payable account increases because the company now owes more money to creditors, and the Purchases account increases because the amount spent on goods to be sold goes up.

Figure 5-4 shows some store purchase transactions as they appear in the company's Purchases journal.

Figure 5-4:
The first point of entry for purchases bought on credit is the Purchases journal.

Cheesecake Shop
Purchases Journal
March 2014

Date	Vendor Account Credited	PR	Invoice Number	Purchases Debit	Accounts Payable Credit
3/1	Supplies from Henry's		1575	$750	$750
3/3	Packaging Boxes from Barry's		1235	$100	$100
3/5	Paper Goods from Helen's		1745	$75	$75

The Purchases journal in Figure 5-4 has six columns of information:

- ✓ **Date:** The date of the transaction.

- ✓ **Vendor Account Credited:** The name of the vendor from whom the purchases were made.

- ✔ **PR (post reference):** Where information about the transaction will be posted at the end of the month. This information is filled in at the end of the month when you do the posting to the General Ledger accounts. If the entry to be posted to the accounts is summarized and totaled at the bottom of the page, you can just put a check mark next to the entry in the PR column. For transactions listed in the General Credit or General Debit columns, you should indicate an account number for the account into which the transaction is posted.

- ✔ **Invoice Number:** The invoice number for the purchase assigned by the vendor.

- ✔ **Purchases Debit:** Additions to the Purchases account.

- ✔ **Accounts Payable Credit:** Increases to the Accounts Payable account.

At the end of the month, the bookkeeper can just total the Purchases and Accounts Payable columns and post the totals to the corresponding General Ledger accounts. She can refer back to the Purchases journal for details if necessary. However, each invoice should be carefully recorded in each vendor's accounts so that there's a running total of outstanding bills for each vendor. Otherwise, the bookkeeper doesn't know who and how much is owed.

Dealing with Transactions that Don't Fit

Not all your transactions fit in one of the four main journals (Cash Receipts, Cash Disbursements, Sales, and Purchases). If you need to establish other special journals as the original points of entry for transactions, go ahead. The sky's the limit!

If you keep your books the old-fashioned way — on paper — be aware that paper is vulnerable to being mistakenly lost or destroyed. In this case, you may want to consider keeping the number of journals you maintain to a minimum.

For transactions that don't fit in the "big four" journals but don't necessarily warrant the creation of their own journals, you should consider keeping a General Journal for miscellaneous transactions. Using columnar paper similar to what's used for the other four journals, create the following columns:

- ✔ **Date:** The date of the transaction.

- ✔ **Account:** The account impacted by the transaction. More detail is needed here because the General Ledger impacts so many different accounts with so many different types of transactions. For example, you will find only sales transactions in the Sales journal and Purchase transactions in the Purchase journal, but you could find any type of transaction in the General journal affecting many less active accounts.

✔ **PR (post reference):** Where information about the transaction will be posted at the end of the month. This information is filled in at the end of the month when you do the posting to the General Ledger accounts. If the entry to be posted to the accounts is summarized and totaled at the bottom of the page, you can just put a check mark next to the entry in the PR column. For transactions listed in the General Credit or General Debit columns, you should indicate an account number for the account into which the transaction is posted.

✔ **General Debit:** Contains most debits.

✔ **General Credit:** Contains most credits.

If you have certain accounts for which you expect a lot of activity, you can start a column for those accounts, too. In Figure 5-5, I added columns for Accounts Payable and Accounts Receivable. The big advantage of having a separate column for an account is that you'll be able to total that column at the end of the month and just put the total in the General Ledger. You won't have to enter each transaction separately.

Many businesses also add columns for Accounts Receivable and Accounts Payable because those accounts are commonly impacted by noncash transactions.

All the transactions in this General journal are noncash transactions. Cash transactions should go into one of the two cash journals: Cash Receipts (see the section "Keeping track of incoming cash") and Cash Disbursements (see the section "Following outgoing cash").

In a General journal, transactions need to be entered on multiple lines because each transaction impacts at least two accounts (and sometimes more than two). For example, in the General journal shown in Figure 5-5, the first transaction listed is the return of a cheesecake by S. Smith. This return of products sold must be posted to the customer's account as a credit as well as to the Accounts Receivable account. Also, the Sales Return account, where the business tracks all products returned by the customer, has to be debited.

March 5 — Return a portion of purchase from Henry's Bakery Supplies, $200, Debit memo 346. When a business returns a product purchased, it is tracked in the Purchase Return account, which is credited. A debit must also be made to the Accounts Payable account, as well as vendor's account, since less money is now owed. Cash does not change hands with this transaction.

March 5 — H.G. transferred car to business, $10,000. This transaction is posted to the Vehicle asset account and the Capital account in Owner's Equity. Rather than deposit cash into the business, H.G. made his personal vehicle a business asset.

					Accounts	Accounts
				General	General	Payable	Receivable
Date	Account		PR	Debit	Credit	Debit	Credit
3/3	Sales Return			$60			
	S. Smith						$60
	Credit Memo 124						
3/5	Henry's Bakery Supplies					$200	
	Purchase Return				$200		
	Debit Memo 346						
3/5	Vehicles			$10,000			
	Owner Capital				$10,000		
	Transfer of Owner's Vehicle to Business						

Cheesecake Shop
General Journal
March 2014

Figure 5-5:
The point of entry for miscellaneous transactions is the General journal.

In addition to the five columns mentioned above, the General journal in Figure 5-5 has the following two columns:

✔ **Accounts Payable Debit:** Decreases to the Accounts Payable account.

The bookkeeper working with this journal anticipated that many of the company's transactions would impact Accounts Payable. She created this column so that she can subtotal it and make just one entry to the Accounts Payable account in the General Ledger.

✔ **Accounts Receivable Credit:** Decreases to the Accounts Receivable account.

At the end of the month, the bookkeeper can just total this journal's Accounts Payable and Accounts Receivable columns and post those totals to the corresponding General Ledger accounts. All transaction details remain in the General journal. However, because the miscellaneous transactions impact General Ledger accounts, the transactions need to be posted to each affected account separately (see "Posting Journal Information to Accounts").

Posting Journal Information to Accounts

When you close your books at the end of the month, you summarize all the journals — that is, you total the columns and post the information to update all the accounts involved.

Posting journal pages is a four-step process:

1. **Number each journal page at the top if it isn't already numbered.**

2. Total any column that's not titled General Debit or General Credit. Any transactions recorded in the General Debit or General Credit columns need to be recorded individually in the General Ledger.

3. Post the entries to the General Ledger account. Each transaction in the General Credit or General Debit column must be posted separately. You just need to post totals to the General Ledger for the other columns in which transactions for more active accounts were entered in the General journal. List the date and journal page number as well as the amount of the debit or credit, so you can quickly find the entry for the original transaction if you need more details.

The General Ledger account only shows debit or credit (whichever is appropriate to the transaction). Only the journals have both sides of a transaction. (I show you how to work with General Ledger accounts in Chapter 4.)

4. In the PR column of the journal, record information about where the entry is posted. If the entry to be posted to the accounts is summarized and totaled at the bottom of the page, you can just put a check mark next to the entry in the PR column. For transactions listed in the General Credit or General Debit columns, you should indicate an account number for the account into which the transaction is posted. This process helps you confirm that you've posted all entries in the General Ledger.

Posting to the General Ledger is done at the end of an accounting period as part of the process of closing the accounts. I cover the closing process in greater detail in Chapter 15.

Figure 5-6 shows a summarized journal page, specifically the Cash Receipts journal. You can see that entries that are listed in the Sales Credit and Cash Debit columns on the Cash Receipts journal are just checked in the PR column. Only one entry was placed in the General Credit column, and that entry has an account number in the PR column. Although I don't list all the transactions for the month, which would of course be a much longer list, I do show how you summarize the journal at the end of the month.

As you can see in Figure 5-6, after summarizing the Cash Receipts journal, there are only four General Ledger accounts (General Credit, Accounts Receivable Credit, Sales Credit, and Cash Debit) and three customer accounts (S. Smith, J. Jones, and P. Perry) into which you need to post entries. Even better, the entries balance: $2,900 in debits and $2,900 in credits! (The customer accounts total $500, which is good news because it's the same amount credited to Accounts Receivable. The Accounts Receivable account is decreased by $500 because payments were received, as is the amount due from the individual customer accounts.)

Cheesecake Shop
Cash Receipts Journal
March 2014

Date	Account Credited	PR	General Credit	Accounts Receivable Credit	Sales Credit	Cash Debit
3/1	Sales	x			$300	$300
3/2	Sales	x			$250	$250
3/3	Ck. 121 from S. Smith	x		$200		$200
3/3	Sales	x			$150	$150
3/4	Owner Capital	3300	$1,500			$1,500
3/5	Ck 125 from J. Jones	x		$100		$100
3/5	Ck 567 from P. Perry	x		$200		$200
3/5	Sales	x			$200	$200
	March Summary		$1,500	$500	$900	$2,900

Figure 5-6:
Summary
of Cash
Receipts
journal
entries after
the first five
days.

Simplifying Your Journaling with Computerized Accounting

The process of posting first to the journals and then to the General Ledger and individual customer or vendor accounts can be a very time-consuming job. Luckily, most businesses today use computerized accounting software, so the same information doesn't need to be entered so many times. The computer does the work for you.

If you're working with a computerized accounting software package (see Chapter 6), you only have to enter a transaction once. All the detail that normally needs to be entered into one of the journal pages, one of the General Ledger accounts, and customer, vendor and other accounts is posted automatically. Voilà!

The method by which you initially enter your transaction varies depending on the type of transaction. To show you what's involved in making entries into a computerized accounting system, the following figures show one entry each from the Cash Receipts journal (see Figure 5-7 for a customer payment), the Cash Disbursements journal (see Figure 5-8 for a list of bills to be paid), and the Sales journal (see Figure 5-9 for an invoice). (The screenshots are all from QuickBooks, a popular computerized bookkeeping system.)

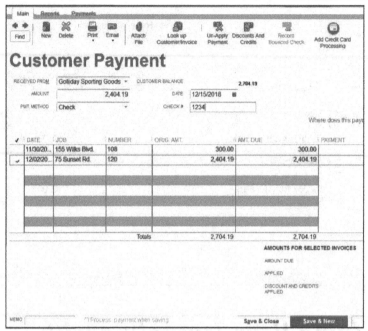

Figure 5-7:
Customer
Payment
entry form.

As you can see in Figure 5-7, to enter the customer payment, all you need to do is type the customer's name in the box labeled Received From. All outstanding invoices then appear. You can put a check mark next to the invoices to be paid, indicate the payment method (in this case, a check), enter the check number, and click Save & Close.

When you use a software package to track your cash receipts, the following accounts are automatically updated:

✔ The Cash account is debited the appropriate amount.

✔ The Accounts Receivable account is credited the appropriate amount.

✔ The corresponding customer account is credited the appropriate amount.

That's much simpler than adding the transaction to the Cash Receipts journal, closing out the journal at the end of the month, adding the transactions to the accounts impacted by the cash receipts, and then (finally!) closing out the books.

Cash disbursements are even easier than cash receipts when you've got a computerized system on your side. For example when paying bills (see Figure 5-8), all you need to do is go to the bill paying screen for QuickBooks. In this example, all the bills due are listed, so all you need to do is select the bills you want to pay, and the system automatically sets the payments in motion.

	DATE DUE	VENDOR	REF. NO.	DISC. DATE	AMT. DUE	DISC. USED	CREDITS USED	AMT. T
	09/01/2019	Conner Garde...			127.20	0.00	0.00	
	12/25/2019	Townley Insura...			427.62	0.00	0.00	
	12/26/2019	Great Statewid...	16		899.12	0.00	0.00	
	12/27/2019	Nolan Hardwar...			610.00	0.00	0.00	
	12/29/2019	Cal Gas & Ele...	12/03		137.50	0.00	0.00	
	01/12/2020	Robert Carr M...			196.25	0.00	0.00	
	01/14/2020	Cal Telephone	12/03		45.00	0.00	0.00	
				Totals	2,242.69	0.00	0.00	

Figure 5-8: List of bills to be paid.

The bill-paying perks of this system include the following:

- ✔ Checks can be automatically printed by the software package.

- ✔ Each of the vendor accounts is updated to show that payment is made.

- ✔ The Accounts Payable account is debited the appropriate amount for your transaction, which decreases the amount due to vendors.

- ✔ The Cash account is credited the appropriate amount for your transaction, which decreases the amount of cash available (because it's designated for use to pay corresponding bills).

When you make the necessary entries into your computerized accounting system for the information that would normally be found in a Sales journal (for example, when a customer pays for your product on credit), you can automatically create an invoice for the purchase. Figure 5-9 shows what that invoice looks like when generated by a computerized accounting system. Adding the customer name in the box marked "Customer" automatically fills in all the necessary customer information. The date appears automatically, and the system assigns a customer invoice number. You add the quantity and select the type of product bought in the "Item Code" section, and the rest of the invoice is calculated automatically. When the invoice is final, you can print it and send it off to the customer.

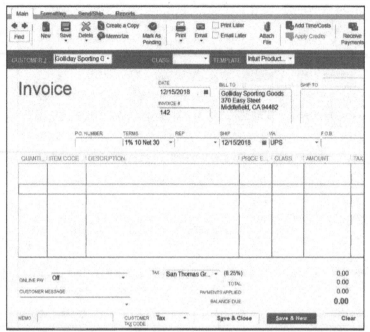

Figure 5-9:
Customer
Invoice
entry form.

Once the customer name is chosen, the system automatically fills in the billing information. If sales taxes are indicated in the customer's information, then those figures are automatically calculated as well. In Figure 5-9, you can see the sales tax percentage of 8.25%. All the bookkeeper needs to do is add shipping information, the P.O. number, and the items ordered. The invoice is then automatically calculated.

Filling out the invoice in the accounting system also updates the affected accounts:

✔ The Accounts Receivable account is debited the appropriate amount, which increases the amount due from customers by that amount.

✔ The Sales account is credited the appropriate amount, which increases the revenue received by that amount.

✔ The invoice is added to the customer's outstanding bills so that when the customer makes a payment, the outstanding invoice appears on the payment screen.

Chapter 6

Computer Options for Your Bookkeeping

In This Chapter
▶ Finding the right accounting software for your business
▶ Getting your computerized books up and running

Some small business owners who have been around a while still do things the old-fashioned way — they keep their books in paper journals and ledgers. However, in this age of technology and instant information, the majority of today's businesses computerize their books.

Not only is computerized bookkeeping easier, it minimizes the chance of errors because most of the work done to a computerized system's ledgers and journals (see Chapters 4 and 5, respectively) involves inputting data on forms that can be understood even by someone without training in accounting or bookkeeping. The person entering the information doesn't need to know whether something is a debit or credit (see Chapter 2 for an explanation of the difference) because the computerized system takes care of everything.

Mobile accounting is also becoming popular, with major accounting software packages now available as online tools that can be accessed from any mobile device. Companies with multiple locations, if they purchase an online accounting software package for multiple users, can allow employees to log on from anywhere and access a central accounting system.

In this chapter, I explore the three top accounting software packages for small businesses, discuss the basics of setting up your own computerized books, talk about how you can customize a program for your business, and give you some pointers on converting your manual bookkeeping system into a computerized one.

Surveying Your Software Options

More than 50 different types of accounting software programs are on the market, and all are designed to computerize your bookkeeping. The more sophisticated ones target specific industry needs, such as food services or utilities, and can cost thousands of dollars. To check out those options, visit http://findaccountingsoftware.com, where you can browse for accounting software that's grouped by industry — 34 industries to be exact, from Agriculture to Food Distribution to Utilities.

Luckily, as a small businessperson, you probably don't need all the bells and whistles offered by the top-of-the-line programs. Instead, the three software programs that I review in this chapter can meet the needs of most small business people. Using one of the three systems I recommend, you can get started with an initial investment of as little as $40. It may not be fancy, but basic computerized accounting software can do a fine job of helping you keep your books. And you can always upgrade to a more expensive program, if needed, as your business grows.

The three programs that meet any small business's basic bookkeeping needs are Bookkeeper, QuickBooks, and Sage 50 (formerly known as Peachtree Accounting). The most affordable of the three is Bookkeeper, which I've seen priced as low as $31 at various Internet sites. QuickBooks and Sage 50 both offer simple systems. QuickBooks Online Simple Start and Sage 50 First Step can get you started for under $100. But if you can afford it, I recommend that you step up at least to QuickBooks Pro 2014 or Sage 50 Pro. The costs vary depending on the number of people you want to have access to the software, but you would need to expect to pay at least $200 more.

 Accounting software packages are updated almost every year. That's because tax laws and laws involving many other aspects of operating a business change so often. In addition, computer software companies are always improving their products to make computerized accounting programs more user-friendly, so be sure that you always buy the most current version of an accounting software package.

 No matter what computerized system you choose, always be sure that you set up a daily backup plan to save your data in another location. This may be an external hard drive or an online backup system. That way if your computer crashes you won't lose all your accounting data.

Bookkeeper 2014

Bookkeeper 2014 (www.avanquest.com/USA/software/bookkeeper-2014-501538) is a cost-effective choice for bookkeeping software if you're just starting up and don't have sophisticated bookkeeping or accounting needs. You can prepare invoices, pay bills, write checks, manage inventory, track receivables, bill customers, and prepare payroll. But there is no online version offered, and it only receives minor updates periodically.

The program includes accounting templates for things like sales orders, quotes, receipts, and other basic needs. More than 125 reports and charts are included that you can customize to your accounting needs.

You can purchase add-ons for processing payroll and credit-card processing. However, the add-on features don't work as well as features that are included in an original software package, such as the ones included as part of QuickBooks.

Bookkeeping 2014 does not offer the ability to scale up, which means as your business grows, you will need to find another package for your business needs. So consider this program only if you plan to keep your business small with only basic accounting needs.

Sage 50 Pro

Sage 50 (`http://na.sage.com/us/sage-50-accounting/pro`) is an excellent software package for your bookkeeping and accounting needs, but it's definitely not recommended if you're a novice. You need to be familiar with accounting jargon just to use the Sage 50 system, and its interface isn't as user-friendly as the ones for Bookkeeper and QuickBooks. I've used this program and didn't like it much because the user interface took much longer to learn and was not as intuitive as QuickBooks, even for someone who knows accounting jargon.

To use Sage 50, you definitely need to know your way around the General Ledger and be comfortable with accounting terms such as Account Reconciliation, Accounts Payable, and Cash Receipts journal. Although Sage 50 offers training options inside the program, it lacks the sophistication of the excellent learning center now offered by QuickBooks. So if you're a beginner, which is probably the case because you bought this book, I don't recommend that you start with this software.

Sage 50 offers inventory-management tools that are the best in its class. New versions of the software even automatically generate purchase orders when inventory reaches a user-specified level. You can also export Sage 50 customer, vendor, and employee databases into Microsoft Word and use the data with Word's mail-merge feature to send emails or letters.

Sage 50 Pro costs around $230, but you may be able to find it cheaper by searching the Internet. Payroll processing is an extra $250 for up to 50 employees. If you want to be able to integrate your shipping with UPS, have more than one user, control users by screen-level security, have advanced inventory or job costing capabilities, or have an audit trail of your work, you need to start with Sage 50 Premium, which starts at around $450. (Multi-user capability for up to five users is a whopping $1,200!) Enterprise and cloud solutions are also available for Sage 50 Premium at additional cost if you want to have mobile access.

Sage 50 offers a utility that makes it easy to use to convert data from Intuit's QuickBooks. You can also import files from Quicken. There's no conversion tool for Microsoft Excel data, but you can import and export Excel files into the program without problems. Check out Jane Kelly's *Sage 50 Accounts for Dummies* (Wiley, 2012) to get a better feel for this program, its capabilities, and how to use it.

QuickBooks Pro

QuickBooks (`http://quickbooks.intuit.com/pro/`) offers the best of both worlds: an easy user interface (for the novice) and extensive bookkeeping and accounting features (for the experienced bookkeeper or accountant). That's why I chose to use QuickBooks to demonstrate various bookkeeping functions throughout this book. Yes, it's my favorite bookkeeping software, but I'm not alone — more small business owners today use QuickBooks than any other small business accounting software package. It is the number one software on the Top Ten Reviews site as well (`http://accounting-software-review.toptenreviews.com/small-business/`). Note that you can check out reviews about other top ten accounting programs at this website.

QuickBooks offers the novice an extensive learning center, which walks you through every type of key transaction with an interactive program that not only shows you how to do the function but also explains the basics of bookkeeping. You don't have to use the tutorial, but the option pops up when you do a task for the first time, so the choice is always yours. You also can go back to the learning center to review at any time. For additional information on this software, check out *QuickBooks 2014 For Dummies* (Wiley, 2013) by Stephen L. Nelson.

Most people have a love/hate relationship with Intuit support (Intuit's the company that makes QuickBooks). Personally, I've had good support experiences not only with QuickBooks but also with its other popular software packages, such as TurboTax and Quicken. But I also know others who have complained loudly about support problems.

QuickBooks Online Simple Start, priced around $50, can meet most of your bookkeeping and accounting needs. The $50 price includes an online monthly subscription that gives you mobile access from your PC, Mac, iPad/iPhone device, or Android phone or tablet. If you want to integrate your bookkeeping with a point-of-sale package, which integrates cash register sales, you need to get QuickBooks Pro, which sells for around $199 for a single user and $650 for up to three users. You also need to upgrade to QuickBooks Pro if you want to do inventory management, generate purchase orders from estimates or sales orders, do job costing and estimates, automatically create a budget, or integrate your data for use with Microsoft Word and Excel programs. Payroll services also can be added for an additional cost, depending on the size of your payroll.

Add-ons and fees

All the accounting programs recommended in this section offer add-ons and features you're likely to need:

✔ **Tax updates:** If you have employees and want up-to-date tax information and forms to do your payroll using your accounting software, you need to buy an update each year.

✔ **Online credit-card processing and electronic bill paying:** Having the capabilities to perform these tasks means additional fees. In fact, QuickBooks advertises its add-ons

in these areas throughout its system; you can see the advertisements pop up on a number of screens.

✔ **Point-of-sale software:** This add-on helps you integrate your sales at the cash register with your accounting software.

Before signing on for one of the add-ons be sure you understand what the fees will be. Usually, you're advised of the additional costs whenever you try to do anything that incurs extra fees.

QuickBooks is the most versatile software if you plan to use other software packages along with it. It can share data with more than 325 popular business software applications. Sales, customer, and financial data can be shared easily too, so you don't have to enter that information twice. To find out if QuickBooks can share data with the business software applications you're currently using or plan to use, call Intuit at 888-729-1996.

Setting Up Your Computerized Books

After you pick your software, the hard work is done because actually setting up the package will probably take you less time than researching your options and picking which one to get. All three packages I just discussed have good start-up tutorials to help you set up the books. QuickBooks even has an interactive interview that asks questions about all aspects of how you want to run your business and then sets up what you'll need based on your answers.

Bookkeeper, Sage 50, and QuickBooks all produce a number of sample Charts of Accounts (see Chapter 3) that automatically appear after you choose the type of business you plan to run and upon which industry that business falls. All three programs ask you to enter a company name, address, and tax identification number to get started. Then they generate a Chart of Accounts for the business type selected. Start with one of the charts offered by the software, like the one in Figure 6-1, and then tweak it to your business's needs.

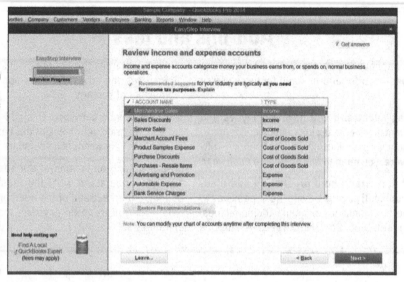

Figure 6-1:
As part of
the initial
interview,
QuickBooks
generates
a Chart of
Accounts
based on
the type of
business
you have.

If you're operating as a sole proprietor or your business is based on a part-nership and you don't have a federal tax ID for the business, you can use your Social Security number. You then select an accounting period (see Figure 6-2). If the calendar year is your accounting period, you don't have to change anything. But if you operate your business based on another period of 12 months, such as September 1 to August 31, you must enter that information.

If you don't change your accounting period to match how you plan to develop your financial statements, then you have to delete the business from the system and start over.

After you set up your business, you can customize the software so that it matches your business's needs.

Fiscal year

Many retail businesses don't close their books at the end of December because the holiday season is not a good time to be closing out for the year. With gift cards and other new ways to give gifts, purchases after the holiday can be very active. So, many retail businesses operate on a fiscal year of February 1 to January 31, so they can close the books well after the holiday season ends.

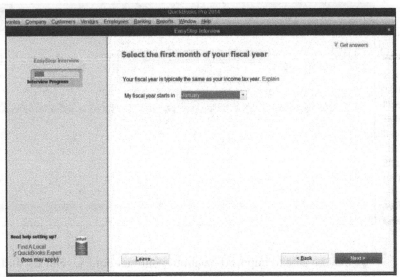

Figure 6-2:
QuickBooks asks whether you plan to operate on a calendar year or fiscal year. If on a fiscal year, you choose the month that you start your business operations each year.

Customizing software to match your operations

With the basics set up (see the preceding section), you can customize the software to fit your business's operations. For example, you're able to pick the type of invoices and other business forms you want to use.

This is also the time to input information about your bank accounts and other key financial data (see Figure 6-3). Your main business bank account is the one that should be used for the first account listed in your software program, Cash in Checking.

After entering your bank and other financial information, you enter data unique to your business. If you want to use the program's budgeting features, you enter your budget information before entering other data. Then you add your vendor and customer accounts so that when you start entering transactions, the information is already in the system. If you don't have any outstanding bills or customer payments due, you can wait and enter vendor and customer information as the need arises.

If you have payments to be made or money to be collected from customers, be sure to input that information so your system is ready when it comes time to pay the bills or input a customer payment. Also, you don't want to forget to pay a bill or collect from a customer!

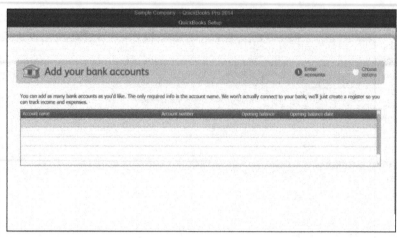

Figure 6-3:
QuickBooks
collects
informa-
tion about
your bank
accounts
as part of
the initial
interview.

You may be able to import data about your customers, vendors, and employees from software packages you're currently using to track that information, such as Microsoft Excel or Access. Full instructions for importing data comes with the software program you choose.

Don't panic about entering everything into your computerized system right away. All programs make it very easy to add customers, vendors, and employees at any time.

Other information collected includes the type of accounting method you'll be using — either cash-basis or accrual accounting. (I talk about both in Chapter 2.) You also need to enter information about whether or not you collect sales taxes from your customers and, if you do, the sales tax rates. Also, you can pick a format for your invoices, set up payroll data, and make arrangements for how you want to pay bills.

Converting your manual bookkeeping to a computerized system

If you're converting a manual bookkeeping system to a computerized system, your conversion will take a bit more time than just starting fresh because you need to be sure your new system starts with information that matches your current books. The process for entering your initial data varies depending on the software you've chosen, so I don't go into detail about that process here. To ensure that you properly convert your bookkeeping system, use the information that comes with your software; read through the manual, review the startup suggestions made as you set up the system, and pick the methods that best match your style of operating.

The best time to convert is at the end of an accounting period. That way, you won't have to do a lot of extra work adding transactions that already occurred during a period. For example, if you decide to computerize your accounting system on March 15, you'd have to add all the transactions that occurred between March 1 and March 15 into your new system. It's just easier to wait until April 1 to get started even if you buy the software on March 15. While you can convert to a computerized accounting system at the end of a month, your best time to do it is at the end of a calendar or fiscal year. Otherwise, you have to input data for all the months of the year that have passed.

Whenever you decide to start your computerized bookkeeping, use the data from your trial balance that you used to close the books at the end of most recent accounting period. (I explain how to prepare a trial balance in Chapter 16.) In the computerized system, enter the balances for each of the accounts in your trial balance. Asset, liability, and equity accounts should have carry-over balances, but income and expense accounts should have zero balances.

Of course, if you're starting a new business, you won't have a previous trial balance. Then you just enter any balances you might have in your cash accounts, any assets your business may own as it starts up, and any liabilities that your business may already owe relating to startup expenses. You also add any contributions from owners that were made to get the business started in the Equity accounts.

After you enter all the appropriate data, run a series of financial reports, such as an income statement and balance sheet, to be sure the data is entered and formatted the way you like it. It's a lot easier to change formatting when the system isn't chock-full of data.

You need to be sure that you've entered the right numbers, so verify that the new accounting system's financial reports match what you created manually. If the numbers are different, now's the time to figure out why. Otherwise the reports you do at the end of the accounting period will be wrong. If the numbers don't match, don't assume the only place an error could be is in the data entered. You may find that the error is in the reports you developed manually. Of course, check your entries first, but if the income statement and balance sheet still don't look right, double-check your trial balances as well.

Chapter 7

Controlling Your Books, Your Records, and Your Money

. . . .

In This Chapter

▶ Protecting your business's cash

▶ Maintaining proper paperwork

▶ Divvying up responsibilities

▶ Insuring your cash handlers

. . . .

*E*very business takes in cash in some form. Whether in the form of dollar bills, checks, credit cards, or electronic payment, it's all eventually deposited as cash into the business's accounts. Before you take in that first penny, controlling that cash and making sure none of it walks out the door improperly should be your first concern as a businessperson.

Finding the right level of cash control while at the same time allowing your employees the flexibility to sell your products or services and provide ongoing customer service can be a monumental task. If you don't have enough controls, you risk theft or embezzlement. Yet if you have too many controls, employees may miss sales or anger customers.

In this chapter, I explain the basic protections you need to put in place to be sure all cash coming into or going out of your business is clearly documented and controlled. I also review the type of paperwork you need to document the use of cash and other business assets. Finally, I tell you how to organize your staff to properly control the flow of your assets and insure yourself against possible misappropriation of those assets.

Putting Controls on Your Business's Cash

Think about how careful you are with your personal cash. You find various ways to protect how you carry it around, you dole it out carefully to your family members, and you may even hide cash in a safe place in the house just in case you need it for unexpected purposes.

If you're that protective of your cash when you're the only one who handles it, consider the vulnerability of business cash. After all, you aren't the only one handling the cash for your business. You have some employees encountering incoming cash at cash registers and others opening the mail and finding checks for orders to purchase products or pay bills and checks from other sources. And don't forget that employees may need petty cash to pay for mail sent COD (Collect on Delivery) or to pay for other unexpected, low-cost needs.

If you were around to watch every transaction in which cash enters your business, you wouldn't have time to do the things you need to do to grow your business. If your business is small enough, you can maintain control of cash going out by signing all checks, but as soon as the business grows, you may not have time for that either.

You can drive yourself crazy with worry about all this cash flow, but the truth is that just putting in place the proper controls for your cash can help protect your business's family jewels. Cash flows through your business in four key ways:

✔ Deposits and payments into and out of your checking accounts

✔ Deposits and payments into and out of your savings accounts

✔ Petty cash funds in critical locations where fast cash may be needed

✔ Transactions made in your cash registers

The following sections cover some key controls for each of these cash flow points.

Checking accounts

Almost every dime that comes into your business flows through your business's checking account (at least that's what *should* happen). Whether it's cash collected at your cash registers, payments received in the mail, cash used to fill the cash registers, petty cash accounts, payments sent out to pay business obligations, or any other cash need, this cash enters and exits your checking account. That's why your checking account is your main tool for protecting your cash flow.

Choosing the right bank

Finding the right bank to help you set up your checking account and the controls that limit access to that account is crucial. When evaluating your banking options, ask yourself the following questions:

✔ Does this bank have a branch that's conveniently located to my business?

- ✔ Does this bank operate at times when I need it most?

- ✔ Does this bank offer secure ways to deposit cash even when the bank is closed?

  Most banks have secure drop boxes for cash so you can deposit receipts as quickly as possible at the end of the business day rather than secure the cash overnight yourself.

Visit local bank branches yourself, and check out the type of business services each bank offers. Pay particular attention to

- ✔ The type of personal attention you receive.

- ✔ What type of charges may be tacked on for this personal attention.

- ✔ How questions are handled.

Some banks require business account holders to call a centralized line for assistance rather than depend on local branches. Some banks are even adding charges today if you use a teller rather than an ATM (automatic teller machine). Other banks charge for every transaction, whether it's a deposit, withdrawal, or a check. Many have charges that differ for business accounts, and most have charges on printing checks. If you're planning to accept credit cards, compare the services offered for that as well.

Deciding on types of checks

After you choose your bank, you need to consider what type of checks you want to use in your business. For example, you need different checks depending upon whether you handwrite each check or print checks from your computerized accounting system.

If you plan to write your checks, you'll most likely use a business voucher check in a three-ring binder; this type of check consists of a voucher on the left and a check on the right (see Figure 7-1). This arrangement provides the best control for manual checks because each check and voucher are numbered. When a check is written, the voucher should be filled out with details about the date, the check's recipient, and the purpose of the check. The voucher also has a space to keep a running total of your balance in the account.

If you plan to print checks from your computerized accounting system, you'll need to order checks that match that system's programming. Each computer software program has a unique template for printing checks. Figure 7-2 shows a common layout for business voucher checks printed by your computerized accounting system. You can see there are actually three sections in a blank computerized check: the check in the middle with two relatively blank sections on either side.

Figure 7-1:
A business
voucher
check is
used by
many busi-
nesses
that manu-
ally write
out their
checks.

Check samples courtesy of Deluxe.com

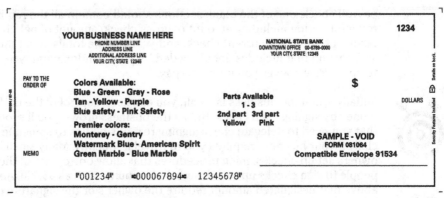

YOUR BUSINESS NAME HERE

PHONE NUMBER LINE
ADDRESS LINE
ADDITIONAL ADDRESS LINE
YOUR CITY, STATE 12345

PAY TO THE
ORDER OF

Colors Available:
Blue - Green - Gray - Rose
Tan - Yellow - Purple
Blue safety - Pink Safety
Premier colors:
Monterey - Gentry
Watermark Blue - American Spirit
Green Marble - Blue Marble

MEMO

NATIONAL STATE BANK
DOWNTOWN OFFICE 00-6789-0000
YOUR CITY, STATE 12345

Parts Available
1 - 3
2nd part 3rd part
Yellow   Pink

$

DOLLARS

SAMPLE - VOID
FORM 081064
Compatible Envelope 91534

1234

⑃"001234⑃" ⑈000067894⑈ 12345678⑃"

YOUR BUSINESS NAME HERE   1234

YOUR BUSINESS NAME HERE   1234

Figure 7-2:
Computer-
printed
checks
usually pre-
print the
business's
name. This
check is
compat-
ible with
QuickBooks.

Check samples courtesy of Deluxe.com

For one of the blank sections, you set up your computer accounting system
to print out the detail you'd expect to find on a manual voucher — the date,
name of the recipient, and purpose of the check. You keep this stub as a control for check use. In the other blank section, you print the information that
the recipient needs. For example, if it's a check to pay an outstanding invoice,
you include all information the vendor needs to properly credit that invoice,
such as the amount, the invoice number, and your account number. If it's a

payroll check, one of the blank sections should contain all the required payroll information including amount of gross check, amount of net check, taxes taken out, totals for current check, and year-to-date totals. Send the check and portion that includes detail needed by your vendor, employee, or other recipient to whoever you intend to pay.

Initially, when the business is small, you can keep control of the outflow of money by signing each check. But as the business grows, you'll probably find that you need to delegate check-signing responsibilities to someone else, especially if your business requires you to travel frequently. Many small business owners set up check-signing procedures that allow one or two of their staff people to sign checks up to a designated amount, such as $5,000. Any checks above that designated amount require the owner's or the signature of an employee and a second designated person, such as an officer of the company.

Arranging deposits to the checking account

Of course, you aren't just withdrawing from your business's checking account (that would be a big problem). You also need to deposit money into that account, and you want to be sure your deposit slips contain all the needed detail as well as documentation to back up the deposit information. Most banks provide printed deposit slips with all the necessary detail to be sure the money is deposited in the appropriate account. They also usually provide you with a "for deposit only" stamp that includes the account number for the back of the checks. (If you don't get that stamp from the bank, be sure to have one made as soon as possible.)

Whoever opens your business mail should be instructed to use that "for deposit only" stamp immediately on the back of any check received in the mail. Stamping "for deposit only" on the back of a check makes it a lot harder for anyone to use that check for other than its intended business purposes. (I talk more about controls for incoming cash in the "Dividing staff responsibilities" section, later in this chapter.) If you get both personal and business checks sent to the same address, you need to set up some instructions for the person opening the mail regarding how to differentiate the types of checks and how each type of check should be handled to best protect your incoming cash, whether for business or personal purposes.

To secure incoming cash even more carefully, some businesses set up lock box services with a bank. Customers or others sending checks to the business mail checks to a post office box number that goes directly to the bank, and a bank employee opens and deposits the checks right into the business's account.

You may think that making bank deposits is as easy as 1-2-3, but when it comes to business deposits and multiple checks, things get a bit more complicated. To properly make deposits to your business's checking account, follow these steps:

1. **Record on the deposit slip the numbers of all checks being deposited as well as the total cash being deposited.**

2. **Make photocopies of all checks being deposited so that you have a record in case something gets lost or misplaced at the bank.**

3. **After you make the deposit, attach the copies of all the checks to the deposit receipt and add any detail regarding the source of the deposited cash; file everything in your daily bank folder.**

   (I talk more about filing in the section "Keeping the Right Paperwork," later in this chapter.)

Savings accounts

Some businesses find they have more cash than they need to meet their immediate plans. Rather than keep that extra cash in a non-interest bearing account, many businesses open a savings account to store the extra cash stash.

If you're a small business owner with few employees, you'll probably be the one to control the flow of money into and out of your savings account. As you grow and find that you need to delegate the responsibility for the business's savings, be sure to think carefully about who gets access and how you will document the flow of funds into and out of the savings account.

Petty cash accounts

Every business needs unexpected cash on almost a weekly basis. Whether it's money to pay the postman when he brings a letter or package COD, money to buy a few emergency stamps to get the mail out, or money for some office supplies needed before the next delivery, businesses need to keep some cash on hand, called *petty cash,* for unexpected expenses.

You certainly don't want to have a lot of cash sitting around in the office, but you should keep $50 to $100 in a petty cash box. If you find that you're faced with cash expenses more or less often than you initially expected, you can adjust the amount kept in petty cash accordingly.

No matter how much you keep in petty cash, be sure you set up a good control system that requires anyone who uses the cash to write a voucher that specifies how much was used and why. If possible, you should also ask that a cash receipt from the store or post office, for example, be attached to the voucher in order to justify the cash withdrawal. In most cases, a staff person buys something for the business and then gets reimbursed for that expense. If the expense is small enough, you can reimburse it by using the petty cash fund. If the expense is more than a few dollars, you'd likely ask the person to fill out an expense account form and get reimbursed by check. Petty cash usually is used for minor expenses of $5 to $10 or less.

The best control for petty cash is to pick one person in the office to manage the use of petty cash. Before giving that person more cash, he or she should be able to prove the absence of cash used and why it was used.

Cash registers

Have you ever gone into a business and tried to pay with a large bill only to find out the cashier can't make change? It's frustrating, but it happens in many businesses, especially when they don't carefully monitor the money in their cash registers. Most businesses empty cash registers each night and put any cash not being deposited in the bank that night into a safe. Some businesses today aren't even using traditional cash registers. They use portable devices to take orders and then a cash drawer to manage cash receipts and disbursements. Even if your business is using something other than a traditional cash register, the basics of cash handling remain the same.

Many businesses instruct their cashiers to periodically deposit their cash in a company safe throughout the day and get a paper voucher to show the cash deposited. These daytime deposits minimize the cash held in the cash draw in case the store is the victim of a robbery.

All these types of controls are necessary parts of modern business operations, but they can have consequences that make customers angry. Most customers will just walk out the door and not come back if they can't buy what they want using the bills they have on hand.

At the beginning of the day, cashiers usually start out with a set amount of cash in the register or cash drawer. As they collect money and give out change, the register records the transactions. At the end of the day, the cashier must count out the amount of change left in the register or cash drawer, run a copy of all transactions that passed through that register, and total the cash collected. Then the cashier must prove that the amount of cash remaining in that register or cash drawer totals the amount of cash at the beginning of the day plus the amount of cash collected during the day. After the cashier balances the register or cash drawer, the staff person in charge of cash deposits (usually the store manager or someone on the accounting or bookkeeping staff) takes all cash out except the amount that will be needed for the next day and deposits it in the bank. (I talk more about separation of staff duties in the section "Dividing staff responsibilities," later in this chapter.)

In addition to having the proper amount of cash on hand necessary to give customers the change they need, you also must make sure that your cashiers are giving the right amount of change and actually recording all sales on their cash registers or other portable devices. Keeping an eye on cashier activities is good business practice, but it's also a way to protect cash theft by your employees. There are three ways cashiers can pocket some extra cash:

✔ **They don't record the sale and instead pocket the cash.** The best deterrent to this type of theft is supervision. You can decrease the likelihood of theft through unrecorded sales by printing up sales tickets that the cashier must use to enter a sale and open the cash drawer. If cash register transactions don't match sales receipts, then the cashier must show a voided transaction for the missing ticket or explain why the cash drawer was opened without a ticket.

✔ **They don't provide a sales receipt and instead pocket the cash.** In this scenario the cashier neglects to give a sales receipt to one customer in line. The cashier gives the next customer the unused sales receipt but doesn't actually record the second transaction in the cash register or other mobile device. Instead, he or she just pockets the cash. In the company's books, the second sale never took place. The customer whose sale wasn't recorded has a valid receipt though it may not match exactly what he bought, so he likely won't notice any problem unless he wants to return something later. Your best defense against this type of deception is to post a sign reminding all customers that they should get a receipt for all purchases and that the receipt is required to get a refund or exchange. Providing numbered sales receipts that include a duplicate copy can also help prevent this problem; cashiers need to produce the duplicates at the end of the day when proving the amount of cash flow that passed through their registers.

In addition to protection from theft by cashiers, the printed sales receipt system can be used to carefully monitor and prevent shoplifters from getting money for merchandise they never bought. For example, suppose a shoplifter took a blouse out of a store, as well as some blank sales receipts. The next day the shoplifter comes back with the blouse and one of the stolen sales receipts filled out as though the blouse had actually been purchased the day before. You can spot the fraud because that sales receipt is part of a numbered batch of sales receipts that you've already identified as missing or stolen. You can quickly identify that the customer never paid for the merchandise and call the police.

✔ **They record a false credit voucher and keep the cash for themselves.** In this case the cashier wrote up a credit voucher for a nonexistent customer and then pocketed the cash themselves. Most stores control this problem by using a numbered credit voucher system, so each credit can be carefully monitored with some detail that proves it's based on a previous customer purchase, such as a sales receipt. Also, stores usually require that a manager reviews the reason for the credit voucher, whether a return or exchange, and approves the transaction before cash or credit is given. When the bookkeeper records the sales return in the books, the number for the credit voucher is recorded with the transaction so that she can easily find the detail about that credit voucher if a question is raised later about the transaction.

Even if cashiers don't deliberately pocket cash, they can do so inadvertently by giving the wrong change. If you run a retail outlet, training and supervising your cashiers is a critical task that you must either handle yourself or hand over to a trusted employee.

Keeping the Right Paperwork

When it comes to handling cash, whether you're talking about the cash register, deposits into your checking accounts, or petty cash withdrawals, you can see that a lot of paper changes hands. In order to properly control the movement of cash into and out of your business, careful documentation is key. And don't forget about organization; you need to be able to find that documentation if questions about cash flow arise later.

Monitoring cash flow isn't the only reason you need to keep loads of paperwork. In order to do your taxes and write off business expenses, you have to have receipts for expenses. You also need details about the money you paid to employees and taxes collected for your employees in order to file the proper reports with government entities. (I discuss taxes in Chapter 21 and dealing with the government relating to employee matters in Chapter 11.) Setting up a good filing system and knowing what to keep and for how long to keep it is very important for any small businessperson.

Some businesses are switching to electronic filing. They scan images of all paperwork and save it on their computers and backup devices. Even if your company has switched to an electronic filing system, the basics of what needs to be kept are the same. Rather than file cabinets, you use external drives and create file folders on those drives. Electronic filing systems can make it easier to find needed paperwork because of their search capabilities. I focus on a traditional filing system here. If your company uses electronic filing, ask your accounting department for a short review on how to make the best use of your company's system.

Creating a filing system

To get started setting up your filing system, you need some supplies, specifically

- **Filing cabinets:** This one's pretty self-explanatory — it's hard to have a filing system with nothing to keep the files in.

- **File folders:** Use these to set up separate files for each of your vendors, employees, and customers who buy on store credit, as well as files for backup information on each of your transactions. Many bookkeepers file transaction information by the date the transaction was added to their journal. If the transaction relates to a customer, vendor, or employee, they add a duplicate copy of the transaction to the individual files as well.

  Even if you have a computerized accounting system, you need to file paperwork related to the transactions you enter into your computer system. You should still maintain employee, vendor, and customer files in hard copy just in case something goes wrong, like if your computer system crashes and you need the originals to restore the data. Of course, you should avoid that type of crisis at all costs and back up your computerized accounting system's data regularly. Daily backups are best; one week is the longest you should ever go without a backup.

✔ **Three-ring binders:** These binders are great for things like your Chart of Accounts (see Chapter 3), your General Ledger (see Chapter 4) and your system of journals (see Chapter 5) because you'll be adding to these documents regularly, and the binders make it easy to add additional pages. Be sure to number the pages as you add them to the binder, so you can quickly spot a missing page. How many binders you need depends on how many financial transactions you have each accounting period. You can keep everything in one binder, or you may want to set up a binder for the Chart of Accounts and General Ledger and then a separate binder for each of your active journals. It's your decision based on what makes your job easier.

✔ **Expandable files:** These are the best way to keep track of current vendor activity and any bills that may be due. Make sure you have

- An alphabetical file: Use this file to track all your outstanding purchase orders by vendor. After you fill the order, you can file all details about that order in the vendor's individual file in case questions about the order arise later.

- A 12-month file: Use this file to keep track of bills that you need to pay. Simply place the bill in the slot for the month that it's due. Many companies also use a 30-day expandable file. At the beginning of the month, the bills are placed in the 30-day expandable file based on the dates that they need to be paid. This approach provides a quick and organized visual reminder for bills that are due.

If you're using a computerized accounting system, you likely don't need the expandable files because your accounting system can remind you when bills are due (as long as you added the information to the system when the bill arrived).

✔ **Blank computer disks or other storage media:** Use these to back up your computerized system on a weekly or, better yet, daily basis. Keep the backup disks in a fire safe or some place that won't be affected if the business is destroyed by a fire. (A fire safe is a must for any business; it's the best way to keep critical financial data safe.)

Figuring out what to keep and for how long

As you can probably imagine, the pile of paperwork you need to hold on to can get very large very quickly. As they see their files getting thicker and thicker, most business people wonder what they can toss, what they really need to keep, and how long they need to keep it.

Generally, you should keep most transaction-related paperwork for as long as the tax man can come and audit your books. For most types of audits, that's three years after you file your return. But if you failed to file taxes or filed taxes fraudulently (and I hope this isn't the case for you), you may be questioned by the IRS at any time because there's no statute of limitations in these cases.

The tax man isn't the only reason to keep records around longer than one year. You may need proof-of-purchase information for your insurance company if an asset is lost, stolen, or destroyed by fire or other accident. Also, you need to hang on to information regarding any business loan until it's paid off, just in case the bank questions how much you paid. After the loan's paid off, be sure to keep proof of payment indefinitely in case a question about the loan ever arises. Information about real estate and other asset holdings also should be kept around for as long as you hold the asset and for at least three years after the asset is sold. And it's necessary to keep information about employees for at least three years after the employee leaves. (If any legal action arises regarding that employee's job tenure after the employee leaves, the statute of limitations for legal action is at most three years.)

Keep the current year's files easily accessible in a designated filing area and keep the most recent past year's files in accessible filing cabinets if you have room. Box up records when they hit the two-year-old mark, and put them in storage. Be sure to date your boxed records with information about what they are, when they were put into storage, and when it's okay to destroy them. So many people forget that detail about when it's safe to destroy the boxes, so they just pile up until total desperation sets in and there's no more room. Then someone must take the time to sort through the boxes and figure out what needs to be kept and what can be destroyed, and that's not a fun job.

Generally, keep information about all transactions around for about three years. After that, make a list of things you want to hold on to longer for other reasons, such as asset holdings and loan information. Check with your lawyer and accountant to get their recommendations on what to keep and for how long.

Protecting Your Business Against Internal Fraud

Many business people start their operations by carefully hiring people they can trust, thinking "We're family — they'll never steal from me." Unfortunately, those who have learned the truth are the ones who put too much trust in just one employee.

Too often a business owner finds out too late that even the most loyal employee may steal from the company if the opportunity arises and the temptation becomes too great — or if the employee finds himself caught up in a serious personal financial dilemma and needs fast cash. After introducing you to the various ways people can steal from a company, I talk about steps you can take to prevent it.

Facing the reality of financial fraud

The four basic types of financial fraud are

- **Embezzlement,** also called *larceny,* which is the illegal use of funds by a person who controls those funds. For example, a bookkeeper may use company money for his own personal needs. Many times, embezzlement stories don't make it into the paper because business people are so embarrassed that they choose to keep the affair quiet instead. They usually settle privately with the embezzler rather than face public scrutiny.

- **Internal theft,** which is the stealing of company assets by employees, such as taking office supplies or products the company sells without paying for them. Internal theft is often the culprit behind inventory shrinkage.

- **Payoffs and kickbacks,** which are situations in which employees accept cash or other benefits in exchange for access to the company's business, often creating a scenario where the company that the employee works for pays more for the goods or products than necessary. That extra money finds its way into the pocket of the employee who helped facilitate the access. For example, say Company A wants to sell its products to Company B. An employee in Company B helps Company A get in the door. Company A prices its product a bit higher and gives the employee of Company B that extra profit in the form of a kickback for helping it out. A payoff is paid before the sale is made, essentially saying "please." A kickback is paid after the sale is made, essentially saying "thank you." In reality, payoffs and kickbacks are a form of bribery, but few companies report or litigate this problem (although sometimes employees are fired when deals are uncovered).

- **Skimming,** which occurs when employees take money from receipts and don't record the revenue on the books.

Although any of these financial crimes can happen in a small business, the one that hits small businesses the hardest is embezzlement. Embezzlement happens most frequently in small businesses when one person has access or control over most of the company's financial activities. For example, a bookkeeper may write checks, make deposits, and balance the monthly bank statement — talk about having your fingers in a very big cookie jar.

Caught with fingers in the cookie jar

Alice is a bookkeeper who's been with Company A a long time. She got promoted to office manager after she was with the company for 20 years. She's like a family member to the business owner, who trusts her implicitly. Because he's so busy with other aspects of running the business, he gives her control of the daily grind of cash flow. The beloved office manager handles or supervises all incoming and outgoing cash, proves out the bank statements, handles payroll, signs all the checks, and files the business's tax returns.

All that control gives her the opportunity, credibility, and access to embezzle a lot of money. At first, the trust was well founded, and Alice handled her new responsibilities very well. But after about three years in the role as office manager, her son was struck with a severe illness, and the medical bills continued to mount.

Alice decides to pay herself more money. She adds her husband or other family members to the payroll and documents the checks for them as consulting expenses. She draws large cash checks to buy nonexistent office supplies and equipment, and then, worst of all, she files the company's tax returns and pockets the money that should go to paying the taxes due. The business owner doesn't find out about the problem until the IRS comes calling, and by then, the office manager is retired and moved away.

Sound far-fetched? Well, it's not. You may not hear this exact scenario, but you're likely to see stories in your local newspaper about similar embezzlement schemes.

Employee embezzlement and theft cost companies more than customer theft

According to the National White Collar Crime Center, internal theft by employees is the largest single component of white-collar crime. You don't hear much about it, though, because many businesses choose to keep it quiet. The reality is that employee theft and embezzlement in the United States are estimated to cost employers over $240 billion per year (when the theft of intellectual property is included) or over $500 million per day. Total cost to businesses is ten times more than the amount lost through all other crimes against businesses combined. Banks, for example, report 95 percent of their theft losses from employee misdeeds as opposed to 5 percent of theft losses from bank robberies and customer theft. Four key situations in the workplace provide opportunities for theft and embezzlement: poor internal controls, too much control given to certain individuals, lax management, and failure to adequately pre-screen employees.

Dividing staff responsibilities

Your primary protection against financial crime is properly separating staff responsibilities when the flow of business cash is involved. Basically, you should never have one person handle more than one of the following tasks:

- ✔ **Bookkeeping:** Involves reviewing and entering all transactions into the company's books. The bookkeeper makes sure that transactions are accurate, valid, appropriate, and have the proper authorization. For example, if a transaction requires paying a vendor, the bookkeeper makes sure the charges are accurate and that someone with proper authority has approved the payment. The bookkeeper can review documentation of cash receipts and the overnight deposits taken to the bank, but he or she shouldn't be the person who actually makes the deposit. Also, if the bookkeeper is responsible for handling payments from external parties, such as customers or vendors, he or she shouldn't be the one to enter those transactions in the books.

- ✔ **Authorization:** Involves being the manager or managers delegated to authorize expenditures for their departments. You may decide that transactions over a certain amount must have two or more authorizations before checks can be sent to pay a bill. Authorization levels should be clearly spelled out and followed by all, even the owner or president of the company. (Remember, as owner, you set the tone for how the rest of the office operates; if you take shortcuts, you set a bad example and undermine the system you put in place.)

- ✔ **Money-handling:** Involves direct contact with incoming cash or revenue, whether check, credit card, or store credit transactions, as well as outgoing cash flow. The person who handles money directly, such as a cashier, shouldn't be the one who prepares and makes bank deposits. Likewise, the person writing checks to pay company bills shouldn't be authorized to sign those checks; to be safe, one person should prepare the checks based on authorized documentation, and a second person should sign those checks after reviewing the authorized documentation.

When setting up your cash-handling systems, try to think like an embezzler to figure out ways someone could take advantage of a system.

- ✔ **Financial report preparation and analysis:** Involves the actual preparation of the financial reports and any analysis of those reports. Financial reports should be prepared by someone who's not involved in the day-to-day entering of transactions in the books. For most small businesses, the bookkeeper turns over the raw reports from the computerized accounting system to an outside accountant who reviews the materials and prepares the financial reports. In addition, he or she does a financial analysis of the business activity results for the previous accounting period.

I realize that you may be just starting up a small business and therefore not have enough staff to separate all these duties. Until you do have that capability, be sure to stay heavily involved in the inflow and outflow of cash in your business.

- ✔ **Open your business's bank statements every month, and keep a close watch on the transactions.** Someone else can be given the responsibility to prove out the statement, but you should still keep an eye on the transactions listed.

- ✔ **Periodically look at your business check voucher system to be sure there aren't missing checks.** A bookkeeper who knows you periodically check the books is less likely to find an opportunity for theft or embezzlement. If you find that a check or page of checks is missing, act quickly to find out if the checks were used legitimately. If you can't find the answer, call your bank and put a stop on the missing check numbers.

- ✔ **Periodically observe cash handling by your cashiers and managers to be sure they're following the rules you've established.** It's known as *management by walking around* — the more often you're out there, the less likely you are to be a victim of employee theft and fraud.

Balancing control costs

As a small businessperson, you'll always be trying to balance the cost of protecting your cash and assets with the cost of adequately separating those duties. It can be a big mistake to put in too many controls that end up costing you money. For example, you may put in inventory controls that require salespeople to contact one particular person who has the key to your product warehouse. This kind of control may prevent employee theft, but it also may result in lost sales because salespeople can't find the key-holder when they're dealing with an interested customer. In the end, the customer gets mad, and you lose the sale.

When you put controls in place, talk to your staff both before and after instituting the controls to see how they're working and to check for any unforeseen problems. Be willing and able to adjust your controls to balance the business needs of selling your products, managing the cash flow, and keeping your eye on making a profit.

Generally, as you make rules for your internal controls, be sure that the cost of protecting an asset is no more than the asset you're trying to protect. For example, don't go overboard to protect office supplies by forcing your staff to sit around waiting for hours to access needed supplies while you and a manager are at a meeting away from the office.

Ask yourself these four questions as you design your internal controls:

- ✔ What exactly do I want to prevent or detect — errors, sloppiness, theft, fraud, or embezzlement?
- ✔ Do I face the problem frequently?
- ✔ What do I estimate the loss to be?
- ✔ What will it cost me to implement the change in procedures to prevent or detect the problem?

You can't answer these questions all by yourself, so consult with your managers and the staff that will be impacted by the changes. Get their answers to these questions, and listen to their feedback.

When you finish putting together the new internal control rule, be sure to document why you decided to implement the rule and the information you collected in developing it. After it's been in place for a while, test your assumptions. Be sure you're in fact detecting the errors, theft, fraud, or embezzlement that you hoped and expected to detect. Check the costs of keeping the rule in place by looking at cash outlay, employee time and morale, and the impact on customer service. If you find any problems with your internal controls, take the time to fix them and change the rule, again documenting the process. With detailed documentation, if two or three years down the road someone questions why he or she is doing something, you'll have the answers and be able to determine if the problem is still a valid one and if the rule is still necessary or needs to be changed.

Insuring Your Cash through Employee Bonding

If you have employees who handle a lot of cash, insuring your business against theft is an absolute must. This insurance, called *fidelity bonds,* helps you protect yourself against theft and reduce your risk of loss. Employee bonding is a common part of an overall business insurance package.

If you carry a fidelity bond on your cash handlers, you're covered for losses sustained by any employee who's bonded. You also have coverage if an employee's act causes losses to a client of your business. For example, if you're a financial consultant and your bookkeeper embezzles a client's cash, you're protected for the loss.

Fidelity bonds are a type of insurance that you can buy through the company that handles your business insurance policies. The cost varies greatly depending on the type of business you operate and the amount of cash or other assets that are handled by the employees you want to bond. If an employee steals from you or one of your customers, the insurance covers the loss.

Employers bond employees who handle cash, as well as employees who may be in a position to steal something other than cash. For example, a janitorial service bonds its workers in case a worker steals something from one of its customers. If a customer reports something missing, the insurance company that bonded the employee covers the loss. Without a bond, an employer must pay back the customer for any loss.

Part III

Tracking Your Day-to-Day Operations with Your Books

It's not your grandfather's cash register anymore — check out the latest in mobile point of sale systems in an online article at www.dummies.com/extras/bookkeeping.

In this part . . .

- ✔ Tracking your inventory purchases.
- ✔ Recording your sales.
- ✔ Paying your employees.
- ✔ Reporting your payroll to the government.

Chapter 8

Buying and Tracking Your Purchases

. . . .

In This Chapter

▶ Tracking inventory and monitoring costs

▶ Keeping your business supplied

▶ Paying your bills

. . . .

*I*n order to make money, your business must have something to sell. Whether you sell products or offer services, you have to deal with costs directly related to the goods or services being sold. Those costs primarily come from the purchase or manufacturing of the products you plan to sell or the items you need in order to provide the services.

All companies must keep careful watch over the cost of the products to be sold or services to be offered. Ultimately, your company's profits depend on how well you manage those costs because, in most cases, costs increase over time rather than decrease. How often do you find a reduction in the price of needed items? Doesn't happen often. If costs increase but the price to the customer remains unchanged, the profit you make on each sale is less.

In addition to the costs to produce products or services, every business has additional expenses associated with purchasing supplies needed to run the business. The bookkeeper has primary responsibility for monitoring all these costs and expenses as invoices are paid and for alerting company owners or managers when vendors increase prices. This chapter covers how to track purchases and their costs, manage inventory, and buy and manage supplies as well as pay the bills for the items your business buys.

Keeping Track of Inventory

Products to be sold are called *inventory*. As a bookkeeper, you use two accounts to track inventory:

✔ **Purchases:** Where you record the actual purchase of goods to be sold. This account is used to calculate the *Cost of Goods Sold,* which is an item on the income statement (see Chapter 19 for more on the income statement).

✔ **Inventory:** Where you track the value of inventory on hand. This value is shown on the balance sheet as an asset in a line item called *Inventory* (see Chapter 18 for more on the balance sheet).

Companies track physical inventory on hand using one of two methods:

✔ **Periodic inventory:** Conducting a physical count of the inventory in the stores and in the warehouse. This count can be done daily, monthly, yearly, or for any other period that best matches your business needs. (Many stores close for all or part of a day when they must count inventory.)

✔ **Perpetual inventory:** Adjusting inventory counts as each sale is made. In order to use this method, you must manage your inventory using a computerized accounting system that's tied into your point of sale (usually cash registers).

Even if you use a perpetual inventory method, it's a good idea to periodically do a physical count of inventory to be sure those numbers match what's in your computer system. Because theft, damage, and loss of inventory aren't automatically entered in your computer system, the losses don't show up until you do a physical count of the inventory you have on hand in your business.

When preparing your income statement at the end of an accounting period (whether that period is for a month, a quarter, or a year), you need to calculate the Cost of Goods Sold in order to calculate the profit made.

In order to calculate the Cost of Goods Sold, you must first find out how many items of inventory were sold. You start with the amount of inventory on hand at the beginning of the month (called Beginning Inventory), as recorded in the Inventory account, and add the amount of purchases, as recorded in the Purchases account, to find the Goods Available for Sale. Then you subtract the Inventory on hand at the end of the month, which is determined by counting remaining inventory.

Here's how you calculate the number of goods sold:

Beginning Inventory + Purchases = Goods available for sale – Ending inventory = Items sold

After you determine the number of goods sold, you compare that number to the actual number of items sold by the company during that accounting period, which is based on sales figures collected throughout the month. If the numbers don't match, you have a problem. The mistake may be in the

inventory count, or items may be unaccounted for because they've been mis-placed or damaged and discarded. In the worst-case scenario, you may have a problem with theft by customers or employees. These differences are usually tracked within the accounting system in a line item called *Inventory Shrinkage*.

Entering initial cost

When your company first receives inventory, you enter the initial cost of that inventory into the bookkeeping system based on the shipment's invoice. In some cases, invoices are sent separately, and only a packing slip is included in the order. If that's the case, you should still record the receipt of the goods because the company incurs the cost from the day the goods are received and must be sure it will have the money to pay for the goods when the invoice arrives and the bill comes due. (You track outstanding bills in the Accounts Payable account.)

Entering the receipt of inventory is a relatively easy entry in the bookkeeping system. For example, if your company buys $1,000 of inventory to be sold, you make the following record in the books:

	Debit	*Credit*
Purchases	$1,000	
Accounts Payable		$1,000

The Purchases account increases by $1,000 to reflect the additional costs, and the Accounts Payable account increases by the same amount to reflect the amount of the bill that needs to be paid in the future.

When inventory enters your business, in addition to recording the actual costs, you need more detail about what was bought, how much of each item was bought, and what each item cost. You also need to track

✔ How much inventory you have on hand.

✔ The value of the inventory you have on hand.

✔ When you need to order more inventory.

Tracking these details for each type of product bought can be a nightmare, especially if you're trying to keep the books for a retail store, because you need to set up a special Inventory journal with pages detailing purchase and sale information for every item you carry. (See Chapter 5 for the scoop on journals.)

However, computerized accounting simplifies this process of tracking inventory. Details about inventory can be entered initially into your computer accounting system in several ways:

✔ If you pay by check or credit card when you receive the inventory, you can enter the details about each item on the check or credit-card form.

✔ If you use purchase orders, you can enter the detail about each item on the purchase order, record receipt of the items when they arrive, and update the information when you receive the bill.

✔ If you don't use purchase orders, you can enter the detail about the items when you receive them and update the information when you receive the bill.

To give you an idea of how this information is collected in a computerized accounting software program, Figure 8-1 shows you how to enter the details in QuickBooks.

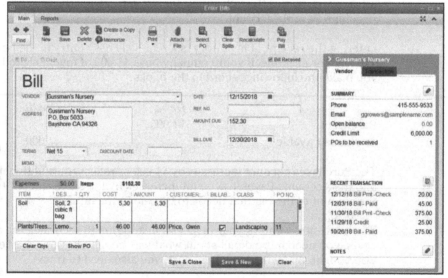

Figure 8-1: Recording of the receipt of inventory with a bill using QuickBooks.

Notice that on the form in Figure 8-1, in addition to recording the name of the vendor, date received, and payment amount, you also record details about the items bought, including the quantity and cost. When you load each item into the computerized accounting system, you can easily track cost details over time. You'll also find recent transaction information, contact details, and credit limit.

Figure 8-2 shows how you initially set up an inventory item in the computerized accounting system. Note that in addition to the item name, two descriptions are added to the system: One is an abbreviated version you can use on purchase transactions, and the other is a longer description that shows on customer invoices (sales transactions). You can input a cost and sales price if you want, or you can leave them at zero and enter the cost and sales prices with each transaction.

If you have a set contract purchase price or sales price on an inventory item, it saves time to enter it on this form so you don't have to enter the price each time you record a transaction. But, if the prices change frequently, it's best to leave the space blank so you don't forget to enter the updated price when you enter a transaction.

Figure 8-2:
Setting up
an Inventory
Item using
QuickBooks.

> New Item
>
> **TYPE**
> Inventory Part ▾   Use for goods you purchase, track as inventory, and resell.
>
> OK
> Cancel
>
> Item Name/Number   ☐ Subitem of   Manufacturer's Part Number
>
> Notes
> Custom Fields
> Spelling
>
> **PURCHASE INFORMATION**   **SALES INFORMATION**
> Description on Purchase Transactions   Description on Sales Transactions
>
> Cost   0.00   Sales Price   0.00
> COGS Account   Cost of Goods Sold ▾   Tax Code   Tax ▾
> Preferred Vendor   Income Account
>
> ☐ Item is inactive
>
> **INVENTORY INFORMATION**
> Asset Account   Reorder Point (Min)   On Hand   Total Value   As of
> Inventory Asset ▾   0.00   0.00   12/15/2018

Notice in Figure 8-2 that information about inventory on hand and when inventory needs to be reordered can also be tracked using this form. To be sure that your store shelves are never empty, for each item you can enter a number that indicates at what point you want to reorder inventory. In Figure 8-2, you can indicate the "Reorder Point" in the section called "Inventory Information." (A nice feature of QuickBooks is that it gives you an inventory reminder when inventory reaches the reorder point.)

After you complete and save the form that records the receipt of inventory in QuickBooks, the software automatically

✔ Adjusts the quantity of inventory you have in stock.

✔ Increases the asset account called Inventory.

✔ Lowers the quantity of items on order (if you initially entered the information as a purchase order).

✔ Averages the cost of inventory on hand.

✔ Increases the Accounts Payable account.

Managing inventory and its value

After you record the receipt of inventory, you have the responsibility of managing the inventory you have on hand. You also must know the value of that inventory. You may think that as long as you know what you paid for the items, the value isn't difficult to calculate. Well, accountants can't let it be that simple, so there are actually five different ways to value inventory:

- ✔ **LIFO (Last In, First Out):** You assume that the last items put on the shelves (the newest items) are the first items to be sold. Retail stores that sell nonperishable items, such as tools, are likely to use this type of system. For example, when a hardware store gets new hammers, workers probably don't unload what's on the shelves and put the newest items in the back. Instead, the new tools are just put in the front, so they're likely to be sold first.

- ✔ **FIFO (First In, First Out):** You assume that the first items put on the shelves (the oldest items) are sold first. Stores that sell perishable goods, such as food stores, use this inventory valuation method most often. For example, when new milk arrives at a store, the person stocking the shelves unloads the older milk, puts the new milk at the back of the shelf, and then puts the older milk in front. Each carton of milk (or other perishable item) has a date indicating the last day it can be sold, so food stores always try to sell the oldest stuff first, while it's still sellable. (They try, but how many times have you reached to the back of a food shelf to find items with the longest shelf life?)

- ✔ **Averaging:** You average the cost of goods received, so there's no reason to worry about which items are sold first or last. This method of inventory is used most often in any retail or services environment where prices are constantly fluctuating and the business owner finds that an average cost works best for managing his Cost of Goods Sold.

- ✔ **Specific Identification:** You maintain cost figures for each inventory item individually. Retail outlets that sell big-ticket items, such as cars, which often have a different set of extras on each item, use this type of inventory valuation method.

- ✔ **LCM (Lower of Cost or Market):** You set inventory value based on whichever is lower: the amount you paid originally for the inventory item (its cost), or the current market value of the item. Companies that deal in precious metals, commodities, or publicly traded securities often use this method because the prices of their products can fluctuate wildly, sometimes even in one day.

After you choose an inventory valuation method, you need to use the same method each year on your financial reports and when you file your taxes. If you decide you want to change the method, you need to explain the reasons for the change to both the IRS and to your financial backers. If you're running a company that's incorporated and has sold stock, you need to explain the change to your stockholders. You also have to go back and show how the change in inventory method impacts your prior financial reporting and adjust your profit margins in previous years to reflect the new inventory valuation method's impact on your long-term profit history.

Figuring out the best method for you

I'm sure you're wondering why it matters so much which inventory valuation method you use. The key to the choice is the impact on your bottom line as well as the taxes your company will pay.

FIFO, because it assumes the oldest (and most likely the lowest priced) items are sold first, results in a low Cost of Goods Sold number. Because Cost of Goods Sold is subtracted from sales to determine profit, a low Cost of Goods Sold number produces a high profit. For more on Cost of Goods Sold, see "Keeping Track of Inventory," earlier in this chapter.

The opposite is true for LIFO, which uses cost figures based on the last price paid for the inventory (and most likely the highest price). Using the LIFO method, the Cost of Goods Sold number is high, which means a larger sum is subtracted from sales to determine profit. Thus, the profit margin is low. The good news, however, is that the tax bill is low, too.

The Averaging method gives a business the best picture of what's happening with inventory costs and trends. Rather than constantly dealing with the ups and downs of inventory costs, this method smoothes out the numbers used to calculate a business's profits. Cost of Goods Sold, taxes, and profit margins for this method fall between those of LIFO and FIFO. If you're operating a business in which inventory prices are constantly going up and down, this is definitely the method you should choose.

The Averaging method always falls between LIFO and FIFO when it comes to cost of goods sold, taxes, and profit margin.

QuickBooks uses the Averaging method to calculate Cost of Goods Sold and Inventory line items on its financial reports, so if you choose this method, you can use QuickBooks and the financial reports it generates. However, if you choose to use one of the other four inventory methods, you can't use the QuickBooks financial report numbers. Instead, you have to print out a report of purchases and calculate the accurate numbers to use on your financial reports for the Cost of Goods Sold and Inventory accounts.

Check with your accountant to see which inventory method he or she thinks is best for you given the type of business you're operating.

Comparing the methods

To show you how much of an impact inventory valuation can have on profit margin, in this section I compare three of the most common methods: FIFO, LIFO, and Averaging. In this example, I assume Company A bought the inventory in question at different prices on three different occasions. Beginning Inventory is valued at $500 (that's 50 items at $10 each).

Here's the calculation for determining the number of items sold (see "Keeping Track of Inventory"):

> Beginning Inventory + Purchases = Goods available for sale – Ending inventory = Items sold
>
> 50 + 500 = 550 – 75 = 475

Here's what the company paid to purchase the inventory:

Date	Quantity	Unit Price
April 1	150	$10
April 15	150	$25
April 30	200	$30

Here's an example of how you calculate the Cost of Goods Sold using the Averaging method:

Beginning Inventory	50	$500
Purchases	150@$10	$1,500
	150@$25	$3,750
	200@$30	$6,000
Total Inventory	550	$11,750
Average Inventory Cost	$11,750 ÷ 550 = $21.36	
Cost of Goods Sold	475 × $21.36 = $10,146	
Ending Inventory	75@$21.36 = $1,602	

Remember, the Cost of Goods Sold number appears on the income statement and is subtracted from Sales. The Ending Inventory number shows up as an asset on the balance sheet. This is true for all three inventory valuation methods.

Here's an example of how you calculate the Cost of Goods Sold using the FIFO method. With this method, you assume that the first items received are the first ones sold, and because the first items received here are those in Beginning Inventory, I start with them:

Beginning Inventory	50@$10	$500
Next in — April 1	150@$10	$1,500
Then — April 15	150@$25	$3,750
Then — April 30	125@$30	$3,750
Cost of Goods Sold	475	$9,500
Ending Inventory	75@$30	$2,250

Note: Only 125 of the 200 units purchased on April 30 are used in the FIFO method. Because this method assumes that the first items into inventory are the first items sold (or taken out of inventory), the first items used are those on April 1. Then the April 15 items are used, and finally the remaining needed items are taken from those bought on April 30. Because 200 were bought on April 30 and only 125 were needed, 75 of the items bought on April 30 would be the ones left in ending inventory.

Here's an example of how you calculate the Cost of Goods Sold using the LIFO method. With this method, you assume that the last items received are the first ones sold, and because the last items received were those purchased on April 30, I start with them:

April 30	200@$30	$6,000
Next April 15	150@$25	$3,750
Then April 1	125@$10	$1,250
Cost of Goods Sold	475	$11,000
Ending Inventory	75@$10	$750

Note: Because LIFO assumes the last items to arrive are sold first, the Ending Inventory includes the 25 remaining units from the April 1 purchase plus the 50 units in Beginning Inventory.

Here's how the use of inventory under the LIFO method impacts the company profits. I assume the items are sold to the customers for $40 per unit, which means total sales of $19,000 for the month (that's $40 × 475 units sold). In this example, I just look at the *Gross Profit,* which is the profit from Sales before considering expenses incurred for operating the company. I talk more about the different profit types and what they mean in Chapter 19. Gross Profit is calculated by the following equation:

Sales – Cost of Goods Sold = Gross Profit

Table 8-1 shows a comparison of Gross Profit for the three methods used in this example scenario.

Table 8-1   **Comparison of Gross Profit Based on Inventory Valuation Method**

Income Statement Line Item	FIFO	LIFO	Averaging
Sales	$19,000	$19,000	$19,000
Cost of Goods Sold	$9,500	$11,000	$10,146
Gross Profit	$9,500	$8,000	$8,854

Looking at the comparisons of gross profit, you can see that inventory valuation can have a major impact on your bottom line. LIFO is likely to give you the lowest profit because the last inventory items bought are usually the most expensive. FIFO is likely to give you the highest profit because the first items bought are usually the cheapest. And the profit produced by the Averaging method is likely to fall somewhere in between the two.

Buying and Monitoring Supplies

In addition to inventory, all businesses must buy supplies that are used to operate the business, such as paper, pens, and paper clips. Supplies that aren't bought in direct relationship to the manufacturing or purchasing of goods or services for sale fall into the category of *expenses.*

When it comes to monitoring the supplies you use, just how closely you want to watch things depends on your business needs. The expense categories you establish may be as broad as "Office supplies" and "Retail supplies," or you may want to set up accounts for each type of supply used. Each additional account is just one more thing that needs to be managed and monitored in the accounting system, so determine whether it's worth your time to keep a very detailed record of supplies.

Your best bet is to carefully track supplies that make a big dent in your budget with an individual account. For example, if you anticipate paper usage will be very high, monitor that usage with a separate account called "Paper expenses."

Many companies don't use the bookkeeping system to manage their supplies. Instead, they designate one or two people as office managers or supply managers and keep the number of accounts used for supplies to a minimum. Other businesses decide they want to monitor supplies by department or division and set up a supply account for each one. That puts the burden of monitoring supplies in the hands of the department or division managers.

Staying on Top of Your Bills

Eventually, you have to pay for both the inventory and the supplies you purchase for your business. In most cases, the bills are posted to the Accounts Payable account when they arrive, and they're paid when due. A large chunk of the cash paid out of your Cash account (see Chapters 5 and 7 for more information on the Cash account and handling cash) is in the form of the checks sent out to pay bills due in Accounts Payable, so you need to have careful controls over the five key functions of Accounts Payable:

✔ Entering the bills to be paid into the accounting system

✔ Preparing checks to pay the bills

✔ Signing checks to pay the bills

✔ Sending out payment checks to vendors

✔ Reconciling the checking account

In your business, it's likely that the person who enters the bills to be paid into the system also prepares the payment checks, but the other tasks should be done by someone else. You should never allow the person who prepares the check to review the bills to be paid and sign the checks, unless of course that person's you, the business owner. The person signing the checks should carefully review what's being paid, verify that proper management approvals for the payment are shown on that paperwork, and confirm that the amount being paid is accurate. You should also separate responsibilities to be sure that the person who reconciles your checking account isn't preparing or signing checks. (I talk more cash control and the importance of separating duties in Chapter 7.)

Properly managing Accounts Payable can save your company a lot of money by avoiding late fees or interest and by taking advantage of discounts offered for paying early. If you're using a computerized accounting system, the bill due date and any discount information should be entered at the time you receive the inventory or supplies (refer to Figure 8-1 for how you record this information).

If you're working with a paper system rather than a computerized accounting system, you need to set up some way to be sure you don't miss bill due dates. Many companies use two accordion files: one that's set up by the month, and the other that's set up by the day. When a bill first comes in, it's put into the first accordion file according to the month in which it's due. On the first day of that month, the Accounts Payable clerk pulls all the bills due that month and puts them in the daily accordion file based on the date the bill is due. Payment checks are then mailed in time to arrive in the vendor's office by the due date.

In some cases, companies offer a discount if their bills are paid early. Suppose the terms of the discount for the vendor is "2% 10 Net 30." That means that if the bill is paid in 10 days, the company can take a 2 percent discount; otherwise, the amount due must be paid in full in 30 days. In addition, many companies state that interest or late fees will be charged if a bill isn't paid in 30 days.

For example, if the bill were for $1,000 and the company pays the bill in ten days, it can take a 2 percent discount, which means they would pay $20 less, or $980. That may not seem like much, but if your company buys $100,000 of inventory and supplies in a month and each vendor offers a similar discount, the company can save $2,000. Over the course of a year, discounts on purchases can save your business a significant amount of money and improve a business's profits.

Chapter 9

Counting Your Sales

· ·

· ·

*E*very business loves to take in money, and that means you, the book-keeper, have a lot to do to make sure sales are properly tracked and recorded in the books. In addition to recording the sales themselves, you must track customer accounts, discounts offered to customers, and customer returns and allowances.

If the company sells products on store credit, you have to carefully monitor customer accounts in Accounts Receivable, including monitoring whether customers pay on time and alerting the sales team if customers are behind on their bills and future purchases on credit need to be denied. Some customers never pay, and in that case, you must adjust the books to reflect nonpayment as a bad debt.

This chapter reviews the basic responsibilities that fall to a business's book-keeping and accounting staff for tracking sales, making adjustments to those sales, monitoring customer accounts, and alerting management to slow-paying customers.

Collecting on Cash Sales

Most businesses collect some form of cash as payment for the goods or services they sell. Cash receipts include more than just bills and coins; checks and credit cards also are considered cash sales for the purpose of bookkeeping. In fact, with electronic transaction processing (that's when a customer's credit card is swiped through a machine), a deposit is usually made to the business's checking account the same day (sometimes within just seconds of the transaction, depending on the type of system the business sets up with the bank).

The only type of payment that doesn't fall under the umbrella of a cash payment is purchases made on store credit. And by *store credit*, I mean credit offered to customers directly by your business rather than through a third party, such as a bank credit card or loan. I talk more about this type of sale in the section "Selling on Credit," later in this chapter.

Discovering the value of sales receipts

Modern businesses generate sales slips in one of three ways: by the cash register or other device used to record payment (such as a tablet and cash drawer), by the credit-card machine, or by hand (written out by the salesperson). Whichever of these three methods you choose to handle your sales transactions, the sales receipt serves two purposes:

✔ It gives the customer proof that the item was purchased on a particular day at a particular price in your store in case he needs to exchange or return the merchandise.

✔ It gives the store a receipt that can be used at a later time to enter the transaction into the company's books. At the end of the day, the receipts also are used to prove out the cash register and ensure that the cashier has taken in the right amount of cash based on the sales made. (In Chapter 7, I talk more about how cash receipts can be used as an internal control tool to manage your cash.)

I'm sure you're familiar with cash receipts, but just to show you how much useable information can be generated for the bookkeeper on a sales receipt here's a sample receipt from a sale at a bakery:

Sales Receipt 4/25/2014			
Item	*Quantity*	*Price*	*Total*
White Serving Set	1@$40	$40	
Cheesecake, Marble	1@$20	$20	
Cheesecake, Blueberry	1@$20	$20	
			$80.00
Sales Tax @ 6%		$4.80	
		$84.80	
Cash Paid		$90.00	
Change		$5.20	

You've probably never thought about how much bookkeeping information is included on a sales receipt. Receipts contain a wealth of information that's collected for your company's accounting system. A look at a receipt tells you the amount of cash collected, the type of products sold, the quantity of products sold, and how much sales tax was collected.

Unless your company uses some type of computerized system at the point of sale (which is usually the cash register) that's integrated into the company's accounting system, sales information is collected throughout the day by the cash register and printed out in a summary form at the end of the day. At that point, you enter the details of the sales day in the books.

If you don't use your computerized system to monitor inventory, you use the data collected by the cash register to simply enter into the books the cash received, total sales, and sales tax collected. Although in actuality you'd have many more sales and much higher numbers at the end of the day, here's what an entry in the Cash Receipts journal would look like for the receipt:

	Debit	*Credit*
Cash in Checking	$84.80	
Sales		$80.00
Sales Tax Collected		$4.80

Cash receipts for April 25, 2014

In this example entry, Cash in Checking is an asset account shown on the balance sheet (see Chapter 18 for more about balance sheets), and its value increases with the debit. The Sales account is a revenue account on the income statement (see Chapter 19 for more about income statements), and its balance increases with a Credit, showing additional revenue. (I talk more about debits and credits in Chapter 2.) The Sales Tax Collected account is a Liability account that appears on the balance sheet, and its balance increases with this transaction.

Businesses pay sales tax to state and local government entities either monthly or quarterly depending on rules set by the states, so your business must hold the money owed in a liability account to be certain that you're able to pay the taxes collected from customers when they're due. I talk more about tax reporting and payment in Chapter 21.

Recording cash transactions in the books

If you're using a computerized accounting system, you can enter more detail from the day's receipts and track inventory sold as well. Most of the computerized accounting systems do include the ability to track the sale of inventory. Figure 9-1 shows you the QuickBooks Sales receipt form that you can use to input data from each day's sales.

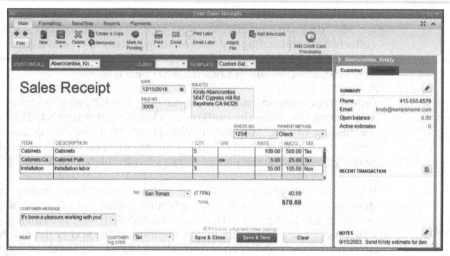

Figure 9-1:
Example
of a sales
receipt in
QuickBooks.

In addition to the information included in the Cash Receipts journal, note that QuickBooks also collects information about the items sold in each transaction. QuickBooks then automatically updates inventory information, reducing the amount of inventory on hand when necessary. When the inventory number falls below the reorder number you set (see Chapter 8), QuickBooks alerts you to pass the word on to whoever is responsible for ordering to order more inventory.

The sales receipt in Figure 9-1 is for an individual customer, so you would find her name in the customer drop-down and automatically populate the name and address in the "Sold To" field. The customer's email information is shown to the right and notes below that show previous emails sent. You can print the receipt and give it to the customer or email it to the customer if the order was made by phone or Internet. You can enter the payment method on the right of the receipt.

If your company accepts credit cards, expect sales revenue to be reduced by the fees paid to credit-card companies. Usually, you face monthly fees as well as fees per transaction; however, each company sets up individual arrangements with its bank regarding these fees. Sales volume impacts how much you pay in fees, so when researching bank services, be sure to compare credit-card transaction fees to find a good deal.

Selling on Credit

Many businesses decide to sell to customers on direct credit, meaning credit offered by the business and not through a bank or credit-card provider. This approach offers more flexibility in the type of terms you can offer your customers, and you don't have to pay bank fees. However, it involves more work for you, the bookkeeper, and more risk if a customer doesn't pay what he or she owes.

If you accept a customer's bank-issued credit card for a sale and the customer doesn't pay the bill, you get your money, and the bank is responsible for collecting from the customer and takes the loss if he or she doesn't pay. That's not the case if you decide to offer credit to your customers directly. If a customer doesn't pay, your business takes the loss.

Deciding whether to offer store credit

The decision to set up your own store credit system depends on what your competition is doing. For example, if you run an office supply store and all other office supply stores allow store credit to make it easier for their customers to get supplies, you probably need to offer store credit to stay competitive.

If you want to allow your customers to buy on store credit, the first thing you need to do is set up some ground rules. You have to decide:

- How you plan to check a customer's credit history
- What the customer's income level needs to be to be approved for credit
- How long you give the customer to pay the bill before charging interest or late fees

The harder you make it to get store credit and the stricter you make the bill-paying rules, the less chance you have of a taking a loss. However, you may lose customers to a competitor with lighter credit rules. For example, you may require a minimum income level of $50,000 and make customers pay in 30 days if they want to avoid late fees or interest charges. Your sales staff reports that these rules are too rigid because your direct competitor down the street allows credit on a minimum income level of $30,000 and gives customers 60 days to pay before late fees and interest charges. Now you have to decide whether you want to change your credit rules to match the competition's. But, if you do lower your credit standards to match your competitor, you could end up with more customers who can't pay on time or at all because you've qualified customers for credit at lower income levels and given them more time to pay. If you loosen your qualification criteria and bill-paying requirements, you have to carefully monitor your customer accounts to be sure they're not falling behind.

The key risk you face is selling products for which you're never paid. For example, if you allow customers 30 days to pay and cut them off from buying goods if their account falls more than 30 days behind, then the most you can lose is the amount purchased over a two-month period (60 days). But if you give customers more leniency, allowing them 60 days to pay and cutting them off after payments are 30 days late, you're faced with three months (90 days) of purchases for which you may never be paid.

Recording store credit transactions in the books

When sales are made on store credit, you have to enter specific information into the accounting system. In addition to inputting information regarding cash receipts (see "Collecting on Cash Sales" earlier in this chapter), you update the customer accounts to be sure each customer is billed and the money is collected. You debit the Accounts Receivable account, an asset account shown on the Balance Sheet (see Chapter 18), which shows money due from customers.

Here's how a journal entry of a sale made on store credit looks:

	Debit	Credit
Accounts Receivable	$84.80	
Sales		$80.00
Sales Tax Collected		$4.80

Credit Sales for April 25, 2014

In addition to making this journal entry, you enter the information into the customer's account so that accurate bills can be sent out at the end of the month. When the customer pays the bill, you update the individual customer's record to show that payment has been received and enter the following into the bookkeeping records:

	Debit	Credit
Cash in Checking	$84.80	
Accounts Receivable		$84.80

Payment from S. Smith on invoice 123.

If you're using QuickBooks, you enter purchases on store credit using an invoice form like the one in Figure 9-2. Most of the information on the invoice form is similar to the sales receipt form (see "Collecting on Cash Sales"), but the invoice form also has space to enter a different address for shipping (the "Ship To" field) and includes payment terms (the "Terms" field). For the sample invoice form shown in Figure 9-2, you can see that payment is due in 30 days. On the right you will see the customer's other recent transactions, as well as contact information for the customer.

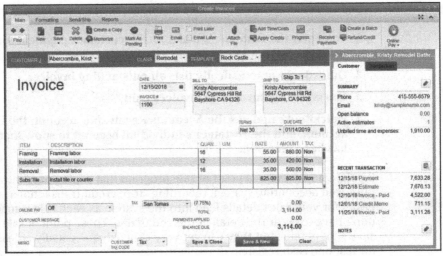

Figure 9-2: QuickBooks sales invoice for purchases made on store credit.

QuickBooks uses the information on the invoice form to update the following accounts:

- ✔ Accounts Receivable
- ✔ Inventory
- ✔ The customer's account
- ✔ Sales Tax Collected

Based on this data, when it comes time to bill the customer at the end of the month, with a little prompting from you (see Figure 9-3), QuickBooks generates statements for all customers with outstanding invoices. You can easily generate statements for specific customers or all customers on the books.

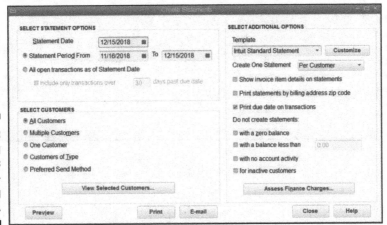

Figure 9-3: Generating statements for customers using QuickBooks.

When you receive payment from a customer, here's what happens:

1. **You enter the customer's name on the customer payment form (shown in Figure 9-4).**

2. **QuickBooks automatically lists all outstanding invoices.**

3. **You select the invoice or invoices paid.**

4. **QuickBooks updates the Accounts Receivable account, the Cash account, and the customer's individual account to show that payment has been received.**

If your company uses a point of sale program that's integrated into the computerized accounting system, recording store credit transactions is even easier for you. Sales details feed into the system as each sale is made, so you don't have to enter the detail at the end of day. These point of sale programs save a lot of time, but they can get very expensive — usually at least $1,000 for just one cash register.

Even if customers don't buy on store credit, point of sale programs provide businesses with an incredible amount of information about their customers and what they like to buy. This data can be used in the future for direct marketing and special sales to increase the likelihood of return business.

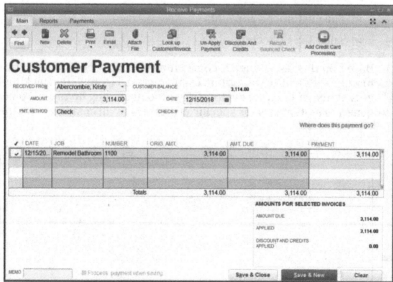

Figure 9-4: In QuickBooks, recording payments from customers who bought on store credit starts with the customer payment form.

Proving Out the Cash Register

To ensure that cashiers don't pocket a business's cash, at the end of each day, cashiers must *prove out* (show that they have the right amount of cash in the register based on the sales transactions during the day) the amount of cash, checks, and charges they took in during the day.

This process of proving out a cash register actually starts at the end of the previous day, when cashier John Doe and his manager agree to the amount of cash left in the John's register drawer. Cash sitting in cash registers or cash drawers is recorded as part of the Cash on Hand account.

When John comes to work the next morning, he starts out with the amount of cash left in the drawer. At the end of the business day, either he or his manager runs a summary of activity on the cash register for the day to produce a report of the total sales taken in by the cashier. John counts the amount of cash in his register as well as totals the checks, credit-card receipts, and store credit charges. He then completes a cash-out form that looks something like this:

Cash Register: John Doe 4/25/2014		
Receipts	*Sales*	*Total*
Beginning Cash		$100
Cash Sales	$400	
Credit-Card Sales	$800	
Store Credit Sales	$200	
Total Sales		$1,400
Sales on Credit		$1,000
Cash Received		$400
Total Cash in Register		$500

A store manager reviews John Doe's cash register summary (produced by the actual register) and compares it to the cash-out form. If John's ending cash (the amount of cash remaining in the register) doesn't match the cash-out form, he and the manager try to pinpoint the mistake. If they can't find a mistake, they fill out a cash-overage or cash-shortage form. Some businesses charge the cashier directly for any shortages, while others take the position that the cashier's fired after a certain number of shortages of a certain dollar amount (say, three shortages of more than $10).

The store manager decides how much cash to leave in the cash drawer or register for the next day and deposits the remainder. He does this task for each of his cashiers and then deposits all the cash and checks from the day in a night deposit box at the bank. He sends a report with details of the deposit to the bookkeeper so that the data makes it into the accounting system. The bookkeeper enters the data on the Cash Receipts form (refer to Figure 9-1) if a computerized accounting system is being used or into the Cash Receipts journal if the books are being kept manually.

Tracking Sales Discounts

Most businesses offer discounts at some point in time to generate more sales. Discounts are usually in the form of a sale with 10 percent, 20 percent, or even more off purchases.

When you offer discounts to customers, it's a good idea to track your sales discounts in a separate account so you can keep an eye on how much you discount sales in each month. If you find you're losing more and more money to discounting, look closely at your pricing structure and competition to find out why it's necessary to frequently lower your prices in order to make sales. You can track discount information very easily by using the data found on a standard sales register receipt. The following receipt from a bakery includes sales discount details.

Sales Receipt 4/25/2014

Item	*Quantity*	*Price*	*Total*
White Serving Set	1	$40	$40
Cheesecake, Marble	1	$20	$20
Cheesecake, Blueberry	1	$20	$20
			$80.00
Sales Discount @ 10%			(8.00)
			$72.00
Sales Tax @ 6%			4.32
			$76.32
Cash Paid			$80.00
Change			$3.68

From this example, you can see clearly that the store takes in less cash when discounts are offered. When recording the sale in the Cash Receipts journal, you record the discount as a debit. This debit increases the Sales Discount account, which is subtracted from the Sales account to calculate the Net Sales. (I walk you through all these steps and calculations when I discuss preparing the income statement in Chapter 19.) Here is what the bakery's entry for this particular sale looks like in the Cash Receipts journal:

	Debit	**Credit**
Cash in Checking	$76.32	
Sales Discounts	$8.00	
Sales		$80.00
Sales Tax Collected		$4.32

Cash receipts for April 25, 2014

If you use a computerized accounting system, add the sales discount as a line item on the sales receipt or invoice, and the system automatically adjusts the sales figures and updates your Sales Discount account.

Recording Sales Returns and Allowances

Most stores deal with *sales returns* on a regular basis. It's common for customers to return items they've purchased because the item is defective, they've changed their minds, or for any other reason. Instituting a no-return policy is guaranteed to produce very unhappy customers, so to maintain good customer relations, you should allow sales returns.

Sales allowances (sales incentive programs) are becoming more popular with businesses. Sales allowances are most often in the form of a gift card. A gift card that's sold is actually a liability for the company because the company has received cash, but no merchandise has gone out. For that reason, gift card sales are entered in a Gift Card liability account. When a customer makes a purchase at a later date using the gift card, the Gift Card liability account is reduced by the purchase amount. Monitoring the Gift Card liability account allows businesses to keep track of how much is yet to be sold without receiving additional cash.

Accepting sales returns can be a more complicated process than accepting sales allowances. Usually, a business posts a set of rules for returns that may include:

- Returns will only be allowed within 30 days of purchase.
- You must have a receipt to return an item.
- If you return an item without a receipt, you can receive only store credit.

You can set up whatever rules you want for returns. For internal control purposes, the key to returns is monitoring how your staff handles them. In most cases, you should require a manager's approval on returns. Also, be sure your staff pays close attention to how the customer originally paid for the item being returned. You certainly don't want to give a customer cash if she paid on store credit — that's just handing over your money! After a return's approved, the cashier either returns the amount paid by cash or credit card. Customers who bought the items on store credit don't get any money back. That's because they didn't pay anything when they purchased the item, but expected to be billed later. Instead, a form is filled out so that the amount of the original purchase can be subtracted from the customer's store credit account

You use the information collected by the cashier who handled the return to input the sales return data into the books. For example, a customer returns a $40 item that was purchased with cash. You record the cash refund in the Cash Receipts Journal like this:

	Debit	Credit
Sales Returns and Allowances	$40.00	
Sales Taxes Collected @ 6%	$2.40	
Cash in Checking		$42.40

To record return of purchase, 4/30/2014.

If the item had been bought with a discount, you'd list the discount as well and adjust the price to show that discount.

In this journal entry,

- The Sales Returns and Allowances account increases. This account normally carries a debit balance and is subtracted from Sales when preparing the income statement, thereby reducing revenue received from customers.

- The debit to the Sales Tax Collected account reduces the amount in that account because sales tax is no longer due on the purchase.

- The credit to the Cash in Checking account reduces the amount of cash in that account.

Monitoring Accounts Receivable

Making sure customers pay their bills is a crucial responsibility of the bookkeeper. Before sending out the monthly bills, you should prepare an *Aging Summary Report* that lists all customers who owe money to the company and how old each debt is. If you keep the books manually, you collect the necessary information from each customer account. If you keep the books in a computerized accounting system, you can generate this report automatically. Either way, your Aging Summary Report should look similar to this example report from a bakery:

Aging Summary — As of May 1, 2014				
Customer	Current	31–60 Days	61–90 Days	>90 Days
S. Smith	$84.32	$46.15		
J. Doe			$65.78	
H. Harris	$89.54			
M. Man				$125.35
Totals	**$173.86**	**$46.15**	**$65.78**	**$125.35**

The Aging Summary quickly tells you which customers are behind in their bills. In the case of this example, customers are cut off from future purchases when their payments are more than 60 days late, so J. Doe and M. Man aren't able to buy on store credit until their bills are paid in full.

Give a copy of your Aging Summary to the sales manager so he can alert staff to problem customers. He can also arrange for the appropriate collections procedures. Each business sets up its own collections process, but usually it starts with a phone call, followed by letters, and possibly even legal action, if necessary.

If you are using a computer accounting system, you can generate an Aging Summary Report in seconds. Figure 9-5 is a sample of an Aging Summary Report from QuickBooks.

Figure 9-5: With QuickBooks you can generate an aging summary report in seconds.

![A/R Aging Summary screenshot from QuickBooks showing Rock Castle Construction A/R Aging Summary as of December 15, 2018, with columns Current, 1-30, 31-60, 61-90, >90, and TOTAL for customers Abercrombie, Kristy; Allard, Robert; Burch, Jason; Campbell, Heather; Cook, Brian; Ecker Designs; and Hendro Riyadi.]

Accepting Your Losses

You may encounter a situation in which your business never gets paid by a customer, even after an aggressive collections process. In this case, you have no choice but to write off the purchase as a *bad debt* and accept the loss.

Most businesses review their Aging Reports every six to 12 months to determine which accounts need to be written off as bad debt. Accounts written off are tracked in a General Ledger account called *Bad Debt*. (See Chapter 2 for more information about the General Ledger.) The Bad Debt account appears as an expense account on the income statement. When you write off a customer's account as bad debt, the Bad Debt account increases, and the Accounts Receivable account decreases.

To give you an idea of how you write off an account, assume that one of your customers never pays the $105.75 due. Here's what your journal entry looks like for this debt:

	Debit	*Credit*
Bad Debt	$105.75	
Accounts Receivable		$105.75

In a computerized accounting system, you enter the information using a customer payment form and allocate the amount due to the Bad Debt expense account.

Chapter 10

Employee Payroll and Benefits

- -

In This Chapter

▶ Hiring employees

▶ Collecting and depositing employee taxes

▶ Keeping track of benefits

▶ Preparing and recording payroll

▶ Finding new ways to deal with payroll responsibilities

- -

*U*nless your business has only one employee (you, the owner), you'll most likely hire employees, and that means you'll have to pay them, offer benefits, and manage a payroll.

Responsibilities for hiring and paying employees usually are shared between the human resources staff and the bookkeeping staff. As the bookkeeper, you must be sure that all government tax-related forms are completed and handle all payroll responsibilities including paying employees, collecting and paying employee taxes, collecting and managing employee benefit contributions, and paying benefit providers. This chapter examines the various employee staffing issues that bookkeepers need to be able to manage.

Staffing Your Business

After you decide that you want to hire employees for your business, you must be ready to deal with a lot of government paperwork. In addition to paperwork, you face many decisions about how employees will be paid and who will be responsible for maintaining the paperwork required by state, local, and federal government entities.

Knowing what needs to be done to satisfy government bureaucracies isn't the only issue you must consider before the first person is hired; you also must decide how frequently you will pay employees and what type of wage and salary scales you want to set up.

Completing government forms

Even before you sign your first employee, you need to start filing government forms related to hiring. If you plan to hire staff, you must first apply for an *Employer Identification Number,* or EIN. Government entities use this number to track your employees and the money you pay them, as well as any taxes collected and paid on their behalf.

Before employees start working for you, they must fill out forms, including the W-4 (tax withholding form) and I-9 (citizenship verification form). The following sections explain each of these forms as well as the EIN.

Employer Identification Number (EIN)

Every company must have an EIN to hire employees. If your company is incorporated (see Chapter 21 for the lowdown on corporations and other business types), which means you've filed paperwork with the state and become a separate legal entity, you already have an EIN. Otherwise, to get an EIN you must complete and submit Form SS-4, which you can see in Figure 10-1.

Luckily, the government offers four ways to submit the necessary information and obtain an EIN. The fastest way is to call the IRS's Business & Specialty Tax Line at 800-829-4933 and complete the form by telephone. IRS officials assign your EIN over the telephone. You can also apply online at www.irs.gov, or you can download Form SS-4 at www.irs.gov/pub/irs-pdf/fss4.pdf and submit it by fax or by mail.

In addition to tracking pay and taxes, most state entities use the EIN number to track the payment of unemployment taxes and workers' compensation taxes, both of which the employer must pay. Some states issue separate ID numbers, so be sure to check with your state tax office. I talk more about state taxes in Chapter 11.

W-4

Every person you hire must fill out a W-4 form called the "Employee's Withholding Allowance Certificate." You've probably filled out a W-4 at least once in your life, if you've ever worked for someone else. You can download this form and make copies for your employees at www.irs.gov/pub/irs-pdf/fw4.pdf.

The W-4 form, shown in Figure 10-2, tells you, the employer, how much to take out of your employees' paychecks in income taxes. On the W-4, employees indicate whether they're married or single. They can also claim additional allowances if they have children or other major deductions that can reduce their tax bills. The amount of income taxes you need to take out of each employee's check depends upon how many allowances he or she claimed on the W-4.

Form **SS-4**
(Rev. January 2010)
Department of the Treasury
Internal Revenue Service

Application for Employer Identification Number

(For use by employers, corporations, partnerships, trusts, estates, churches, government agencies, Indian tribal entities, certain individuals, and others.)

► See separate instructions for each line.   ► Keep a copy for your records.

OMB No. 1545-0003

EIN

Type or print clearly.

1	Legal name of entity (or individual) for whom the EIN is being requested

2	Trade name of business (if different from name on line 1)	3	Executor, administrator, trustee, "care of" name

4a	Mailing address (room, apt., suite no. and street, or P.O. box)	5a	Street address (if different) (Do not enter a P.O. box.)
4b	City, state, and ZIP code (if foreign, see instructions)	5b	City, state, and ZIP code (if foreign, see instructions)

6	County and state where principal business is located

7a	Name of responsible party	7b	SSN, ITIN, or EIN

8a Is this application for a limited liability company (LLC) (or a foreign equivalent)? . . . . ☐ Yes ☐ No   8b If 8a is "Yes," enter the number of LLC members . . . . ►

8c If 8a is "Yes," was the LLC organized in the United States? . . . . ☐ Yes ☐ No

9a **Type of entity** (check only one box). **Caution.** If 8a is "Yes," see the instructions for the correct box to check.

☐ Sole proprietor (SSN) _____
☐ Partnership
☐ Corporation (enter form number to be filed) ►_____
☐ Personal service corporation
☐ Church or church-controlled organization
☐ Other nonprofit organization (specify) ►_____
☐ Other (specify) ►

☐ Estate (SSN of decedent) _____
☐ Plan administrator (TIN) _____
☐ Trust (TIN of grantor) _____
☐ National Guard   ☐ State/local government
☐ Farmers' cooperative   ☐ Federal government/military
☐ REMIC   ☐ Indian tribal governments/enterprises
Group Exemption Number (GEN) if any ►

9b If a corporation, name the state or foreign country (if applicable) where incorporated | State | Foreign country

10 **Reason for applying** (check only one box)
☐ Started new business (specify type) ►_____
☐ Hired employees (Check the box and see line 13.)
☐ Compliance with IRS withholding regulations
☐ Other (specify) ►

☐ Banking purpose (specify purpose) ►_____
☐ Changed type of organization (specify new type) ►_____
☐ Purchased going business
☐ Created a trust (specify type) ►_____
☐ Created a pension plan (specify type) ►_____

11 Date business started or acquired (month, day, year). See instructions.   12 Closing month of accounting year

13 Highest number of employees expected in the next 12 months (enter -0- if none).
If no employees expected, skip line 14.

14 If you expect your employment tax liability to be $1,000 or less in a full calendar year **and** want to file Form 944 annually instead of Forms 941 quarterly, check here. (Your employment tax liability generally will be $1,000 or less if you expect to pay $4,000 or less in total wages.) If you do not check this box, you must file Form 941 for every quarter. ☐

Agricultural	Household	Other

15 First date wages or annuities were paid (month, day, year). **Note.** If applicant is a withholding agent, enter date income will first be paid to nonresident alien (month, day, year) . . . . ►

16 Check **one** box that best describes the principal activity of your business.
☐ Construction ☐ Rental & leasing ☐ Transportation & warehousing ☐ Accommodation & food service ☐ Wholesale-other ☐ Retail
☐ Real estate ☐ Manufacturing ☐ Finance & insurance ☐ Other (specify)
☐ Health care & social assistance ☐ Wholesale-agent/broker

17 Indicate principal line of merchandise sold, specific construction work done, products produced, or services provided.

18 Has the applicant entity shown on line 1 ever applied for and received an EIN? ☐ Yes ☐ No
If "Yes," write previous EIN here ►

Third Party Designee	Complete this section **only** if you want to authorize the named individual to receive the entity's EIN and answer questions about the completion of this form.	
	Designee's name	Designee's telephone number (include area code) ( )
	Address and ZIP code	Designee's fax number (include area code) ( )

Under penalties of perjury, I declare that I have examined this application, and to the best of my knowledge and belief, it is true, correct, and complete. | Applicant's telephone number (include area code) ( )

Name and title (type or print clearly) ►

Signature ►   Date ► | Applicant's fax number (include area code) ( )

For Privacy Act and Paperwork Reduction Act Notice, see separate instructions.   Cat. No. 16055N   Form **SS-4** (Rev. 1-2010)

Figure 10-1: You must file IRS Form SS-4 to get an Employer Identification Number before hiring employees.

It's a good idea to ask an employee to fill out a W-4 immediately, but you can allow him to take the form home if he wants to discuss allowances with his spouse or accountant. If an employee doesn't complete a W-4, you must take income taxes out of his check based on the highest possible amount for that person. I talk more about taking out taxes in the section "Collecting Employee Taxes" later in this chapter.

Figure 10-2:
IRS Form W-4 should be completed by all employees when they're hired so that you know how much to take out of their paychecks for taxes.

---- Separate here and give Form W-4 to your employer. Keep the top part for your records. ----

Form **W-4**	**Employee's Withholding Allowance Certificate**	OMB No. 1545-0074
Department of the Treasury Internal Revenue Service	► Whether you are entitled to claim a certain number of allowances or exemption from withholding is subject to review by the IRS. Your employer may be required to send a copy of this form to the IRS.	20**14**

1 Your first name and middle initial	Last name	2 Your social security number

Home address (number and street or rural route)	3 ☐ Single ☐ Married ☐ Married, but withhold at higher Single rate. Note. If married, but legally separated, or spouse is a nonresident alien, check the "Single" box.
City or town, state, and ZIP code	4 If your last name differs from that shown on your social security card, check here. You must call 1-800-772-1213 for a replacement card. ► ☐

5	Total number of allowances you are claiming (from line H above **or** from the applicable worksheet on page 2)	5
6	Additional amount, if any, you want withheld from each paycheck	6 $
7	I claim exemption from withholding for 2014, and I certify that I meet **both** of the following conditions for exemption.
	• Last year I had a right to a refund of **all** federal income tax withheld because I had **no** tax liability, **and**
	• This year I expect a refund of **all** federal income tax withheld because I expect to have **no** tax liability.
	If you meet both conditions, write "Exempt" here . . . . ►	7

Under penalties of perjury, I declare that I have examined this certificate and, to the best of my knowledge and belief, it is true, correct, and complete.

Employee's signature
(This form is not valid unless you sign it.) ►   Date ►

8	Employer's name and address (Employer: Complete lines 8 and 10 only if sending to the IRS.)	9 Office code (optional)	10 Employer identification number (EIN)

For Privacy Act and Paperwork Reduction Act Notice, see page 2.   Cat. No. 10220Q   Form **W-4** (2014)

An employee can always fill out a new W-4 to reflect life changes that impact the tax deduction. For example, if the employee was single when she started working for you and gets married a year later, she can fill out a new W-4 and claim her spouse, lowering the amount of taxes that must be deducted from her check. Another common life change that can reduce an employee's tax deduction is the birth or adoption of a baby.

I-9

All employers in the United States must verify that any person they intend to hire is a U.S. citizen or has the right to work in the United States. As an employer, you verify this information by completing and keeping on file an I-9 form from the U.S. Citizenship and Immigration Services (USCIS). The new hire fills out Section 1 of the form by providing information about his name and address, birth history, Social Security number, and U.S. Citizenship or work permit.

You then fill out Section 2, which requires you to check for and copy documents that establish identity and prove employment eligibility. For a new hire who's a U.S. citizen, you make a copy of one picture ID (usually a driver's license but maybe a military ID, student ID, or other state ID) and an ID that proves work eligibility, such as a Social Security card, birth certificate, or citizen ID card. A U.S. passport can serve as both a picture ID and proof of employment eligibility. Instructions provided with the form list all acceptable documents you can use to verify work eligibility.

Figure 10-3 shows a sample I-9 form. You can download the form and its instructions from the U.S. Citizenship and Immigration Services website at www.uscis.gov/i-9.

Employment Eligibility Verification

Department of Homeland Security
U.S. Citizenship and Immigration Services

USCIS
Form I-9
OMB No. 1615-0047
Expires 03/31/2016

▶ START HERE. Read instructions carefully before completing this form. The instructions must be available during completion of this form.
ANTI-DISCRIMINATION NOTICE: It is illegal to discriminate against work-authorized individuals. Employers CANNOT specify which document(s) they will accept from an employee. The refusal to hire an individual because the documentation presented has a future expiration date may also constitute illegal discrimination.

Section 1. Employee Information and Attestation *(Employees must complete and sign Section 1 of Form I-9 no later than the first day of employment, but not before accepting a job offer.)*

Last Name *(Family Name)* | First Name *(Given Name)* | Middle Initial | Other Names Used *(if any)*

Address *(Street Number and Name)* | Apt. Number | City or Town | State | Zip Code

Date of Birth *(mm/dd/yyyy)* | U.S. Social Security Number | E-mail Address | Telephone Number

I am aware that federal law provides for imprisonment and/or fines for false statements or use of false documents in connection with the completion of this form.

I attest, under penalty of perjury, that I am (check one of the following):

☐ A citizen of the United States

☐ A noncitizen national of the United States *(See instructions)*

☐ A lawful permanent resident (Alien Registration Number/USCIS Number):

☐ An alien authorized to work until (expiration date, if applicable, mm/dd/yyyy) _____ . Some aliens may write "N/A" in this field. *(See instructions)*

For aliens authorized to work, provide your Alien Registration Number/USCIS Number OR Form I-94 Admission Number:

1. Alien Registration Number/USCIS Number:

OR

2. Form I-94 Admission Number:

If you obtained your admission number from CBP in connection with your arrival in the United States, include the following:

Foreign Passport Number:

Country of Issuance:

Some aliens may write "N/A" on the Foreign Passport Number and Country of Issuance fields. *(See instructions)*

3-D Barcode
Do Not Write in This Space

Signature of Employee: | Date *(mm/dd/yyyy)*:

Preparer and/or Translator Certification *(To be completed and signed if Section 1 is prepared by a person other than the employee.)*

I attest, under penalty of perjury, that I have assisted in the completion of this form and that to the best of my knowledge the information is true and correct.

Signature of Preparer or Translator: | Date *(mm/dd/yyyy)*:

Last Name *(Family Name)* | First Name *(Given Name)*

Address *(Street Number and Name)* | City or Town | State | Zip Code

🛑 *Employer Completes Next Page* 🛑

Form I-9 03/08/13 N | Page 7 of 9

Figure 10-3:
U.S. employers must verify a new hire's eligibility to work in the United States by completing Form I-9.

Picking pay periods

Deciding how frequently you'll pay employees is an important point to work out before hiring staff. Most businesses choose one or more of these four pay periods:

- ✓ **Weekly:** Employees are paid every week, and payroll must be done 52 times a year.

- ✓ **Biweekly:** Employees are paid every two weeks, and payroll must be done 26 times a year.

- ✓ **Semimonthly:** Employees are paid twice a month, commonly on the 15th and last day of the month, and payroll must be done 24 times a year.

- ✓ **Monthly:** Employees are paid once a month, and payroll must be done 12 times a year.

You can choose to use any of these pay periods, and you may even decide to use more than one type. For example, some companies will pay hourly employees (employees paid by the hour) weekly or biweekly and pay salaried employees (employees paid by a set salary regardless of how many hours they work) semimonthly or monthly. Whatever your choice, decide on a consistent pay period policy and be sure to make it clear to employees when they're hired.

Determining wage and salary types

You have a lot of leeway regarding the level of wages and salary you pay your employees, but you still have to follow the rules laid out by the U.S. Department of Labor. When deciding on wages and salaries, you have to first categorize your employees. Employees fall into one of two categories:

Keeping time with time sheets

For each employee who's paid hourly, you need to have some sort of time sheet to keep track of work hours. These time sheets are usually completed by the employees and approved by their managers. Completed and approved time sheets are then sent to the bookkeeper so that checks can be calculated based on the exact number of hours worked.

✔ **Exempt employees** are exempt from the Fair Labor Standards Act (FLSA), which sets rules for minimum wage, equal pay, overtime pay, and child labor laws. Executives, administrative personnel, managers, professionals, computer specialists, and outside salespeople can all be exempt employees. They're normally paid a certain amount per pay period with no connection to the number of hours worked. Often, exempt employees work well over 40 hours per week without extra pay. Prior to new rules from the Department of Labor effective in 2004, only high-paid employees fell in this category; today, however, employees making as little as $23,600 can be placed in the exempt category.

✔ **Nonexempt employees** must be hired according to rules of the FLSA, meaning that companies with gross sales of over $500,000 per year must pay a minimum wage per hour of $7.25. Smaller companies with gross sales under $500,000 do not have to pay this minimum wage as long as they do not operate across state lines. For new employees who are under the age of 20 and need training, an employer can pay as little as $4.25 for the first 90 days. Also, any nonexempt employee who works over 40 hours in a seven-day period must be paid time and one-half for the additional hours. Minimum wage doesn't have to be paid in cash. The employer can pay some or all the wage in room and board provided it doesn't make a profit on any noncash payments. Also, the employer can't charge the employee to use its facilities if the employee's use of a facility is primarily for the employer's benefit.

Exempt or nonexempt

You're probably wondering how to determine whether to hire exempt or nonexempt employees. Of course, most businesses would prefer to exempt all their employees from the overtime laws. You don't have a choice if your employees earn less than $23,660 per year or $455 per week. All employees lower than this earning range must be paid overtime if they work more than 40 hours in a week. These employees are nonexempt employees — in other words, not exempt from the Fair Labor Practices Act, which governs who must be paid overtime.

You have more flexibility with employees earning more than $23,660 per year. You can classify employees who work as executives, administrative personnel, professionals, computer specialists, and outside salespeople as exempt. Also those who perform office or nonmanual work earning over $100,000 per year can be exempt. Blue-collar workers in manual labor positions cannot be exempt employees and must be paid overtime. Also police, fire fighters, paramedics, and other first responders cannot be exempt employees and must be paid overtime.

For more details about who can be designated an exempt employee, visit the U.S. Department of Labor's website at www.dol.gov/whd/regs/compliance/ca_main.htm.

The federal government hasn't adjusted the minimum wage law since 1997. Many states require minimum wages above those set by the federal government. You can see a detailed breakdown by state at the website of the National Conference of State Legislators (`www.ncsl.org/research/labor-and-employment/state-minimum-wage-chart.aspx`).

If you plan to hire employees who are under the age of 18, you must pay attention to child labor laws. Federal and state laws restrict what kind of work children can do, when they can do it, and how old they have to be to do it, so be sure you become familiar with the laws before hiring employees who are younger than 18. For minors below the age of 16, work restrictions are even tighter than for teens aged 16 and 17. (You can hire your own child without worrying about these restrictions.)

Collecting Employee Taxes

In addition to following wage and salary guidelines set for your business, when calculating payroll, you, the bookkeeper, must also be familiar with how to calculate the employee taxes that must be deducted from each employee's paycheck. These taxes include Social Security; Medicare; and federal, state, and local withholding taxes.

Sorting out Social Security tax

Employers and employees share the Social Security tax equally: Each must pay 6.2 percent (0.062) toward Social Security up to a cap of $117,000 per year per person (as of this writing). After an employee earns $117,000, no additional Social Security taxes are taken out of his check. The federal government adjusts the cap each year based on salary level changes in the marketplace. Essentially, the cap gradually increases as salaries increase.

The calculation for Social Security taxes is relatively simple. For example, for an employee who makes $1,000 per pay period, you calculate Social Security tax this way:

$$\$1,000 \times 0.062 = \$62$$

The bookkeeper deducts $62 from this employee's gross pay, and the company pays the employer's share of $62. Thus, the total amount submitted in Social Security taxes for this employee is $124.

Making sense of Medicare tax

Employees and employers also share Medicare taxes, which are 1.45 percent each. However, unlike Social Security taxes, the federal government places no cap on the amount that must be paid in Medicare taxes. So even if someone makes $1 million per year, 1.45 percent is calculated for each pay period and paid by both the employee and the employer. Here's an example of how you calculate the Medicare tax for an employee who makes $1,000 per pay period:

$1,000 × 0.0145 = $14.50

The bookkeeper deducts $14.50 from this employee's gross pay, and the company pays the employer's share of $14.50. Thus, the total amount submitted in Medicare taxes for this employee is $29.

Figuring out federal withholding tax

Deducting federal withholding taxes is a much more complex task for bookkeepers than deducting Social Security or Medicare taxes. You not only have to worry about an employee's tax rate, but you also must consider the number of withholding allowances the employee claimed on her W-4 and whether she's married or single. Under the 2013 tax law still in effect as of this writing, the first $8,925 of an unmarried person's taxable income (the first $17,850 for a married couple) is taxed at 10 percent. Other tax rates depending on income are 15 percent, 25 percent, 28 percent, 33 percent, 35 percent and 39.6 percent.

Trying to figure out taxes separately for each employee based on his or her tax rate and number of allowances would be an extremely time-consuming task, but luckily, you don't have to do that. The IRS publishes tax tables in Publication 15, "Employer's Tax Guide," that let you just look up an employee's tax obligation based on the taxable salary and withholdings. You can access the IRS Employer's Tax Guide online at www.irs.gov/pub/irs-pdf/p15. pdf. You can find tables for calculating withholding taxes at www.irs.gov/pub/irs-pdf/p15a.pdf.

The IRS's tax tables give you detailed numbers up to ten withholding allowances. Table 10-1 shows a sample tax table with only seven allowances because of space limitations. But even with seven allowances, you get the idea — just match the employee's wage range up with the number of allowances he or she claims, and the box where they meet contains the amount of that employee's tax obligation. For example, if you're preparing a paycheck for a married employee whose taxable income is $1,000 per weekly pay period, and he claims three withholding allowances — one for himself, one for his wife, and one for his children — then the amount of federal income taxes you deduct from his pay is $75.

Table 10-1		Portion of an IRS Tax Table for Employers						
If Wages Are:		**And the Number of Allowances Claimed Is:**						
At Least	**But Less Than**	**1**	**2**	**3**	**4**	**5**	**6**	**7**
1,000	1,010	98	86	75	63	52	41	31
1,010	1,020	99	88	76	65	53	42	32
1,020	1,030	101	89	78	66	55	44	33

Settling up state and local withholding taxes

In addition to the federal government, most states have income taxes, and some cities even have local income taxes. You can find all state tax rates and forms online at www.payroll-taxes.com. If your state or city has income taxes, they need to be taken out of each employee's paycheck.

Determining Net Pay

Net pay is the amount a person is paid after subtracting all tax and benefit deductions. In other words after all deductions are subtracted from a person's gross pay, you are left with the net pay.

After you figure out all the necessary taxes to be taken from an employee's paycheck, you can calculate the check amount. Here's the equation and an example of how you calculate the net pay amount:

Gross pay – (Social Security + Medicare + Federal withholding tax + State withholding tax + Local withholding tax) = Net pay

$$1,000 - (62 + 14.50 + 75 + 45 + 0) = 803.50$$

This net pay calculation doesn't include any deductions for benefits. Many businesses offer their employees health, retirement, and other benefits but expect the employees to share a portion of those costs. The fact that some of these benefits are tax deductible and some are not makes a difference in when you deduct the benefit costs. If an employee's benefits are tax deductible and taken out of the check before federal withholding taxes are calculated, the federal tax rate may be lower than if the benefits were deducted after calculating federal withholding taxes. Many states follow the federal government's lead on tax-deductible benefits, so the amount deducted for state taxes will be lower as well. For example, the federal government allows employers to consider health insurance premiums as nontaxable, so the states do so also.

Surveying Your Benefits Options

Benefits include programs that you provide your employees to better their life, such as health insurance and retirement savings opportunities. Most benefits are tax-exempt, which means that the employee isn't taxed for them. However, some benefits are taxable, so the employee has to pay taxes on the money or the value of the benefits received. This section reviews the different tax-exempt and taxable benefits you can offer your employees.

Tax-exempt benefits

Most benefits are tax-exempt, or not taxed. Healthcare and retirement benefits are the most common of this type of benefit. In fact, accident and health benefits and retirement benefits make up the largest share of employers' pay toward employees' benefits. Luckily, not only are these benefits tax-exempt, but anything an employee pays toward them can be deducted from the gross pay, so the employee doesn't have to pay taxes on that part of his salary or wages.

For example, if an employee's share of health insurance is $50 per pay period and he makes $1,000 per pay period, his taxable income is actually $1,000 minus the $50 health insurance premium contribution, or $950. As the bookkeeper, you calculate taxes in this situation on $950 rather than $1,000.

The money that an employee who contributes to the retirement plan you offer is tax deductible, too. For example, if an employee contributes $50 per pay period to your company's 401(k) retirement plan, that $50 can also be subtracted from the employee's gross pay before you calculate net pay. So if an employee contributes $50 to both health insurance and retirement, the $1,000 taxable pay is reduced to only $900 taxable pay. (According to the tax table for that pay level, his federal withholding taxes are only $71, a savings of $15 over a taxable income of $1,000, or 15 percent of his health and retirement costs.)

Employer obligations for providing healthcare benefits changed with the passage of the Patient Protection and Affordable Care Act in 2010. There are now four sets of rules regarding who must provide what benefits. Smaller employers also may be eligible for government assistance to provide health benefits for their employees. The four levels include

- Employers with 50 or more employees
- Employers with up to 50 employees
- Employers with fewer than 25 employees
- Self-employed

The U.S. Small Business Administration offers webinars for small business owners to learn more about how the new law impacts their business. You can find out more about the new law and sign up for these webinars at www.sba. gov/healthcare.

You can offer a myriad of other tax-exempt benefits to employees, as well, including:

- **Adoption assistance:** You can provide up to $12,970 per child that an employee plans to adopt without having to include that amount in gross income for the purposes of calculating federal withholding taxes in the current tax year. The value of this benefit must be included when calculating Social Security and Medicare taxes, however. Additional benefits can be an unused tax credit that can be carried forward for up to five tax years. You must develop a written plan for adoption assistance that meets the rules of the IRS, which you can find in Publication 15-B, "Employer's Tax Guide to Fringe Benefits" (www.irs.gov/pub/irs-pdf/p15b.pdf).

- **Athletic facilities:** You can offer your employees the use of a gym on premises that your company owns or leases without having to include the value of the gym facilities in gross pay. In order for this benefit to qualify as tax-exempt, the facility must be operated by the company primarily for the use of employees, their spouses, and their dependent children.

- **Dependent care assistance:** You can help your employees with dependent care expenses, which can include children and elderly parents, provided you offer the benefit in order to make it possible for the employee to work.

- **Education assistance:** You can pay employees' educational expenses up to $5,250 without having to include that payment in gross income. Any amounts provided in addition to $5,250 would be taxable.

- **Employee discounts:** You can offer employees discounts on the company's products without including the value of the discounts in their gross pay, provided the discount is not more than 20 percent less than what's charged to customers. If you only offer this discount to high-paid employees, then the value of these discounts must be included in gross pay of those employees.

- ✔ **Group term life insurance:** You can provide group term life insurance up to a coverage level of $50,000 to your employees without including the value of this insurance in their gross pay. Premiums for coverage above $50,000 must be added to calculations for Social Security and Medicare taxes.

- ✔ **Meals:** Meals that have little value (such as coffee and doughnuts) don't have to be reported as taxable income. Also, occasional meals brought in so employees can work late also don't have to be reported in employees' income.

- ✔ **Moving expense reimbursements:** If you pay moving expenses for employees, you don't have to report these reimbursements as employee income as long as the reimbursements are for items that would qualify as tax-deductible moving expenses on an employee's individual tax return. Employees who have been reimbursed by their employers can't deduct moving expenses for which the employer paid.

Taxable benefits

You may decide to provide some benefits that are taxable. These include the personal use of a company automobile, life insurance premiums for coverage over $50,000, and benefits that exceed allowable maximums. For example, if you pay $10,250 toward an employee's education expenses, then $5,000 of that amount must be reported as income because the federal government's cap is $5,250.

Dealing with cafeteria plans

When I mention cafeteria plans, I'm not talking about offering a lunch spot for your employees. Cafeteria plans are benefit plans that offer employees a choice of benefits based on cost. Employees can pick and choose from those benefits and put together a benefit package that works best for them within the established cost structure.

Cafeteria plans are becoming more popular among larger businesses, but not all employers decide to offer their benefits this way. Primarily, this decision is because managing a cafeteria plan can be much more time consuming for the bookkeeping and human resources staff. Many small business employers that do choose to offer a cafeteria plan for benefits do so by outsourcing benefit management services to an outside company that specializes in managing cafeteria plans.

For example, a company tells its employees that it will pay up to $5,000 in benefits per year and values its benefit offerings this way:

Health insurance	$4,600
Retirement	$1,200
Child care	$1,200
Life insurance	$800

Joe, an employee, then picks from the list of benefits until he reaches $5,000. If Joe wants more than $5,000 in benefits, he pays for the additional benefits with a reduction in his paycheck.

The list of possible benefits could be considerably longer, but in this case, if Joe chooses health insurance, retirement, and life insurance, the total cost is $6,600. Because the company pays up to $5,000, Joe needs to copay $1,600, a portion of which is taken out in each paycheck. If Joe gets paid every two weeks for a total of 26 paychecks per year, the deduction for benefits from his gross pay is $61.54 ($1,600 ÷ 26).

Preparing Payroll and Posting It in the Books

Once you know the details about your employees' withholding allowances and their benefit costs, you can then calculate the final payroll and post it to the books.

Calculating payroll for hourly employees

When you're ready to prepare payroll for nonexempt employees, the first thing you need to do is collect time records from each person being paid hourly. Some companies use time clocks, and some use time sheets to produce the required time records, but whatever the method used, usually the manager of each department reviews the time records for each employee she supervises and then sends those time records to you, the bookkeeper.

With time records in hand, you have to calculate gross pay for each employee. For example, if a nonexempt employee worked 45 hours and is paid $12 an hour, you calculate gross pay like so:

40 regular hours × $12 per hour = $480

5 overtime hours × $12 per hour × 1.5 overtime rate = $90

$480 + $90 = $570

In this case, because the employee isn't exempt from the FLSA (see "Determining wage and salary types" earlier in this chapter), overtime must be paid for any hours worked over 40 in a seven-day workweek. This employee worked five hours more than the 40 hours allowed, so he needs to be paid at time plus one-half.

Doling out funds to salaried employees

In addition to employees paid based on hourly wages, you also must prepare payroll for salaried employees. Paychecks for salaried employees are relatively easy to calculate — all you need to know are their base salaries and their pay period calculations. For example, if a salaried employee makes $30,000 per year and is paid twice a month (totaling 24 pay periods), that employee's gross pay is be $1,250 for each pay period.

Totaling up for commission checks

Running payroll for employees paid based on commission can involve the most complex calculations. To show you a number of variables, in this section I calculate a commission check based on a salesperson who sells $60,000 worth of products during one month.

For a salesperson on a straight commission of 10 percent, you calculate pay using this formula:

Total amount sold × Commission percentage = Gross pay

$60,000 × 0.10 = $6,000

For a salesperson with a guaranteed base salary of $2,000 plus an additional 5 percent commission on all products sold, you calculate pay using this formula:

Base salary + (Total amount sold × Commission percentage) = Gross pay

$2,000 + ($60,000 × 0.05) = $5,000

Although this employee may be happier having a base salary he can count on each month, he actually makes less with a base salary because the commission rate is so much lower. By selling $60,000 worth of products he made only $3,000 in commission at 5 percent. Without the base pay, he would have made 10 percent on the $60,000 or $6,000, so he actually got paid $1,000 less with a base pay structure that includes a lower commission pay rate.

If he has a slow sales month of just $30,000 worth of products sold, his pay would be:

$30,000 × 0.10 = $3,000 on straight commission of 10 percent

and

$30,000 × 0.05 = $1,500 plus $2,000 base salary, or $3,500

For a slow month, the salesperson would make more money with the base salary rather than the higher commission rate.

There are many other ways to calculate commissions. One common way is to offer higher commissions on higher levels of sales. Using the figures in this example, this type of pay system encourages salespeople to keep their sales levels over $30,000 to get the best commission rate.

With a graduated commission scale, a salesperson can make a straight commission of 5 percent on his first $10,000 in sales, then 7 percent on his next $20,000, and finally 10 percent on anything over $30,000. Here's what his gross pay calculation looks like using this commission pay scale:

($10,000 × 0.05) + ($20,000 × 0.07) + (<u>$30,000</u> × <u>0.10</u>) = $4,900 Gross pay

One other type of commission pay system involves a base salary plus tips. This method is common in restaurant settings in which servers receive between $2.50 and $5 per hour plus tips.

Businesses that pay less than minimum wage must prove that their employees make at least minimum wage when tips are accounted for. Today, that's relatively easy to prove because most people pay their bills with credit cards and include tips on their bills. Businesses can then come up with an average tip rate using that credit-card data.

Employees must report tips to their employers on an IRS Form 4070, Employee's Report of Tips to Employer, which is part of IRS Publication 1244, "Employees Daily Record of Tips and Report to Employer." If your employees receive tips and you want to supply the necessary paperwork, you can download it at www.irs.gov/pub/irs-pdf/p1244.pdf. The publication provides details about what the IRS expects you and your employees to do if they work in an environment where tipping is common.

As an employer, you must report an employee's gross taxable wages based on salary plus tips. Here's how you calculate gross taxable wages for an employee whose earnings are based on tips and wages:

Base wage + Tips = Gross taxable wages

($3 × 40 hours per week) + $300 = $420

If your employees are paid using a combination of base wage plus tips, you must be sure that your employees are earning at least the minimum wage rate of $7.25 per hour. Checking this employee's gross wages, the hourly rate earned is $10.50 per hour.

Hourly wage = $10.50 ($420 ÷ 40)

Taxes due are calculated on the base wage plus tips, so the check you prepare for the employee in this example is for the base wage minus any taxes due.

After calculating paychecks for all your employees, you prepare the payroll, make up the checks, and post the payroll to the books. In addition to Cash, many accounts are impacted by payroll, including:

✔ Accrued Federal Withholding Payable, which is where you record the liability for future federal tax payments.

✔ Accrued State Withholding Payable, which is where you record the liability for future state tax payments.

✔ Accrued Employee Medical Insurance Payable, which is where you record the liability for future medical insurance premiums.

✔ Accrued Employee Elective Insurance Payable, which is where you record the liability for miscellaneous insurance premiums, such as life or accident insurance.

When you post the payroll entry, you indicate the withdrawal of money from the Cash account as well as record liabilities for future cash payments that will be due for taxes and insurance payments. Just for the purposes of giving you an example of the proper setup for a payroll journal entry, I assume the total payroll is $10,000 with $1,000 set aside for each type of withholding payable. In reality, your numbers will be much different, and I doubt your payables will ever all be the same. Here's what your journal entry for posting payroll should look like:

	Debit	*Credit*
Salaries and Wages Expense	$10,000	
Accrued Federal Withholding Payable		$1,000
Accrued State Withholding Payable		$1,000
Accrued Medical Insurance Payable		$1,000
Accrued Elective Insurance Payable		$1,000
Cash		$6,000

To record payroll for May 27, 2014.

In this entry, you increase the expense account for salaries and wages as well as all the accounts in which you accrue future obligations for taxes and employee insurance payments. You decrease the amount of the Cash account; when cash payments are made for the taxes and insurance payments in the future, you post those payments in the books. Here's an example of the entry you would post to the books after making the federal withholding tax payment:

	Debit	Credit
Accrued Federal Withholding Payable	$1,000	
Cash in Checking		$1,000

To record the payment of May federal taxes for employees.

Depositing Employee Taxes

The IRS used to accept employee taxes using a Federal Tax Deposit Coupon, numbered Form 8109 and 8109-B. This form of payment became no longer accepted as of December 31, 2010. The IRS recommends that all businesses use the Electronic Federal Tax Payment System.

You can find out more about getting set up on this system by calling the IRS at 800-434-7338. Or sign up at the EFTPS website: www.eftps.gov/eftps.

For the purposes of tax payments collected from employees for the federal government, you must complete Form 941, which is shown in Figures 10-4 and 10-5. This form summarizes the tax payments made on behalf of employees. You can get instructions and Form 941 online www.irs.gov/pub/irs-pdf/i941.pdf. (I talk more about the various forms employers must file in Chapter 11.)

During the first year as an employer, the company will have to make monthly deposits of employee taxes. Monthly payments must be made by the 15th day of the month following when the taxes were taken. For example, taxes collected from employees in April must be paid by May 15. If the date the deposit is due falls on a weekend or bank holiday, the payment is due on the next day the banks are open.

As your business gets larger, you'll need to make more frequent deposits. Large employers that accumulate taxes of $100,000 or more in a day must deposit the funds on the next banking day.

Form 941 for 2014: Employer's QUARTERLY Federal Tax Return

(Rev. January 2014) — Department of the Treasury — Internal Revenue Service

950114

OMB No. 1545-0029

Employer identification number (EIN)

Name (not your trade name)

Trade name (if any)

Address — Number, Street, Suite or room number, City, State, ZIP code

Foreign country name, Foreign province/county, Foreign postal code

Report for this Quarter of 2014 (Check one.)

- ☐ 1: January, February, March
- ☐ 2: April, May, June
- ☐ 3: July, August, September
- ☐ 4: October, November, December

Instructions and prior year forms are available at www.irs.gov/form941.

Read the separate instructions before you complete Form 941. Type or print within the boxes.

Part 1: Answer these questions for this quarter.

1. Number of employees who received wages, tips, or other compensation for the pay period including: *Mar. 12* (Quarter 1), *June 12* (Quarter 2), *Sept. 12* (Quarter 3), or *Dec. 12* (Quarter 4) — **1**

2. Wages, tips, and other compensation — **2**

3. Federal income tax withheld from wages, tips, and other compensation — **3**

4. If no wages, tips, and other compensation are subject to social security or Medicare tax ☐ Check and go to line 6.

	Column 1	Column 2
5a Taxable social security wages	× .124 =	
5b Taxable social security tips	× .124 =	
5c Taxable Medicare wages & tips	× .029 =	
5d Taxable wages & tips subject to Additional Medicare Tax withholding	× .009 =	

5e. Add Column 2 from lines 5a, 5b, 5c, and 5d — **5e**

5f. Section 3121(q) Notice and Demand—Tax due on unreported tips (see instructions) — **5f**

6. Total taxes before adjustments. Add lines 3, 5e, and 5f — **6**

7. Current quarter's adjustment for fractions of cents — **7**

8. Current quarter's adjustment for sick pay — **8**

9. Current quarter's adjustments for tips and group-term life insurance — **9**

10. Total taxes after adjustments. Combine lines 6 through 9 — **10**

11. Total deposits for this quarter, including overpayment applied from a prior quarter and overpayments applied from Form 941-X, 941-X (PR), 944-X, 944-X (PR), or 944-X (SP) filed in the current quarter — **11**

12. Balance due. If line 10 is more than line 11, enter the difference and see instructions — **12**

13. Overpayment. If line 11 is more than line 10, enter the difference — Check one: ☐ Apply to next return ☐ Send a refund.

▶ You MUST complete both pages of Form 941 and SIGN it.

For Privacy Act and Paperwork Reduction Act Notice, see the back of the Payment Voucher. — Cat. No. 17001Z — Form **941** (Rev. 1-2014)

Figure 10-4: Employers must file Form 941 to report taxes collected on behalf of employees.

950214

Name *(not your trade name)*	Employer identification number (EIN)

Part 2: Tell us about your deposit schedule and tax liability for this quarter.

If you are unsure about whether you are a monthly schedule depositor or a semiweekly schedule depositor, see Pub. 15 (Circular E), section 11.

14 Check one: ☐ Line 10 on this return is less than $2,500 or line 10 on the return for the prior quarter was less than $2,500, and you did not incur a $100,000 next-day deposit obligation during the current quarter. If line 10 for the prior quarter was less than $2,500 but line 10 on this return is $100,000 or more, you must provide a record of your federal tax liability. If you are a monthly schedule depositor, complete the deposit schedule below; if you are a semiweekly schedule depositor, attach Schedule B (Form 941). Go to Part 3.

☐ **You were a monthly schedule depositor for the entire quarter.** Enter your tax liability for each month and total liability for the quarter, then go to Part 3.

Tax liability: Month 1 [.   ]

Month 2 [.   ]

Month 3 [.   ]

Total liability for quarter [.   ]   Total must equal line 10.

☐ **You were a semiweekly schedule depositor for any part of this quarter.** Complete Schedule B (Form 941), Report of Tax Liability for Semiweekly Schedule Depositors, and attach it to Form 941.

Part 3: Tell us about your business. If a question does NOT apply to your business, leave it blank.

15 If your business has closed or you stopped paying wages . . . . ☐ Check here, and

enter the final date you paid wages [/   /   ] .

16 If you are a seasonal employer and you do not have to file a return for every quarter of the year . . ☐ Check here.

Part 4: May we speak with your third-party designee?

Do you want to allow an employee, a paid tax preparer, or another person to discuss this return with the IRS? See the instructions for details.

☐ Yes. Designee's name and phone number [   ]   [   ]

Select a 5-digit Personal Identification Number (PIN) to use when talking to the IRS. ☐ ☐ ☐ ☐ ☐

☐ No.

Part 5: Sign here. You MUST complete both pages of Form 941 and SIGN it.

Under penalties of perjury, I declare that I have examined this return, including accompanying schedules and statements, and to the best of my knowledge and belief, it is true, correct, and complete. Declaration of preparer (other than taxpayer) is based on all information of which preparer has any knowledge.

X **Sign your name here** [   ]

Print your name here [   ]

Print your title here [   ]

Date [/   /   ]   Best daytime phone [   ]

Paid Preparer Use Only   Check if you are self-employed . . . ☐

Preparer's name	[ ]	PTIN	[ ]
Preparer's signature	[ ]	Date	[/ /]
Firm's name (or yours if self-employed)	[ ]	EIN	[ ]
Address	[ ]	Phone	[ ]
City	[ ] State [ ]	ZIP code	[ ]

Figure 10-5: Form 941 (continued).

Page **2**   Form **941** (Rev. 1-2014)

Outsourcing Payroll and Benefits Work

Given all that's required of you to prepare payroll, you may think it's a good idea for your small company to outsource the work of payroll and benefits. I don't disagree. Many companies outsource the work because it's such a specialized area and requires extensive software to manage both payroll and benefits.

If you don't want to take on payroll and benefits, you can also pay for a monthly payroll service from the software company that provides your accounting software. For example, QuickBooks provides various levels of payroll services starting at $79 per month plus $2 per employee.

Chapter 11

Employer-Paid Taxes and Government Payroll Reporting

. . . .

In This Chapter

▶ Tallying up the employer's share of Social Security and Medicare

▶ Filing and paying unemployment taxes

▶ Figuring out workers' compensation

▶ Keeping accurate employee records

. . . .

*Y*ou may think that employees will make your job as a business owner easier, but I'm afraid you're wrong on that one. It's really a mixed bag. While employees help you keep your business operating and enable you to grow, they also add a lot of government paperwork.

After your company hires employees, you need to complete regular reports for the government regarding the taxes you must pay toward the employees' Social Security and Medicare, as well as unemployment taxes. In every state except Texas, employers also are required to buy workers' compensation insurance based on employees' salary and wages.

This chapter reviews the federal, state, and local government reporting requirements for employers as well as the records you, the bookkeeper, must keep in order to complete these reports. You also find out how to calculate the various employee taxes and how to buy workers' compensation insurance.

In Chapter 10, I show you how to calculate the employee side of Social Security and Medicare taxes. This chapter looks at the employer side of these taxes, as well as other employer-paid government taxes.

Paying Employer Taxes on Social Security and Medicare

In the United States, both employers and employees must contribute to the Social Security and Medicare systems. In fact, employers share equally with employees the tax obligation for both Social Security and Medicare.

As I discuss in greater detail in Chapter 10, the employer and the employee each must pay 6.2 percent of an employee's compensation for Social Security, up to a salary of $117,000 in 2014. The percentage paid toward Medicare is 1.45 percent for both the employer and employee. There is no salary cap related to the amount that must be paid toward Medicare, so even if your employee makes $1 million (don't you wish your business was that successful?), you still must pay Medicare taxes on that amount.

When you finish calculating payroll checks, you calculate the employer's portion of Social Security and Medicare. When you post the payroll to the books, the employer's portion of Social Security and Medicare is set aside in an accrual account.

Filing Form 941

Each quarter you must file federal Form 941, *Employer's Federal Tax Return,* which details the number of employees who received wages, tips, or other compensation for the quarter. In Chapter 10, you can see what the form looks like. Below, Table 11-1, tells what months are reported during each quarter and when the report is due:

Table 11-1	Filing Requirements for Employer's Quarterly Federal Tax Return (Form 941)
Months in Quarter	*Report Due Date*
January, February, March	On or before April 30
April, May, June	On or before July 31
July, August, September	On or before October 31
October, November, December	On or before January 31

Form 941 was revised for 2014, so be sure you're using the newest version, the one dated 2014. The new form requires more detail than older versions, so you definitely don't want to be working from an old form or you could find yourself in big trouble.

The following key information must be included on Form 941:

- ✔ Number of employees who received wages, tips, or other compensation in the pay period
- ✔ Total of wages, tips, and other compensation paid to employees
- ✔ Total tax withheld from wages, tips, and other compensation
- ✔ Taxable Social Security and Medicare wages
- ✔ Tax due on unreported tips
- ✔ Adjustment for sick pay
- ✔ Adjustments for tips and group term life insurance
- ✔ Total deposits for the quarter

Knowing how often to file

As an employer, you file Form 941 on a quarterly basis, but you probably have to pay taxes more frequently. Employers make deposits online using the IRS's Electronic Federal Tax Payment System (EFTPS). For more information on EFTPS, go to www.eftps.gov.

Employers on a monthly payment schedule (usually small companies) must deposit all employment taxes due by the 15th day of the following month. For example, the taxes for the payroll in April must be paid by May 15th. Larger employers must pay taxes more frequently. For example, employers whose businesses accumulate $100,000 or more in taxes due on any day during a deposit period must deposit those taxes on the next banking day. If you hit $100,000 due when you're a monthly depositor, you must start paying taxes semiweekly for at least the remainder of the current tax year.

After you become a semiweekly payer, you must deposit your taxes on Wednesday or Friday, depending on your payday:

- ✔ **If you pay employees on Wednesday, Thursday, or Friday,** you must deposit the taxes due by the next Wednesday.
- ✔ **If you pay employees on Saturday, Sunday, Monday, or Tuesday,** you must deposit the taxes due by the next Friday.

Still larger employers, that is, those with tax payments due of $200,000 or more, must deposit these taxes electronically using EFTPS according to the semiweekly payment schedule. Electronic tax payments for employers with tax payments under $200,000 are voluntary.

However you're required to pay your payroll-based taxes, one thing you definitely don't want to do is underpay. Interest and penalty charges for late payment can make your tax bite even higher — and I'm sure you're convinced it's high enough already. If you find it hard to accurately estimate your quarterly tax payment, your best bet is to pay a slightly higher amount in the first and second month of a quarter. Then, if you've paid a bit more than needed, you can cut back the payment for the third month of the quarter. This strategy lets you avoid the possibility of underpaying in the first two months of a quarter and risking interest and penalty charges.

Completing Unemployment Reports and Paying Unemployment Taxes

If you ever faced unemployment, I'm sure you were relieved to get a weekly check while you looked for a job — meager as it may have been. Did you realize that unemployment compensation was partially paid by your employer? In fact, an employer pays his share of unemployment compensation based on his record of firing or laying off of employees. So think for a moment of your dear employees and your own past experiences, and you'll see the value of paying toward unemployment compensation.

The fund that used to be known simply as Unemployment is now known as the Federal Unemployment Tax Act (FUTA) fund. Employers contribute to the fund, but states also collect taxes to fill their unemployment fund coffers.

For FUTA, employers pay a federal rate of 6.0 percent on the first $7,000 that each employee earns. Luckily, you don't just have to add the state rate on top of that; the federal government allows you to subtract up to 5.4 percent of the first $7,000 per employee, if that amount is paid to the state. Essentially, the amount you pay to the state can serve as a credit toward the amount you must pay to the federal government.

Each state sets its own unemployment tax rate. Many states also charge additional fees for administrative costs and job-training programs. You can check out the full charges for your state at `http://payroll-taxes.com`, but to give you an idea of how taxes vary state to state, check out the sampling shown in Table 11-2.

Table 11-2	Sampling of Unemployment Tax Rates		
State	*Percentage Range*	*For a Salary Up To*	*New Employee Percentage*
California	1.6 to 6.2	$7,000	3.4
Florida	0.59 to 5.4	$8,000	2.7
Nevada	0.25 to 5.4	$27,400	2.95
New York	2.025 to 9.825	$10,300	4.025
Rhode Island	1.69 to 9.79	$20,600	2.85

The percentage an employer must pay isn't a set amount but instead is a percentage range. The employee income amount upon which this percentage is charged also varies from state to state. The percentage range is based on the company's employment history and how frequently its employees collect unemployment.

How states calculate the FUTA tax rate

States use four different methods to calculate how much you may need to pay in FUTA taxes:

- ✔ **Benefit ratio formula:** The state looks at the ratio of benefits collected by former employees to your company's total payroll over the past three years. States also adjust your rate depending upon the overall balance in the state unemployment insurance fund.

- ✔ **Benefit wage formula:** The state looks at the proportion of your company's payroll that's paid to workers who become unemployed and receive benefits, and then divides that number by your company's total taxable wages.

- ✔ **Payroll decline ratio formula:** The state looks at the decline in your company's payrolls from year to year or from quarter to quarter.

- ✔ **Reserve ratio formula:** The state keeps track of your company's balance in the unemployment reserve account, which gives a cumulative representation of its use by your former employees that were laid off and paid unemployment. This record-keeping dates back from the date you were first subject to the state unemployment rate. The reserve account is calculated by adding up all your contributions to the account and then subtracting total benefits paid. This amount is then divided by your company's total payroll. The higher the reserve ratio, the lower the required contribution rate.

These formulas can be very complicated, so your best bet is to meet with your state's unemployment office to review how your company's unemployment rate will be set. In addition to getting a better idea of what may impact your FUTA tax rate, you can also discuss how best to minimize that rate.

Calculating FUTA tax

After you know what your rate is, calculating the actual FUTA tax you owe isn't difficult.

As an example, consider a new company that's just getting started in the state of Florida; it has ten employees, and each employee makes more than $8,000 per year. For state FUTA taxes, I use the new employer rate of 2.7 percent on the first $8,000 of income. The federal FUTA is the same for all employers — 6.0 percent. Here's how you calculate the FUTA tax for this company:

State unemployment taxes:

$8,000 × 0.027 = $216 per employee

$216 × 10 employees = $2,160

Federal unemployment taxes:

$7,000 × 0.060 = $420

$420 × 10 employees = $4,200

The company doesn't have to pay the full federal amount because it can take up to a 5.4 percent credit for state taxes paid ($7,000 × 0.054 = $378). Since state taxes in Florida are 2.7 percent of $8,000, this employer can't subtract the full amount of Florida FUTA taxes from the federal FUTA tax. It can only subtract 2.7 percent of the first 7,000 or $189 per employee for a total of $1,890:

$4,200 − $1,890 = $2,310

So this company only needs to pay $2,310 to the federal government in FUTA taxes. Any company paying more than $378 per employee to the state is only able to reduce its federal bill by the maximum of $378 per employee. So, every employer pays at least $56 per employee into the Federal FUTA pool.

Each year, you must file IRS Form 940, *Employer's Annual Federal Unemployment (FUTA) Tax Return.* The first page of Form 940 is shown in Figure 11-1, and the second page is shown in Figure 11-2. You can also find it online at www.irs. gov/pub/irs-pdf/f940.pdf.

Form **940 for 2013:** Employer's Annual Federal Unemployment (FUTA) Tax Return	850113

Department of the Treasury — Internal Revenue Service

OMB No. 1545-0028

Employer identification number (EIN)

Name (not your trade name)

Trade name (if any)

Address

Number   Street   Suite or room number

City   State   ZIP code

Foreign country name   Foreign province/county   Foreign postal code

Type of Return
(Check all that apply.)

- a. Amended
- b. Successor employer
- c. No payments to employees in 2013
- d. Final: Business closed or stopped paying wages

Instructions and prior-year forms are available at *www.irs.gov/form940*.

Read the separate instructions before you complete this form. Please type or print within the boxes.

Part 1: Tell us about your return. If any line does NOT apply, leave it blank.

1a If you had to pay state unemployment tax in one state only, enter the state abbreviation . **1a**

1b If you had to pay state unemployment tax in more than one state, you are a multi-state employer . . . . **1b** ☐ Check here. Complete Schedule A (Form 940).

2 If you paid wages in a state that is subject to CREDIT REDUCTION . . . . **2** ☐ Check here. Complete Schedule A (Form 940).

Part 2: Determine your FUTA tax before adjustments for 2013. If any line does NOT apply, leave it blank.

3 Total payments to all employees **3**

4 Payments exempt from FUTA tax **4**

Check all that apply: 4a ☐ Fringe benefits   4c ☐ Retirement/Pension   4e ☐ Other
4b ☐ Group-term life insurance   4d ☐ Dependent care

5 Total of payments made to each employee in excess of $7,000 . . . . **5**

6 Subtotal (line 4 + line 5 = line 6) **6**

7 Total taxable FUTA wages (line 3 – line 6 = line 7) (see instructions) **7**

8 FUTA tax before adjustments (line 7 x .006 = line 8) **8**

Part 3: Determine your adjustments. If any line does NOT apply, leave it blank.

9 If ALL of the taxable FUTA wages you paid were excluded from state unemployment tax, multiply line 7 by .054 (line 7 x .054 = line 9). Go to line 12 . . . . . **9**

10 If SOME of the taxable FUTA wages you paid were excluded from state unemployment tax, OR you paid ANY state unemployment tax late (after the due date for filing Form 940), complete the worksheet in the instructions. Enter the amount from line 7 of the worksheet . . **10**

11 If credit reduction applies, enter the total from Schedule A (Form 940) **11**

Part 4: Determine your FUTA tax and balance due or overpayment for 2013. If any line does NOT apply, leave it blank.

12 Total FUTA tax after adjustments (lines 8 + 9 + 10 + 11 = line 12) **12**

13 FUTA tax deposited for the year, including any overpayment applied from a prior year . **13**

14 Balance due (if line 12 is more than line 13, enter the excess on line 14.)
- If line 14 is more than $500, you must deposit your tax.
- If line 14 is $500 or less, you may pay with this return. (see instructions) **14**

15 Overpayment (If line 13 is more than line 12, enter the excess on line 15 and check a box below.) **15**
► You MUST complete both pages of this form and SIGN it.   Check one: ☐ Apply to next return.   ☐ Send a refund.

Next ►

For Privacy Act and Paperwork Reduction Act Notice, see the back of Form 940-V, Payment Voucher.   Cat. No. 11234O   Form **940** (2013)

Figure 11-1:
Employers report their FUTA tax on Form 940. This is page 1.

You can pay taxes for Form 940 electronically using EFTPS. Most employers pay unemployment taxes quarterly, but if the amount you must pay is less than $100 in any one quarter, you can wait until at least $100 is due. For example, if you owe $50 in federal unemployment taxes in one quarter, you can wait two quarters before making the payment.

Form 940-V, Payment Voucher

Purpose of Form

Complete Form 940-V, Payment Voucher, if you are making a payment with Form 940, Employer's Annual Federal Unemployment (FUTA) Tax Return. We will use the completed voucher to credit your payment more promptly and accurately, and to improve our service to you.

Making Payments With Form 940

To avoid a penalty, make your payment with your 2013 Form 940 **only if** your FUTA tax for the fourth quarter (plus any undeposited amounts from earlier quarters) is $500 or less. If your total FUTA tax after adjustments (Form 940, line 12) is more than $500, you must make deposits by electronic funds transfer. See *When Must You Deposit Your FUTA Tax?* in the Instructions for Form 940. Also see sections 11 and 14 of Pub. 15 (Circular E), Employer's Tax Guide, for more information about deposits.

Caution. *Use Form 940-V when making any payment with Form 940. However, if you pay an amount with Form 940 that should have been deposited, you may be subject to a penalty. See Deposit Penalties in section 11 of Pub. 15 (Circular E).*

Specific Instructions

Box 1—Employer Identification Number (EIN). If you do not have an EIN, you may apply for one online. Go to IRS.gov and click on the *Apply for an EIN Online* link under *Tools*. You may also apply for an EIN by calling 1-800-829-4933, or you can fax or mail Form SS-4, Application for Employer Identification Number, to the IRS. If you have not received your EIN by the due date of Form 940, write "Applied For" and the date you applied in this entry space.

Box 2—Amount paid. Enter the amount paid with Form 940.

Box 3—Name and address. Enter your name and address as shown on Form 940.

• Enclose your check or money order made payable to the "United States Treasury." Be sure to enter your EIN, "Form 940," and "2013" on your check or money order. Do not send cash. Do not staple Form 940-V or your payment to Form 940 (or to each other).

• Detach Form 940-V and send it with your payment and Form 940 to the address provided in the Instructions for Form 940.

Note. You must also complete the entity information above Part 1 on Form 940.

✂ ▼ **Detach Here and Mail With Your Payment and Form 940.** ▼ ✂

Form **940-V**	Payment Voucher	OMB No. 1545-0028
Department of the Treasury Internal Revenue Service	▶ Do not staple or attach this voucher to your payment.	20**13**

1 Enter your employer identification number (EIN).

2 **Enter the amount of your payment.** ▶
Make your check or money order payable to "**United States Treasury**"

Dollars | Cents

3 Enter your business name (individual name if sole proprietor).

Enter your address.

Enter your city, state, and ZIP code or your city, foreign country name, foreign province/county, and foreign postal code.

Figure 11-2: Page 2 of Form 940 features the payment voucher.

Filing and paying unemployment taxes to state governments

States collect their unemployment taxes on a quarterly basis, and many states allow you to pay your unemployment taxes online. Check with your state to find out how to file and make unemployment tax payments.

Skipping out on state taxes isn't a good idea. If you don't pay your state taxes, you may end up with a lien filed against your business. You may also end up facing penalties and interest charges for late payments. And if the state has to take you to court to collect back taxes, you'll have to pay court and processing costs in addition to the back taxes, penalties, and interest.

Unfortunately, the filing requirements for state unemployment taxes are much more difficult to complete than those for federal taxes (see the discussion of Federal Form 940 above). States require you to detail each employee by name and Social Security number because that's how unemployment records are managed at the state level. The state must know how much an employee was paid each quarter in order to determine his or her unemployment benefit, if the need arises. Some states also require you to report the number of weeks an employee worked in each quarter because the employee's unemployment benefits are calculated based on the number of weeks worked.

Each state has its own form and filing requirements. Some states require a detailed report as part of your quarterly wage and tax reports. Other states allow a simple form for state income tax and a more detailed report with your unemployment tax payment. Nine states — Alaska, Florida, Nevada, New Hampshire, South Dakota, Tennessee, Texas, Washington, and Wyoming — have no income tax on wages. (New Hampshire and Tennessee do have a state income tax on dividends and interest, however.)

Carrying Workers' Compensation Insurance

Taxes aren't the only thing you need to worry about when figuring out your state obligations after hiring employees. Every state (except Texas) requires employers to carry *workers' compensation insurance,* which covers your employees in case they're injured on the job. Texas doesn't require this insurance but permits employees injured on the job to sue their employers in civil court to recoup the costs of injuries.

If an employee gets hurt on the job, workers' compensation covers costs of lost income, medical expenses, vocational rehabilitation, and, if applicable, death benefits. Each state sets its own rules regarding how much medical coverage you must provide. If the injury also causes the employee to miss work, the state determines the percentage of the employee's salary you must pay and how long you pay that amount. If the injury results in the employee's death, the state also sets the amount you must pay toward funeral expenses and the amount of financial support you must provide the employee's family.

The state also decides who gets to pick the physician that will care for the injured employee; options are the employer, the employee, the state agency, or a combination of these folks. Most states allow either the employer or the injured employee to choose the physician.

Each state makes up its own rules about how a company must insure itself against employee injuries on the job. Some states create state-based workers' compensation funds to which all employers must contribute. Other states allow you the option of participating in a state-run insurance program or buying insurance from a private company. A number of states permit employers to use HMOs, PPOs, or other managed-care providers to handle workers' claims. If your state doesn't have a mandatory state pool, you'll find that shopping around for the best private rates doesn't help you much. States set the requirements for coverage, and premiums are established by either a national rating bureau called the National Council on Compensation Insurance (NCCI) or a state rating bureau. For the lowdown on NCCI and workers' compensation insurance, visit `www.irmi.com/online/insurance-glossary/terms/n/national-council-on-compensation-insurance-ncci.aspx`.

You may find lower rates over the long term if your state allows you to buy private workers' compensation insurance. Many private insurers give discounts to companies with good safety standards in place and few past claims. So the best way to keep your workers' compensation rates low is to encourage safety and minimize your company's claims.

Your company's rates are calculated based on risks identified in two areas:

- ✔ **Classification of the business:** These classifications are based on historic rates of risk in different industries. For example, if you operate a business in an industry that historically has a high rate of employee injury, such as a construction business, your base rate for workers' compensation insurance is higher than that of a company in an industry without a history of frequent employee injury, such as an office that sells insurance.

- ✔ **Classification of the employees:** The NCCI publishes classifications of over 700 jobs in a book called the *Scopes Manual*. Most states use this manual to develop the basis for their classification schedules. For example, businesses that employ most workers at desk jobs pay less in workers' compensation than businesses with a majority of employees operating heavy machinery because more workers are hurt operating heavy machinery than working at desks.

Be careful how you classify your employees. Many small businesses pay more than needed for workers' compensation insurance because they misclassify employees. Be sure you understand the classification system and properly classify your employee positions before applying for workers' compensation insurance. A specialist in selling business insurance can assist you with classification.

When computing insurance premiums for a company, the insurer (whether the state or a private firm) looks at employee classifications and the rate of pay for each employee. For example, consider the position of a secretary who earns $25,000 per year. If that job classification is rated at 29 cents per $100 of income, the workers' compensation premium for that secretary is $72.50.

Most states allow you to exclude any overtime paid when calculating workers' compensation premiums. You may also be able to lower your premiums by paying a *deductible* on claims. A deductible is the amount you would have to pay before the insurance company pays anything. Deductibles can lower your premium by as much as 25 percent, so consider that as well to keep your upfront costs low.

Maintaining Employee Records

One thing that's abundantly clear when you consider all the state and federal filing requirements for employee taxes is that you must keep very good employee records. Otherwise, you'll have a hard time filling out all the necessary forms and providing quarterly details on your employees and your payroll. The best way to track employee information using a manual bookkeeping system is to set up an employee journal and create a separate journal page for each employee. (Chapter 5 gets into how to set up journals.)

The detailed individual records you keep on each employee should include the following basic information, most of which is collected or determined as part of the hiring process:

- ✔ Name, address, phone number, and Social Security number
- ✔ Department or division within the company
- ✔ Start date with the company
- ✔ Pay rate
- ✔ Pay period (weekly, biweekly, semimonthly, or monthly)
- ✔ Whether hourly or salaried
- ✔ Whether exempt or nonexempt
- ✔ W-4 withholding allowances
- ✔ Benefits information
- ✔ Payroll deductions
- ✔ All payroll activity

If an employee asks to change the number of withholding allowances and file a new W-4 or asks for benefits changes, his or her record must be updated to reflect such changes.

The personal detail that doesn't change each pay period should appear at the top of the journal page. Then, you divide the remaining information into at least seven columns. Here's a sample of what an employee's journal page may look like:

Name: **SS#:**
Address:
Tax Info: Married, 2 WH
Pay Information: $8 hour, nonexempt, biweekly
Benefits: None

The sample journal page contains only seven columns: date of check, taxable wages, Social Security tax, Medicare tax, benefits withholding, federal withholding, state withholding, and net check amount. (The state tax in the sample is zero because this particular employee works in a non-income tax state.)

Date	Taxable Wages	SS	Fed Med	State WH	WH	Check
4/8/2005	$640	39.68	9.28	8.62		$582.42
4/22/2005	$640	38.68	9.28	8.62		$582.42

You may want to add other columns to your employee journal to keep track of things such as:

- **Nontaxable wages,** such as health or retirement benefits that are paid before taxes are taken out
- **Benefits:** If the employee receives benefits, you need at least one column to track any money taken out of the employee's check to pay for those benefits. In fact, you may want to consider tracking each benefit in a separate column.
- **Sick time**
- **Vacation time**

Clearly, these employee journal sheets can get very lengthy very quickly. That's why many small businesses use computerized accounting systems to monitor both payroll and employee records. Figures 11-3 and 11-4 show you how a new employee is added to the QuickBooks system.

Figure 11-3: New employee personal and contact information can be added in QuickBooks to make it easier to keep track of employees.

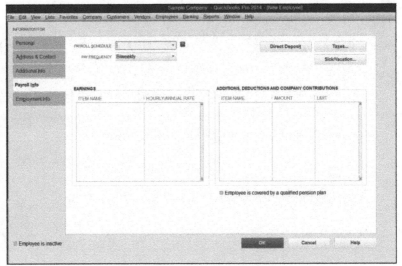

Figure 11-4: QuickBooks enables you to track salary and deduction information, as well as information about sick time and vacation time.

Part IV

Preparing the Books for Year's (or Month's) End

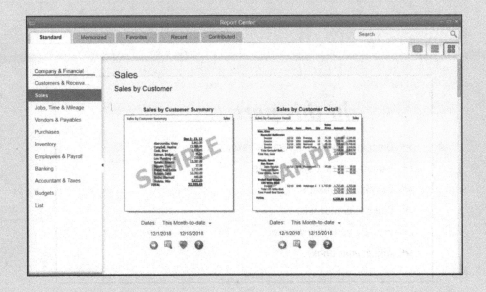

Tracking and managing cash sales in retail environments are becoming easier and safer thanks to mobile devices. See the online article on this topic at www.dummies.com/extras/bookkeeping.

In this part . . .

- ✔ Discover how to depreciate assets.
- ✔ Explore interest calculations.
- ✔ Check your cash.
- ✔ Close your journals.
- ✔ Prepare your trial balance.
- ✔ Adjust your books.

Chapter 12

Depreciating Your Assets

All businesses use equipment, furnishings, and vehicles that last more than a year. Any asset that has a lifespan of more than a year is called a fixed asset. They may last longer than other assets, but even fixed assets eventually get old and need replacing.

And because your business should match its expenses with its revenue, you don't want to write off the full expense of a fixed asset in one year. After all, you'll certainly be making use of the asset for more than one year.

Imagine how bad your income statement would look if you wrote off the cost of a $100,000 piece of equipment in just one year? It would sure look as if your business wasn't doing well. Imagine the impact on a small business — $100,000 could eat up its entire profit or maybe even put it in the position of reporting a loss.

Instead of writing off the full amount of a fixed asset in one year, you use an accounting method called depreciation to write off the asset as it gets used up. In this chapter, I introduce you to the various ways you can depreciate your assets and explain how to calculate depreciation, how depreciation impacts both the income statement and your tax bill, and how to record depreciation in your books.

Defining Depreciation

You may think of depreciation as something that happens to your car as it loses value. In fact, most new cars depreciate 20 to 30 percent or even more as soon as you drive them off the lot. But when you're talking about accounting, the definition of depreciation is a bit different.

Essentially, accountants use depreciation as a way to allocate the costs of a fixed asset over the period in which the asset is useable to the business. You, the bookkeeper, record the full transaction when the asset is bought, but the value of the asset is gradually reduced by subtracting a portion of that value as a depreciation expense each year. Depreciation expenses don't involve the exchange of cash; they're solely done for accounting purposes. Most companies enter depreciation expenses into the books once a year just before preparing their annual reports, but others calculate depreciation expenses monthly or quarterly.

One key reason to write off assets is to lower your tax bill, so the IRS gets involved in depreciation, too. As a business owner, you can't write off the cost of all major purchases in one year. Instead the IRS has strict rules about how you can write off assets as tax-deductible expenses. I talk more about the IRS's rules in the section, "Tackling Taxes and Depreciation," later in this chapter.

Knowing what you can and can't depreciate

Businesses don't depreciate all assets. Low-cost items or items that aren't expected to last more than one year are recorded in expense accounts rather than asset accounts. For example, office supplies are expense items and not depreciated, but that office copier, which you'll use for more than one year, is recorded in the books as a fixed asset and depreciated each year.

Lifespan isn't the deciding factor for depreciation, however. Some assets that last many years are never depreciated. One good example is land; you can always make use of land, so its value never depreciates. You also can't depreciate any property that you lease or rent, but if you make improvements to leased property, you can depreciate the cost of those improvements. In that case, you write off the lease or rent as an expense item and depreciate the lease improvements over their estimated useful life.

You can't depreciate any items that you use outside your business, such as your personal car or home computer, but if you use these assets for both personal needs and business needs, you can depreciate a portion of them based on the percentage of time or other measurement that proves how much you use the car or computer for business. For example, the portion of a car that can be depreciated is based on the miles driven for business versus the miles driven for personal use. If you drive your car a total of 12,000 miles in a year and have records showing that 6,000 of those miles were for business purposes, you can depreciate 50 percent of the cost of the car. That percentage is allocated over the anticipated useful life of the car.

Another example of depreciation of a dual-usage asset is a room in your home designated exclusively for your business. You may be able to depreciate a portion of your home's cost as part of your business expenses. The amount you can depreciate is based on the portion of your home used for business.

Figuring out the useful life of a fixed asset

You're probably wondering how you figure out the useful life of a fixed asset. Well, the IRS has done the dirty work for you by creating a chart that spells out the recovery periods allowed for business equipment (see Table 12-1). Recovery periods are the anticipated useful lifespan of a fixed asset. For example, cars have a five-year recovery period because the IRS anticipates that they'll have a useful lifespan of five years. While the car will probably run longer than that, you're not likely to continue using that car for business purposes after the first five years. You're more likely to trade it in and get a new car.

You can use the IRS chart to determine your fixed asset's useful life, or you can develop a chart that makes more sense for your business. For example, if you run a trucking company, you may determine that your trucks get used up more quickly than those used by a business for occasional deliveries. Although the IRS says that five years is the normal useful life for a truck, you may determine that trucks in your business are only useable for three years. You may need to justify the shorter useful life to the IRS, so be sure that you have the data to back up your decision.

Most accountants use the IRS estimates of useful life unless there's something unique about the way the business uses its fixed assets.

Table 12-1	Depreciation Recovery Periods for Business Equipment
Property Class Recovery Period	*Business Equipment*
3-year property	Tractor units and horses over 2 years old
5-year property	Cars, taxis, buses, trucks, computers, office machines (faxes, copiers, calculators, and so on), research equipment, and cattle
7-year property	Office furniture and fixtures

(continued)

Table 12-1 *(continued)*	
Property Class Recovery Period	Business Equipment
10-year property	Water transportation equipment, single-purpose agricultural or horticultural structures, and fruit- or nut-bearing vines and trees
15-year property	Land improvements, such as shrubbery, fences, roads, and bridges
20-year property	Farm buildings that are not agricultural or horticultural structures
27.5-year property	Residential rental property, not including the value of land

Delving into cost basis

In order to calculate depreciation for an asset, you need to know the cost basis of that asset. The equation for cost basis is:

Cost of the fixed asset + Sales tax + Shipping and delivery costs + Installation charges + Other costs = Cost basis

✔ **Cost of the fixed asset:** What you paid for the equipment, furniture, structure, vehicle, or other asset.

✔ **Sales tax:** What you were charged in sales tax to buy the fixed asset.

✔ **Shipping and delivery:** Any shipping or delivery charges you paid to get the fixed asset.

✔ **Installation charges:** Any charges you paid in order to have the equipment, furniture, or other fixed asset installed on your business's premises.

✔ **Other costs:** Any other charges you need to pay to make the fixed asset usable for your business. For example, if you buy a new computer and need to set up certain hardware in order to use that computer for your business, those setup costs can be added as part of the cost basis of the fixed asset (the computer).

Reducing the Value of Assets

After you decide on the useful life of an asset and calculate its cost basis (see the preceding sections), you have to decide how to go about reducing the asset's value according to accounting standards.

Evaluating your depreciation options

When calculating depreciation of your assets each year, you have a choice of four methods: Straight-Line, Sum-of-Years-Digits, Double-Declining Balance, and Units of Production. In this section, I explain these methods as well as the pros and cons of using each one.

To show you how the methods handle assets differently, I calculate the first year's depreciation expense using the purchase of a truck on January 1, 2005, with a cost basis of $25,000. I assume that the truck can be sold in five years for $5,000. This is called the salvage value. I show you how to use the salvage value as part of the calculations for three of the depreciation methods. The fourth method I cover, Units of Production, is used primarily in manufacturing, so the truck example doesn't work. But you'll still get the idea of how to use that method, don't worry.

Straight-Line

When depreciating assets using the Straight-Line method, you spread the cost of the asset evenly over the number of years the asset will be used. Straight-Line is the most common method used for depreciation of assets, and it's also the easiest one to use. Another advantage of this method is that you can use it for both accounting purposes and tax purposes. (If you use any of the other methods, you have to keep separate depreciation records — one for your financial reports and one for the tax man.

The formula for calculating Straight-Line depreciation is:

(Cost of fixed asset − Salvage) ÷ Estimated useful life = Annual depreciation expense

For the truck in this example, the cost basis is $25,000, the salvage value is $5,000, and I'm using the IRS estimate of useful life of five years. With these figures, the calculation for finding the annual depreciation expense of this truck based on the Straight-Line depreciation method is:

($25,000 − $5,000) ÷ 5 = $4,000

Each year, the business's Income Statement should include $4,000 as a depreciation expense for this truck. You add this $4,000 depreciation expense to the accumulated depreciation account for the truck. This accumulated depreciation account is shown below the truck's original value on the Balance Sheet. You subtract the accumulated depreciation from the cost basis of the truck to show a net asset value, which is the value remaining on the truck.

Sum-of-Years-Digits

If you think your asset loses a greater portion of its useful life in the early years, you can speed up its depreciation by using the *Sum-of-Years-Digits (SYD) method*. This method allows you to write off higher depreciation expenses in the earlier years of useful life and lower depreciation in later years. When you use Sum-of-Years-Digits, you assume that the fixed asset will be used less in later years.

One big disadvantage of writing off assets quickly is that the higher depreciation expense lowers your business's net income.

Sum-of-Years-Digits requires a three-step calculation:

1. **Find the SYD using this formula, with *n* representing the number of years of estimated useful life remaining as of the start of the fiscal year:**

   $n(n+1) \div 2 = SYD$

2. **Find the applicable fraction using this formula:**

   $n \div SYD = $ Applicable fraction

3. **Calculate the depreciation expense using this formula:**

   (Cost − Salvage value) × Applicable fraction = Depreciation expense

To calculate the first year of the depreciation expense on the truck, this formula works like so:

SYD: $5(5+1) \div 2 = 15$

Applicable fraction: $5 \div 15 = \frac{1}{3}$

Depreciation expense: $20,000 × ⅓ = $6,666.67

The depreciation expense written off during the truck's first year of life is $2,666.67 higher than it is when I calculate it using the Straight-Line depreciation method. If I do the same calculation for the remaining years of useful life, I get the following results:

Year 2: $5,333.33

Year 3: $4,000.00

Year 4: $2,666.67

Year 5: $1,333.33

By Year 3, I've written off $16,000, 80 percent of the depreciable amount for the truck.

Double-Declining Balance

The Double-Declining Balance method of depreciation allows you to write off an asset even more quickly than the Sum-of-Years-Digits (see the preceding section). This method is ideal for assets whose primary usefulness is in the early years of life.

You calculate the depreciation using the Declining Balance method using this formula:

> 2 × (1 ÷ Estimated useful life) × Book value at the beginning of the year = Depreciation expense

The calculation for the truck's depreciation expense using the Declining Balance method is:

> 2 × (1 ÷ 5) × $25,000 = $10,000

As you can see, the depreciation expense for the first year of using the truck is $10,000. If I do the same calculation for the remaining years of useful life, I get the following results:

> Year 2: $6,000
>
> Year 3: $3,600
>
> Year 4: $400
>
> Year 5: $0

Eighty percent of the value of the truck is written off in the first two years. Clearly, the Double-Declining Balance method of depreciation reduces the value of an asset even faster than the Sum-of-Years-Digits.

Units of Production

The Units of Production (UOP) method of depreciation works well primarily in a manufacturing environment because it calculates depreciation based on the number of units produced in a year. Companies whose machinery usage varies greatly each year depending on the market and the number of units needed for sale make use of this depreciation method.

The formula for calculating depreciation using Units of Production is a two-step process:

1. **Find the UOP rate using this formula:**

   (Cost – Salvage value) ÷ Estimated number of units to be produced during estimated useful life = UOP rate

2. **Find the depreciation expense using this formula:**

   Units produced during the year × UOP rate = Depreciation expense

You only need to use the Units of Production depreciation method if you're manufacturing the products you sell and if the usage of your equipment fluctuates widely from year to year.

Tackling Taxes and Depreciation

Depreciation calculations for tax purposes are a completely different animal than the calculations used to record depreciation for accounting purposes. You can use Straight-Line depreciation to calculate your depreciation expense for tax purposes, but most businesses prefer to write off the highest expense legally permissible and reduce their tax bills by the greatest amount.

In addition to Straight-Line depreciation, two other acceptable IRS methods for writing off assets are: Section 179 and Modified Accelerated Cost Recovery System (MACRS). The big advantage of the Section 179 Deduction is that you can write off up to 100 percent of the cost basis of qualifying property. (I talk more about what qualifies in the following section.) If the property doesn't qualify, most businesses choose to use MACRS rather than Straight-Line depreciation.

Section 179

Section 179, which gets its name from a section of the tax code, is a great boon for companies. Businesses can write off up to $25,000 in newly purchased property that qualifies for the deduction up to 100 percent of the cost basis of the property. This amount could be increased if Congress changes the law. A law passed in 2012 allowed up to $500,000 for the Section 179 deduction, but it expired at the end of 2013.

The primary reason for this part of the tax code is to encourage businesses to buy new property in order to stimulate the economy. That's why only certain types of property are included, and there are limits on the amount that can be deducted for some types of property.

Basically, Section 179's qualifying property includes tangible property such as machines, equipment, and furniture. In addition, some storage facilities qualify, as do some single-purpose agricultural and horticultural structures. All cars and SUVs between 6,000 and 14,000 pounds can't be fully written off under Section 179. You also can't write off property held for the production of income (such as rental property), most real property, property acquired as a gift or inheritance, and property held outside the United States.

You can get full details about Section 179 by ordering a copy of IRS Publication 946, How to Depreciate Property, from the IRS or accessing it online at www.irs.gov/pub/irs-pdf/p946.pdf. At the time of this writing, the rules for 2014 were not yet published, because the IRS was waiting for congressional action regarding the limits and rules for Section 179. Be sure to work with your accountant to determine what's eligible and how much of the cost basis is eligible for the Section 179 deduction.

MACRS

The most common type of depreciation write-off used by businesses is Modified Accelerated Cost Recovery System, or MACRS. The recovery period shown in Table 12-1 is the basis for this depreciation method. After you know what type of property you have (three-year, five-year, and so on), you use the MACRS table in IRS Publication 946, "How to Depreciate Property," to figure out the depreciation expense you can write off. Luckily, you can leave MACRS calculations for your accountant to do when he prepares your business tax forms.

Setting Up Depreciation Schedules

In order to keep good accounting records, you need to track how much you depreciate each of your assets in some form of a schedule. After all, your financial statements include only a total value for all your assets and a total accumulated depreciation amount. Most businesses maintain depreciation schedules in some type of spreadsheet program that exists outside their accounting systems. Usually, one person is responsible for managing assets and their depreciation. However, in a large company, these tasks can turn into full-time jobs for several people.

The best way to keep track of depreciation is to prepare a separate schedule for each asset account that you depreciate. For example, set up depreciation schedules for buildings, furniture and fixtures, office equipment, and so on. Your depreciation schedule should include all the information you need to determine annual depreciation, such as the original purchase date, original cost basis, and recovery period. You can add columns to track the actual depreciation expenses and calculate the current value of each asset. Here's a sample depreciation schedule for vehicles:

Depreciation Schedule: Vehicles

Date Put in Service	Description	Cost	Recovery Period	Annual Depreciation
1/5/2013	Black car	$30,000	5 years	$5,000
1/1/2014	Blue truck	$25,000	5 years	$4,000

If you use a different method of depreciation for tax purposes (see "Tackling Taxes and Depreciation"), you should prepare schedules for tax purposes as well.

Depreciation can be more than just a mathematical exercise. Keeping track of depreciation is a good way to monitor the age of your assets and know when you should plan for their replacement. As your assets age, they'll incur greater repair costs, so keeping depreciation schedules can help you plan repair and maintenance budgets as well.

Recording Depreciation Expenses

Recording a depreciation expense calls for a rather simple entry into your accounting system.

After calculating your depreciation expense, no matter which method you used to calculate that expense, here is how you would record a depreciation expense of $4,000:

	Debit	*Credit*
Depreciation Expense	$4,000	
Accumulated Depreciation: Vehicles		$4,000

The Depreciation Expense account increases by the debit, and the Accumulated Depreciation: Vehicles account increases by the credit. On the income statement, you subtract the Depreciation Expense from sales, and on the balance sheet, you subtract the Accumulated Depreciation: Vehicles from the value of Vehicles.

Chapter 13

Paying and Collecting Interest

. . . .

In This Chapter

▶ Understanding interest calculations

▶ Making the most of interest income

▶ Calculating loan interest

. . . .

*F*ew businesses are able to make major purchases without taking out loans. Whether loans are for vehicles, buildings, or other business needs, businesses must pay *interest,* a percentage of the amount loaned, to whoever loans them the money.

Some businesses loan their own money and receive interest payments as income. In fact, a savings account can be considered a type of loan because by placing your money in the account, you're giving the bank the opportunity to loan that money to others. So the bank pays you for the use of your money by paying interest, which is a type of income for your company.

This chapter reviews different types of loans and how to calculate and record interest expenses for each type. In addition, I discuss how you calculate and record interest income in your business's books.

Deciphering Types of Interest

Any time you make use of someone else's money, such as a bank, you have to pay interest for that use — whether you're buying a house, a car, or some other item you want. The same is true when someone else is using your money. For example, when you buy a bond or deposit money in a money market account, you're paid interest for allowing the use of your money while it's on deposit.

The financial institution that has your money will likely combine your money with that of other depositors and loan it out to other people to make more interest than it's paying you. That's why when the interest rates you have to pay on loans are low, the interest rates you can earn on savings are even lower.

Banks actually use two types of interest calculations:

- ✔ **Simple interest** is calculated only on the principal amount of the loan.
- ✔ **Compound interest** is calculated on the principal and on interest earned.

Simple interest

Simple interest is simple to calculate. Here's the formula for calculating simple interest:

Principal × interest rate × n = interest

To show you how interest is calculated, I assume that someone deposited $10,000 in the bank in a money market account earning 3 percent (0.03) interest for 3 years. So the interest earned over 3 years is $10,000 × .03 × 3 = $900.

Compound interest

Compound interest is computed on both the principal and any interest earned. You must calculate the interest each year and add it to the balance before you can calculate the next year's interest payment, which will be based on both the principal and interest earned.

Here's how you would calculate compound interest:

Principal × interest rate	= interest for year one
(Principal + interest earned) × interest rate	= interest for year two
(Principal + interest earned) × interest rate	= interest for year three

You repeat this calculation for all years of the deposit or loan. The one exception could be with a loan. If you pay the total interest due each month or year (depending on when your payments are due), there would be no interest to compound.

To show you how this impacts earnings, I calculated the three-year deposit of $10,000 at 3 percent (0.03):

$10,000 × .03	=	$300 — Year One interest
($10,000 + 300) × .03	=	$309 — Year Two Interest
($10,000 + 300 +309) × .03	=	$318.27 — Year Three Interest
Total Interest Earned	=	$927.27

You can see that you'd earn an extra $27.27 during the first three years of that deposit if the interest is compounded. When working with much larger sums or higher interest rates for longer periods of time, compound interest can make a big difference in how much you earn or how much you pay on a loan.

Ideally, you want to find a savings account, certificate deposit, or other savings instrument that earns compound interest. But, if you want to borrow money, look for a simple interest loan.

Also, not all accounts that earn compound interest are created equally. Watch carefully to see how frequently the interest is compounded. The preceding example shows a type of account for which interest is compounded annually. But, if you can find an account where interest is compounded monthly, the interest you earn will be even higher. Monthly compounding means that interest earned will be calculated each month and added to the principle each month before calculating the next month's interest, which results in a lot more interest than a bank that compounds interest just once a year.

Handling Interest Income

The income that your business earns from its savings accounts, certificates of deposits, or other investment vehicles is called *interest income*. As the bookkeeper, you're rarely required to calculate interest income using the simple interest or compounded interest formulas described in the earlier sections of this chapter. In most cases, the financial institution sends you a monthly, quarterly, or annual statement that has a separate line item reporting interest earned.

When you get your monthly statement, you then reconcile the books. *Reconciliation* is a process in which you prove out whether the amount the bank says you have in your account is equal to what you think you have in your account. I talk more about reconciling bank accounts in Chapter 14. The reason I mention it now is that the first step in the reconciliation process involves recording any interest earned or bank fees in the books so that your balance matches what the bank shows. Figure 13-1 shows you how to record $25 in Interest Income.

If you're keeping the books manually, a journal entry to record interest would look similar to this:

	Debit	Credit
Cash	XXXX	
Interest Income		XXXX

To record interest income from American Savings Bank.

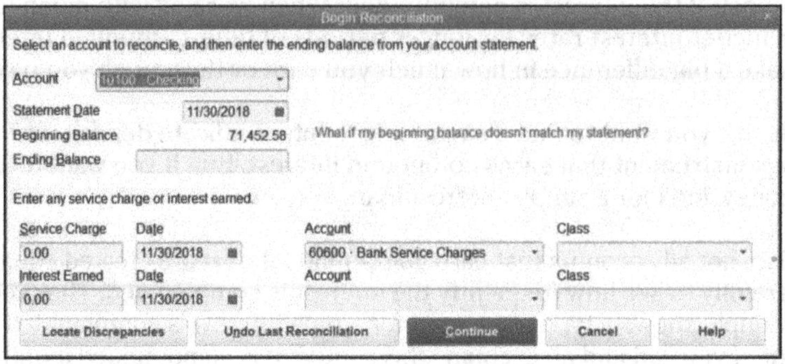

Figure 13-1:
In
QuickBooks,
you enter
interest
income at
the begin-
ning of the
account
recon-
ciliation
process.

When preparing financial statements, you show Interest Income on the income statement (see Chapter 19 for more information about the income statement) in a section called Other Income. Other Income includes any income your business earned that was not directly related to your primary business activity — selling your goods or services.

Delving into Loans and Interest Expenses

Businesses borrow money for both *short-term periods* (periods of less than 12 months) and *long-term periods* (periods of more than one year). Short-term debt usually involves some form of credit-card debt or line-of-credit debt. Long-term debt can include a 5-year car loan, 20-year mortgage, or any other type of debt that is paid over more than one year.

Short-term debt

Any money due in the next 12-month period is shown on the balance sheet as short-term or current debt. Any interest paid on that money is shown as an Interest Expense on the income statement.

In most cases, you don't have to calculate your interest due. The financial institution sending you a bill gives you a breakdown of the principal and interest to be paid.

How credit-card interest is calculated

For example, when you get a credit-card bill at home, a line always shows you new charges, the amount to pay in full to avoid all interest, and the amount of interest charged during the current period on any money not paid from the previous bill. If you don't pay your credit in full, interest on most cards is calculated using a daily periodic rate of interest, which is compounded each day based on the unpaid balance. Yes, credit cards are a type of compounded interest. When not paid in full, interest is calculated on the unpaid principal balance plus any unpaid interest. Table 13-1 shows what a typical interest calculation looks like on a credit card.

Table 13-1	Credit-Card Interest Calculation				
	Avg. Daily Balance	Daily Periodic Rate	Corresponding Annual Rate	Finance Charges	
				Daily Rate	Transaction Fees
Purchases	$XXX	0.034076%	12.40%	$XXX	$XXX
Cash	$XXX	0.0452%	16.49%	$XXX	$XXX

On many credit cards, you start paying interest on new purchases immediately, if you haven't paid your balance due in full the previous month. When opening a credit-card account for your business, be sure you understand how interest is calculated and when the bank starts charging on new purchases. Some issuers give a grace period of 20 to 30 days before charging interest, while others don't give any type of grace period at all.

In Table 13-1, the Finance Charges include the daily rate charged in interest based on the daily periodic rate plus any transaction fees. For example, if you take a cash advance from your credit card, many credit-card companies charge a transaction fee of 2 to 3 percent of the total amount of cash taken. This fee can be true when you transfer balances from one credit card to another. Although the company entices you with an introductory rate of 1 or 2 percent to get you to transfer the balance, be sure to read the fine print. You may have to pay a 3 percent transaction fee on the full amount transferred, which makes the introductory rate much higher.

Using credit lines

As a small business owner, you get better interest rates using a line of credit with a bank rather than a credit card. Interest rates are usually lower on lines of credit. Typically, a business owner uses a credit card for purchases, but if he can't pay the bill in full, he draws money from his line of credit rather than carry over the credit-card balance.

When the money is first received from the credit line, you record the cash receipt and the liability. Just to show you how this transaction works, I record the receipt of a credit line of $1,500. Here is what the journal entry would look like:

	Debit	**Credit**
Cash	1,500	
Credit Line Payable		1,500

To record receipt of cash from credit line.

In this entry, you increase the Cash account and the Credit Line Payable account balances. If you're using a computerized accounting program, you record the transaction using the deposit form, as shown in Figure 13-2.

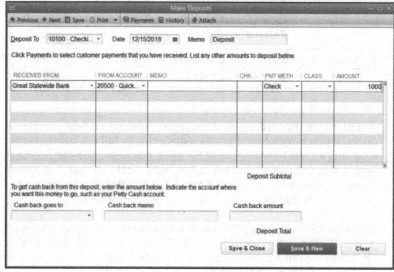

Figure 13-2:
Recording receipt of cash from credit line.

When you make your first payment, you must record the use of cash, the amount paid on the principal of the loan, and the amount paid in interest. Here is what that journal entry looks like:

	Debit	**Credit**
Credit Line Payable	150	
Interest Expense	10	
Cash		160

To make monthly payment on credit line.

This journal entry reduces the amount due in the Credit Line Payable account, increases the amount paid in the Interest Expense account, and reduces the amount in the Cash account.

If you're using a computerized system, you simply complete a check form and indicate which accounts are impacted by the payment, and the system updates the accounts automatically. Figure 13-3 shows you how to record a loan payment in QuickBooks.

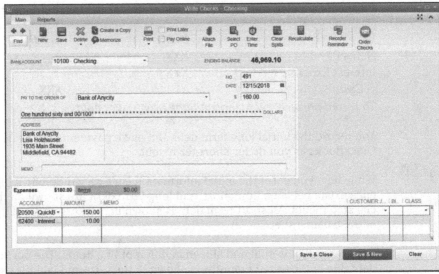

Figure 13-3:
Recording
a loan pay-
ment in
QuickBooks.

As you can see in Figure 13-3, at the same time that you prepare the check for printing, you can add the accounts that are impacted by that payment by splitting the detail expense information. I indicate $150 of that payment should be recorded in the Bank Credit Card Payable account, and $10 should be recorded as Interest Expense. At the top of the check, I indicate which account will be used to pay the bill. QuickBooks can then print the check and update all affected accounts. You don't need to do any additional postings to update your books.

Long-term debt

Most companies take on some form of debt that will be paid over a period of time that is longer than 12 months. This debt may include car loans, mortgages, or promissory notes. A *promissory note* is a written agreement where you agree to repay someone a set amount of money at some point in the future at a particular interest rate. It can be monthly, yearly, or some other term specified in the note. Most installment loans are types of promissory notes.

Recording a debt

When the company first takes on the debt, it's recorded in the books in much the same way as a short-term debt:

	Debit	**Credit**
Cash	XXX	
Notes Payable		XXX

To record receipt of cash from American Bank promissory note.

Payments are also recorded in a manner similar to short-term debt:

	Debit	Credit
Notes Payable	XXX	
Interest Expense	XXX	
Cash		XXX

To record payment on American Bank promissory note.

You record the initial long-term debt and make payments the same way in QuickBooks as you do for short-term debt.

While how you enter the initial information isn't very different, a big difference exists between how short- and long-term debt are shown on the financial statements. All short-term debt is shown in the Current Liability section of the balance sheet.

Long-term debt is split and shown in different line items. The portion of the debt due in the next 12 months is shown in the Current Liabilities section, which is usually a line item named something like "Current Portion of Long-Term Debt." The remaining balance of the long-term debt due beyond the next 12 months appears in the Long-Term Liability section of the balance sheet as Notes Payable.

Major purchases and long-term debt

Sometimes a long-term liability is set up at the same time as you make a major purchase. You may pay some portion of the amount due in cash as a down payment and the remainder as a note. To show you how to record such a transaction, I assume that a business has purchased a truck for $25,000, made a down payment of $5,000, and took a note at an interest rate of 6 percent for $20,000. Here's how you record this purchase in the books:

	Debit	Credit
Vehicles	25,000	
Cash		5,000
Notes Payable – Vehicles		20,000

To record payment for the purchase of the blue truck.

You then record payments on the note in the same way as any other loan payment:

	Debit	Credit
Notes Payable – Vehicles	XXX	
Interest Expense	XXX	
Cash		XXX

To record payment on note for blue truck.

When recording the payment on a long-term debt for which you have a set installment payment, you may not get a breakdown of interest and principal with every payment. For example, many times when you take out a car loan, you get a coupon book with just the total payment due each month. Each payment includes both principal and interest, but you don't get any breakdown detailing how much goes toward interest and how much goes toward principal.

Separating principal and interest

Why is this lack of separation a problem for recording payments? Each payment includes a different amount for principal and for interest. At the beginning of the loan, the principal is at its highest amount, so the amount of interest due is much higher than later in the loan payoff process when the balance is lower. Many times in the first year of notes payable on high-price items, such as a mortgage on a building, you're paying more interest than principal.

In order to record long-term debt for which you don't receive a breakdown each month, you need to ask the bank that gave you the loan for an amortization schedule. An *amortization schedule* lists the total payment, the amount of each payment that goes toward interest, the amount that goes toward principal, and the remaining balance to be paid on the note.

Some banks provide an amortization schedule automatically when you sign all the paperwork for the note. If your bank can't give you one, you can easily get one online using an amortization calculator. You can find one online at www.amortization-calc.com.

Using that calculator, I list the principal/interest breakdown for the first six months of payment on the truck in a six-month amortization chart. You can see from Table 13-2 that the amount paid to principal on a long-term note gradually increases, while the amount of interest paid gradually decreases as the note balance is paid off. The calculator did calculate payments for all 60 months, but I don't include them all here.

Table 13-2	Six-Month Amortization Chart for Truck Payments		
Total Payment	*Principal*	*Interest*	*Remaining Note Balance*
$386.66	$286.66	100.00	$19,713.34
$386.66	$288.09	98.57	$19,425.25
$386.66	$289.53	97.13	$19.135.72
$386.66	$290.98	95.68	$18,844.75
$386.66	$292.43	94.23	$18,552.32
$386.66	$293.89	92.77	$18,258.42

Looking at the six-month amortization chart, I developed what you would need to record in the books for the first payment on the truck:

	Debit	Credit
Notes Payable – Vehicles	286.66	
Interest Expense	100.00	
Cash		386.66

To record payment on note for blue truck.

In reading the amortization chart in Table 13-2, notice how the amount paid toward interest is slightly less each month as the balance on the note still due is gradually reduced. Also, the amount paid toward the principal of that note gradually increases as less of the payment is used to pay interest.

By the time you start making payments for the final year of the loan, interest costs drop dramatically because the balance is so much lower. For the first payment of Year 5, the amount paid in interest is $22.47, and the amount paid on principal is $364.19. The balance remaining after that payment is $4,128.34.

As you lower your principal balance, much less of your payment goes toward interest and much more goes toward reducing principal. That's why many financial specialists advice you to pay down principal as fast as possible if you want to reduce the term of a loan.

Chapter 14

Proving Out the Cash

*A*ll business owners — whether the business is a small, family-owned candy store or a major international conglomerate — like to periodically test how well their businesses are doing. They also want to be sure that the numbers in their accounting systems actually match what's physically in their stores and offices. After they check out what's in the books, these business owners can prepare financial reports to determine the company's financial success or failure during the last month, quarter, or year. This process of verifying the accuracy of your cash is called *proving out.*

The first step in proving out the books involves counting the company's cash and verifying that the cash numbers in your books match the actual cash on hand at a particular point in time. This chapter explains how you can test to be sure the cash counts are accurate, finalize the cash journals for the accounting period, prove out the bank accounts, and post any adjustments or corrections to the General Ledger.

Why Prove Out the Books?

You're probably thinking that proving out the books sounds like a huge task that takes lots of time. You're right — it's a big job, but it's also a very necessary one to do periodically so you can be sure that what's recorded in your accounting system realistically measures what's actually going on in your business.

With any accounting system, mistakes can be made, and, unfortunately, any business can fall victim to incidents of theft or embezzlement. The only way to be sure that none of these problems exist in your business is to periodically prove out the books. The process of proving out the books is a big part of the accounting cycle, which I discuss in detail in Chapter 2. The first three steps of the accounting cycle — recording transactions, making journal entries, and posting summaries of those entries to the General Ledger — involve tracking the flow of cash throughout the accounting period. All three steps are part of the process of recording a business's financial activities throughout the entire accounting period. The rest of the steps in the accounting cycle are conducted at the end of the period and are part of the process of proving out the accuracy of your books. They include running a trial balance (see Chapter 16), creating a work-sheet (see Chapter 16), adjusting journal entries (see Chapter 17), creating financial statements (see Chapters 18 and 19), and closing the books (see Chapter 22). Most businesses prove out their books every month.

Of course, you don't want to shut down your business for a week while you prove out the books, so you should select a day during each accounting period on which you'll take a financial snapshot of the state of your accounts. For example, if you're preparing monthly financial reports at the end of the month, you test the amount of cash your business has on hand as of that certain time and day, such as 6 p.m. on June 30 after your store closes for the day. The rest of the testing process — running a trial balance, creating a work-sheet, adjusting journal entries, creating financial statements, and closing the books — is based on what happened before that point in time. When you open the store and sell more products the next day and buy new things to run your business, those transactions and any others that follow the point in time of your test become part of the next accounting cycle.

Making Sure Ending Cash Is Right

Testing your books starts with counting your cash. Why start with cash? Because the accounting process starts with transactions, and transactions occur when cash exchanges hands either to buy things you need to run the business or to sell your products or services. Before you can even begin to test whether the books are right, you need to know if your books have cap-tured what's happened to your company's cash and if the amount of cash shown in your books actually matches the amount of cash you have on hand.

I'm sure you've heard the well-worn expression, "Show me the money!" Well, in business, that idea is the core of your success. Everything relies on your cash profits that you can take out of your business or use to expand your business.

In Chapter 9, I discuss how a business proves out the cash taken in by each of its cashiers. That daily process gives a business good control of the point at which cash comes into the business from customers who buy the company's products or services. It also measures any cash refunds that were given to customers who returned items. But the points of sale and return aren't the only times cash comes into or goes out of the business.

If your business sells products on store credit (see Chapter 9), some of the cash from customers is actually collected at a later point in time by the book-keeping staff responsible for tracking customer credit accounts. And when your business needs something, whether products to be sold or supplies needed by various departments, you must pay cash to vendors, suppliers, and contractors. Sometimes cash is paid out on the spot, but many times the bill is recorded in the Accounts Payable account and paid at a later date. All these transactions involve the use of cash, so the amount of cash on hand in the business at any one time includes not only what's in the cash registers but also what's on deposit in the company's bank accounts. You need to know the balances of those accounts and test those balances to be sure they're accurate and match what's in your company's books. I talk more about how to do that in the section "Reconciling Bank Accounts" later in this chapter.

So your snapshot in time includes not only the cash on hand in your cash registers but also any cash you may have in the bank. Some departments may also have petty cash accounts, which means you total that cash as well. The total cash figure is what you show as an asset named "Cash" on the first line of your company's financial statement, the *balance sheet*. The balance sheet shows all that the company owns (its assets) and owes (its liabilities) as well as the equity the owners have in the company. (I talk more about the balance sheet and how you prepare one in Chapter 18.)

The actual cash you have on hand is just one tiny piece of the cash moving through your business during the accounting period. The true detail of what cash has flowed into and out of the business is in your cash journals. Closing those are the next step in the process of figuring out how well your business did.

Closing the Cash Journals

As I explain in Chapter 5, if you keep the books manually, you can find a record of every transaction that involves cash in one of two cash journals: the Cash Receipts journal (cash that comes into the business) and the Cash Disbursements journal (cash that goes out of the business).

If you use a computerized accounting system, you don't have these cash journals, but you have many different ways to find out the same detailed information that they contain. You can run reports of sales by customer, by item, or by sales representative. Figure 14-1 shows the types of sales reports that QuickBooks can automatically generate for you. You can also run reports that show you all the company's purchases by vendor or by item as well as list any purchases still on order. Figure 14-2 shows the various purchase reports that QuickBooks can automatically run for you. These reports can be run by the week, the month, the quarter, or the year, or you can customize the reports to show a particular period of time that you're analyzing. For example, if you want to know what sales occurred between June 5 and 10, you can run a report specifying the exact dates.

In addition to the sales and purchase reports shown in Figures 14-1 and 14-2, you can generate other transaction detail reports including customers and receivables; jobs, time, and mileage; vendors and payables; inventory; employees and payroll; and banking (see the options listed on the left side of Figure 14-1). One big advantage of a computerized accounting system when you're trying to prove out your books is the number of different ways you can develop reports to check for accuracy in your books if you suspect an error.

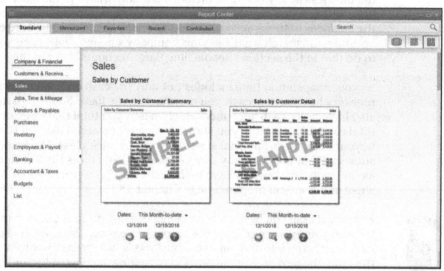

Figure 14-1:
Using QuickBooks, you can easily generate reports showing your company's cash receipts organized by customer, items sold, or sales representative.

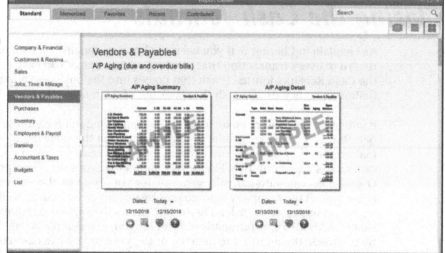

Figure 14-2:
Using QuickBooks, you can produce reports showing your company's cash disbursements by vendor or by items bought.

Finalizing cash receipts

If all your books are up-to-date, when you summarize the Cash Receipts journal on whatever day and time you choose to prove out your books, you should come up with a total of all cash received by the business at that time. Unfortunately, in the real world of bookkeeping, things don't come out so nice and neat. In fact, you probably wouldn't even start entering the transactions from that particular day into the books until the next day, when you enter the cash reports from all cashiers and others who handle incoming cash (such as the accounts receivable staff who collect money from customers buying on credit) into the Cash Receipts journal.

After entering all the transactions from the day in question, the books for the period you're looking at may still be incomplete. Sometimes, adjustments or corrections must be made to the ending cash numbers. For example, monthly credit-card fees and interest received from the bank may not yet be recorded in your cash journals. As the bookkeeper, you must be sure that all bank fees related to cash receipts as well as any interest earned are recorded in the Cash Receipts journal before you summarize the journals for the period you're analyzing.

Remembering credit-card fees

When your company allows customers to use credit cards, you must pay fees to the bank that processes these transactions, which is probably the same bank that handles all your business accounts. These fees actually lower the amount you take in as cash receipts, so the amount you record as a cash receipt must be adjusted to reflect those costs of doing business. Monthly credit-card fees vary greatly depending upon the bank you're using, but here are some of the most common fees your company may be charged:

- ✔ **Address verification service (AVS) fee** is a fee companies pay if they want to avoid accepting fraudulent credit card sales. Businesses that use this service take orders by phone or email and therefore don't have the credit card in hand to verify a customer's signature. Banks charge this fee for every transaction that's verified.

- ✔ **Discount rate** is a fee all companies that use credit cards must pay; it's based on a percentage of the sale or return transaction. The rate your company may be charged varies greatly depending on the type of business you conduct and the volume of your sales each month. Companies that use a terminal to swipe cards and electronically send transaction information usually pay lower fees than companies that use paper credit-card transactions because the electronic route creates less work for the bank and eliminates the possibility of key-entry errors by employees.

- ✔ **Secure payment gateway fee,** which allows the merchant to process transactions securely, is charged to companies that transact business over the Internet. If your business sells products online, you can expect to pay this fee based on a set monthly amount.

- ✔ **Customer support fee** is charged to companies that want bank support for credit-card transactions for 24 hours a day, 365 days a year. Companies such as mail-order catalogs that allow customers to place orders 24 hours a day look for this support. Sometimes companies even want this support in more than one language if they sell products internationally.

- ✔ **Monthly minimum fee** is the least a business is required to pay for the ability to offer its customers the convenience of using credit cards to buy products. This fee usually varies between $10 and $30 per month.

Even if your company doesn't generate any credit-card sales during a month, you're still required to pay this minimum fee. As long as enough sales are generated to cover the fee, you shouldn't have a problem. For example, if the fee is $10 and your company pays 2 percent per sale in discount fees, you need to sell at least $500 worth of products each month to cover that $10 fee. When deciding whether to accept credit cards as a payment option, be sure you're confident that you'll generate enough business through credit-card sales to cover that fee. If not, you may find that accepting credit cards costs you more than the sales you generate by offering that convenience.

- ✔ **Transaction fee** is a standard fee charged to your business for each credit-card transaction you submit for authorization. You pay this fee even if the cardholder is denied and you lose the sale.

- ✔ **Equipment and software fees** are charged to your company based on the equipment and computer software you use in order to process credit-card transactions. You have the option of buying or leasing credit-card equipment and related software.

- ✔ **Chargeback and retrieval fees** are charged if a customer disputes a transaction.

When deciding whether to accept credit cards as a form of payment, you must consider what your competition is doing. If all your competitors offer the convenience of using credit cards and you don't, you may lose sales if customers take their business elsewhere.

Reconciling your credit-card statements

Each month, the bank that handles your credit-card sales will send you a statement listing

- ✔ All your company's transactions for the month.

- ✔ The total amount your company sold through credit-card sales.

- ✔ The total fees charged to your account.

If you find a difference between what the bank reports was sold on credit cards and what the company's books show regarding credit-card sales, it's time to play detective and find the reason for the difference. In most cases, the error involves the charging back of one or more sales because a customer disputes the charge. In this case, the Cash Receipts journal is adjusted to reflect that loss of sale, and the bank statement and company books should match up.

For example, suppose $200 in credit-card sales was disputed. The original entry of the transaction in the books should look like this:

	Debit	Credit
Sales	$200	
Cash		$200

To reverse disputed credit sales recorded in June.

This entry reduces the total Sales for the month as well as the amount of the Cash account. If the dispute is resolved and the money is later retrieved, the sale is then reentered when the cash is received.

You also record any fees related to credit-card fees in the Cash Disbursements journal. For example, if credit-card fees for the month of June total $200, the entry in the books should look like this:

	Debit	Credit
Credit-Card Fees	$200	
Cash		$200

To record credit-card fees for the month of June.

Summarizing the Cash Receipts journal

When you're sure that all cash receipts as well as any corrections or adjustments to those receipts have been properly entered in the books (see the previous two sections), you summarize the Cash Receipts journal as I explain in detail in Chapter 5. After summarizing the Cash Receipts journal for the accounting period you're analyzing, you know the total cash that was taken into the business from sales as well as from other channels.

In the Cash Receipts journal, sales usually appear in two columns:

✔ **Sales:** The cash shown in the Sales column is cash received when the customer purchases the goods using cash, check, or bank credit card.

✔ **Accounts Receivable:** The Accounts Receivable column is for sales in which no cash was received when the customer purchased the item. Instead, the customer bought on credit and intends to pay cash at a later date. (I talk more about Accounts Receivable and collecting money from customers in Chapter 9.)

After you add all receipts to the Cash Receipts journal, entries for items bought on store credit can be posted to the Accounts Receivable journal and the individual customer accounts. You then send bills to customers that reflect all transactions from the month just closed as well as any payments still due from previous months. Billing customers is a key part of the closing process that occurs each month.

In addition to the Sales and Accounts Receivable columns, your Cash Receipts journal should have at least two other columns:

✔ **General:** The General column lists all other cash received, such as owner investments in the business.

✔ **Cash:** The Cash column contains the total of all cash received by the business during an accounting period.

Finalizing cash outlays

After you close the Cash Receipts journal (see "Summarizing the Cash Receipts journal"), the next step is to close the Cash Disbursements journal. Any adjustments related to outgoing cash receipts, such as bank credit-card fees, should be added to the Cash Disbursements journal.

Before you close the journal, you must also be certain that any bills paid at the end of the month have been added to the Cash Disbursements journal.

Bills that are related to financial activity for the month being closed but that haven't yet been paid have to be *accrued,* which means recorded in the books, so they can be matched to the revenue for the month. These accruals are only necessary if you use the accrual accounting method. If you use the cash-basis accounting method, you only need to record the bills when cash is actually paid. For more on the accrual and cash-basis methods, flip to Chapter 2.

You accrue bills yet to be paid in the Accounts Payable account. For example, suppose that your company prints and mails fliers to advertise a sale during the last week of the month. A bill for the fliers totaling $500 hasn't been paid yet. Here's how you enter the bill in the books:

	Debit	*Credit*
Advertising	$500	
Accounts Payable		$500

To accrue the bill from Jack's printing for June sales flyers.

This entry increases advertising expenses for the month and increases the amount due in Accounts Payable. When you pay the bill, the Accounts Payable account is debited (to reduce the liability), and the Cash account is credited (to reduce the amount in the cash account). You make the actual entry in the Cash Disbursements journal when the cash is paid out.

When proving out the cash, you should also review any accounts in which expenses are accrued for later payment, such as Sales Taxes Collected, to be sure all accrual accounts are up-to-date. These tax accounts are actually liability accounts for taxes that will need to be paid in the future. If you use the accrual accounting method, the expenses related to these taxes must be matched to the revenues collected for the month they're incurred.

Using a Temporary Posting Journal

Some companies use a Temporary Posting journal to record payments that are made without full knowledge of how the cash outlay should be posted to the books and which accounts will be impacted. For example, a company using a payroll service probably has to give that service a certain amount of cash to cover payroll even if it's not yet known exactly how much is needed for taxes and other payroll-related costs.

In this payroll example, cash must be disbursed, but transactions can't be entered into all affected accounts until the payroll is done. Suppose a company's payroll is estimated to cost $15,000 for the month of May. The company sends a check to cover that cost to the payroll service and posts the payment to the Temporary Posting journal, and after the payroll is calculated and completed, the company receives a statement of exactly how much was paid to employees and how much was paid in taxes. After the statement arrives, allocating the $15,000 to specific accounts such as Payroll Expenses or Tax Expenses, that information is posted to the Cash Disbursements journal.

If you decide to keep a Temporary Posting journal to track cash coming in or going out, before summarizing your Cash Disbursements journal and closing the books for an accounting period, be sure to review the transactions listed in this journal that may need to be posted in the Cash Disbursements journal.

Reconciling Bank Accounts

Part of proving out cash involves checking that what you have in your bank accounts actually matches what the bank thinks you have in those accounts. This process is called *reconciling* the accounts.

Before you tackle reconciling your accounts with the bank's records, it's important to be sure that you've made all necessary adjustments to your books. When you make adjustments to your cash accounts, you identify and correct any cash transactions that may not have been properly entered into the books. You also make adjustments to reflect interest income or payments, bank fees, and credit-card chargebacks.

If you've done everything right, your accounting records should match the bank's records when it comes to how much cash you have in your accounts. The day you close your books probably isn't the same date as the bank sends its statements, so do your best at balancing the books internally without actually reconciling your checking account. Correcting any problems during the process of proving out, will minimize problems you may face reconciling the cash accounts when that bank statement actually does arrive.

You've probably reconciled your personal checking account at least a few times over the years, and you'll be happy to hear that reconciling business accounts is a similar process. Table 14-1 shows one common format for reconciling your bank account:

Table 14-1	Bank Reconciliation			
Transactions	Beginning Balance	Deposits	Disbursements	Ending Balance
Balance per bank statement	$	$	$	$
Deposits in transit (those not shown on statement)		$		$
Outstanding checks (checks that haven't shown up yet)			($)	($)
Total	$	$	$	$
Balance per checkbook or Cash in Checking (which should be the same)				$

Tracking down errors

Ideally, your balance and the bank's balance adjusted by transactions not yet shown on the statement should match. If they don't, you need to find out why.

✔ **If the bank balance is higher than your balance,** check to be sure that all the deposits listed by the bank appear in the Cash account in your books. If you find that the bank lists a deposit that you don't have, you need to do some detective work to figure out what that deposit was for and add the detail to your accounting records. Also, check to be sure that all checks have cleared. Your balance may be missing a check that should have been listed in outstanding checks.

✔ **If the bank balance is lower than your balance,** check to be sure that all checks listed by the bank are recorded in your Cash account. You may have missed one or two checks that were written but not properly recorded. You also may have missed a deposit that you have listed in your Cash account and you thought the bank already should have shown as a deposit, but it was not yet on the statement. If you notice a missing deposit on the bank statement, be sure you have your proof of the deposit and check with the bank to be sure the cash is in the account.

✔ **If all deposits and checks are correct but you still see a difference,** your only option is to check your math and make sure all checks and deposits were entered correctly.

Sometimes, you have to decide whether rooting out every little difference is really worth the time it takes. If it's just a matter of pennies, you probably don't need to waste your time trying to find the error, and you can just adjust the balance in your books. But if the difference is a significant amount for your business, you should try to track it down. You never know exactly what accounts are impacted by an error or how that difference may impact your profit or loss.

Using a computerized system

If you use a computerized accounting system, reconciliation should be much easier than keeping your books manually. In QuickBooks, for example, when you start the reconciliation process, a screen pops up in which you can add the ending bank statement balance and any bank fees or interest earned. Figure 14-3 shows you that screen. In this example, I've added $60,000 as the ending balance and $60 in bank fees. (The bank fees are automatically added to the bank fees expense account.)

After you click Continue, you get a screen that lists all checks written since the last reconciliation as well as all deposits. You put a check mark next to the checks and deposits that have cleared on the bank statement, as I've done in Figure 14-4, and then click Reconcile Now.

Figure 14-3:
When you
start the
recon-
ciliation
process in
QuickBooks,
you indicate
the bank's
ending bal-
ance and
any bank
service
charges
or interest
earned on
a particular
account.

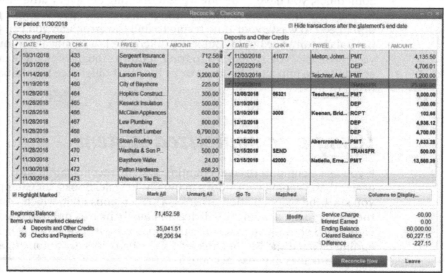

Figure 14-4:
To reconcile
check-
ing using
QuickBooks,
you put a
check mark
next to all
the checks
and deposits
that have
cleared the
account
and click
Reconcile
Now.

QuickBooks automatically reconciles the accounts and provides reports that indicate any differences. It also provides a *reconciliation summary,* shown in Figure 14-5, that includes the beginning balance, the balance after all cleared transactions have been recorded, and a list of all uncleared transactions. QuickBooks also calculates what your check register should show when the uncleared transactions are added to the cleared transactions.

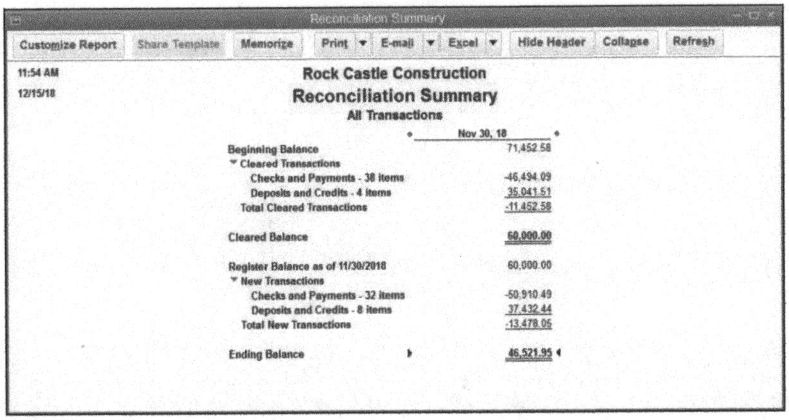

Figure 14-5:
After reconciling your accounts, QuickBooks automatically provides a reconciliation summary.

Posting Adjustments and Corrections

After you close out the Cash Receipts and Cash Disbursements journals as well as reconcile the bank account with your accounting system, you post any adjustments or corrections that you uncover to any other journals that may be impacted by the change, such as the Accounts Receivable or Accounts Payable. If you make changes that don't impact any journal accounts, you post them directly to the General Ledger.

For example, if you find that several customer payments haven't been entered in the Cash Receipts journal, you also need to post those payments to the Accounts Receivable journal and the customers' accounts. The same is true if you find payments on outstanding bills that haven't been entered into the books. In this case, you post the payments to the Accounts Payable journal as well as to the individual vendors' accounts.

Chapter 15

Closing the Journals

- -

In This Chapter

▶ Making sure your journals are correct

▶ Gathering journal information for closing

▶ Posting adjustments to the General Ledger

▶ Examining your journals in a computerized system

- -

*A*s the old saying goes, "The devil is in the details." When it comes to your bookkeeping, especially if you keep your books manually, those details are in the journals you keep. And those small details can get you every time.

If you use a computerized accounting system to do your books, you don't need to close out your journals, but you can still run a series of reports to verify that all the information in the computer accounting system matches what you have on paper. I talk about how to do that briefly in this chapter.

This chapter focuses primarily on how to prove out your journals and close them at the end of an accounting period. (Chapter 14 looks at this process for cash journals in particular, if you're interested.) You also find out how to post all corrections and adjustments to the General Ledger after you make them in the appropriate journal. (To find out how to set up your journals, flip to Chapter 5.)

Prepping to Close: Checking for Accuracy and Tallying Things Up

As you prepare to close the books, you first need to total what is in your journals, which is called *summarizing the journals*. During the process, it's a good idea to look for blatant errors and be sure that the entries accurately reflect the transactions during the accounting period.

Even the smallest error in a journal can cause a lot of frustration when you try to run a trial balance and close out your books, so it's best to do a thorough search for errors as you close out each journal for the month. It's much easier to find an error at this point in the closing process than to try to track it back through all your various accounts.

Paying attention to initial transaction details

Do a quick check to be sure the transaction details in your journals are accurate. Chapter 14 tells you how to do this type of check with the cash journals, but when you follow the rules of accrual accounting, not all transactions involve cash.

In accrual accounting, noncash transactions can include customer purchases made on store credit (which you track in the Accounts Receivable journal) and bills you will pay in the future (which you track in the Accounts Payable journal). You may also have created other journals to track transactions in your most active accounts, and you probably also keep details about sales in the Sales journal and payroll in the Payroll journal.

In the Payroll journal, make sure that all payrolls for the month have been added with all the proper details about salaries, wages, and taxes. Also verify that you've recorded all employer taxes that need to be paid. These taxes include the employer's portion of Medicare and Social Security as well as unemployment taxes. (I talk more about employer tax obligations in Chapter 11.)

Summarizing journal entries

The first step in checking for accuracy in your journals is summarizing them, which I explain in Chapter 5, which is primarily totaling all the columns in the journal. This summary process gives you totals for the accounts being tracked by each journal. For example, summarizing the Accounts Receivable journal gives you a grand total of all transactions for that period that involved customer credit accounts. Figure 15-1 shows a summary of an Accounts Receivable journal.

The Accounts Receivable journal includes transactions from the Sales journal (where customer purchases on store credit first appear) and the Cash Receipts journal (where customers' payments toward their store credit accounts first appear) as well as any credit memos for customer returns. The example in Figure 15-1 is only a few lines long, but, in most companies, the Accounts Receivable journal is very active with transactions posted every day the store is open during the month. When you summarize the Accounts Receivable journal, you get a *closing balance,* a balance that shows the total of all financial activity recorded in that journal. Figure 15-1 shows a closing balance of $2,240, which is the amount outstanding from customers.

Figure 15-1:
A sample
Accounts
Receivable
journal
summary.

			Cheesecake Shop Accounts Receivable March 2014			
Date	Description		Ref. #	Debit	Credit	Balance
	Opening Balance					$2,000
3/31	From Cash Receipts Journal		Journal P2		$500	$1,500
3/31	From Sales Journal		Journal P3	$800		$2,300
3/31	Credit Memo 124 (General Journal)		Journal P3		$60	$2,240
	March Closing Balance					$2,240

Each transaction in the journal should have a reference number next to it, which tells you where the detail for that transaction first appears in the books. You may need to review this information later when you're proving out the books. When you check for errors in the journal, you may need to review the original source information used to enter some transactions in order to double-check that entry's accuracy.

In addition to the Accounts Receivable journal, you also have individual journal pages for each customer; these pages detail each customer's purchases on store credit and any payments made toward those purchases. At the end of an accounting period, prepare an *Aging Summary* detailing all outstanding customer accounts. This report shows you what money is due from customers and how long it has been due. (I talk more about managing customer accounts in Chapter 9.)

For the purpose of proving out the books, the aging report is a quick summary that ensures that the customer accounts information matches what's in the Accounts Receivable journal.

Table 15-1 shows what an aging summary would look like for the time period.

Table 15-1	Aging Summary: Accounts Receivable as of March 31, 2014			
Customer	*Current*	*31–60 Days*	*61–90 Days*	*>90 Days*
S. Smith	$300			
J. Doe	$100	$300	$200	
H. Harris	$500	$240		
M. Man	$400	$200		
Total	$1,300	$740	$200	

In this sample Accounts Receivable Aging Summary, the total amount outstanding from customers matches the balance total in the Accounts Receivable journal. Therefore, all customer accounts have been accurately entered in the books, and the bookkeeper shouldn't encounter any errors related to customer accounts when running a trial balance, which I explain in Chapter 16.

If you find a difference between the information in your journal and your aging summary, review your customer account transactions to find the problem. An error may be the result of

- Recording a sales transaction without recording the details of that transaction in the customer's account.
- Recording a purchase directly into the customer's account without adding the purchase amount to the Accounts Receivable journal.
- Recording a customer's payment in the customer's account without recording the cash receipt in the Accounts Receivable journal.
- Recording a customer's payment in the Accounts Receivable journal without recording the cash receipt in the customer's account record.

The process of summarizing and closing out the Accounts Payable journal is similar to that of the Accounts Receivable journal. For Accounts Payable, you can prepare an aging summary for your outstanding bills as well.

That summary should look something like Table 15-2.

Table 15-2	Aging Summary: Accounts Payable as of March 31, 2014			
Vendor	*Current*	*31–60 Days*	*61–90 Days*	*>90 Days*
American Bank	$150			
Carol's Realty	$800			

Vendor	Current	31–60 Days	61–90 Days	>90 Days
Helen's Paper Goods		$250		
Henry's Bakery Supplies		$500		
Plates Unlimited	$400	$200		
Total	**$1,350**	**$950**		

The total of outstanding bills on the Accounts Payable Aging Summary should match the total shown on the Accounts Payable journal summary for the accounting period. If yours match, you're ready for a trial balance. If they don't, you must figure out the reason for the difference before closing out the Accounts Payable journal. The problem may be the result of

✔ Recording a bill due in the Accounts Payable journal without recording it in the vendor's account.

✔ Recording a bill due in the vendor's account without recording it in the Accounts Payable journal.

✔ Making a payment to the vendor without recording it in the Accounts Payable journal.

✔ Making a payment to the vendor and recording it in the Accounts Payable journal but neglecting to record it in the vendor's account.

Correct any problems you find before closing out the journal. If you know that you may be working with incorrect data, you don't want to try to do a trial balance because you know that balance will be filled with errors and you won't be able to generate accurate financial reports. Also, if you know errors exist, it's likely the books won't balance anyway, so it's just a wasted exercise to do a trial balance.

Analyzing summary results

You may be wondering how you can find problems in your records by just reviewing a page in a journal. Well, that skill comes with experience and practice. As you summarize your journals each month, you'll become familiar with the expected level of transactions and the types of transactions that occur month after month. If you don't see a transaction that you expect to find, take the time to research the transaction to find out why it's missing. It's possible that the transaction didn't take place, but it's also possible that someone forgot to record it.

For example, suppose that when summarizing the Payroll journal, you notice that the payroll for the 15th of the month seems lower than normal. As you check your details for that payroll, you find that the amount paid to hourly employees was recorded, but someone didn't record the amount paid to salaried employees. For that particular payroll, the payroll company experienced a computer problem after running some checks and as a result sent the final report on two separate pages. The person who recorded the payroll numbers didn't realize there was a separate page for salaried employees, so the final numbers entered into the books didn't reflect the full amount paid to employees.

As you close the books each month, you'll get an idea of the numbers you can expect for each type of journal. After a while, you'll be able to pick out problems just by scanning a page — no detailed research required!

Planning for cash flow

The process you go through each month as you prepare to close your books helps you plan for future cash flow. Reviewing the Accounts Receivable and Accounts Payable Aging Summaries tells you what additional cash you can expect from customers during the next few months and how much cash you'll need in order to pay bills for the next few months.

If you notice that your Accounts Payable Aging Summary indicates that more and more bills are slipping into past-due status, you may need to find another source for cash, such as a credit line from the bank. For example, the Accounts Payable Aging Summary reveals that three key vendors — Helen's Paper Goods, Henry's Bakery Supplies, and Plates Unlimited — haven't been paid on time.

Late payments can hurt your business's working relationship with vendors; they may refuse to deliver goods unless cash is paid upfront. And if you can't get the raw materials you need, you may have trouble filling customer orders on time. The lesson here is to act quickly and find a way to improve cash flow before your vendors cut you off. (For more on Accounts Payable management, check out Chapter 8.)

You may also find that your Accounts Receivable Aging Summary reveals that certain previously good customers are gradually becoming slow or nonpaying customers. For example, J. Doe's account is past due, and at least some portion of his account is overdue by more than 60 days. The bookkeeper dealing with these accounts may need to consider putting a hold on that account until payment is received in full. (For more on Accounts Receivable management, check out Chapter 9.)

Posting to the General Ledger

An important part of closing your books is posting to the General Ledger any corrections or adjustments you find as you close the journals. This type of posting consists of a simple entry that summarizes any changes you found.

For example, suppose you find that a customer purchase was recorded directly in the customer's account record but not in the Accounts Receivable journal. You have to research how that transaction was originally recorded. If the only record was a note in the customer's account, both the Sales account and the Accounts Receivable account are affected by the mistake, and the correcting entry looks like this:

	Debit	*Credit*
Accounts Receivable	$100	
Sales		$100

To record sale to J. Doe on 3/15/2014 — corrected 3/31/2014.

If you find this type of error, the Sales transaction record for that date of sale isn't accurate, which means that someone bypassed your standard bookkeeping process when recording the sale. You may want to research that part of the issue as well because there may be more than just a recording problem behind this incident. Someone in your company may be allowing customers to take product, purposefully not recording the sale appropriately in your books, and pocketing the money instead. It's also possible that a salesperson recorded a sale for a customer that never took place. If that's the case and you bill the customer, he would likely question the bill, and you'd find out about the problem at that point.

The process of proving out your journals, or any other part of your bookkeeping records, is a good opportunity to review your internal controls as well. As you find errors during the process of proving out the books, keep an eye out for ones (probably similar errors that appear frequently) that may indicate bigger problems than just bookkeeping mistakes. Repeat errors may call for additional staff training to be sure your bookkeeping rules are being followed to a T. Or such errors may be evidence that someone in the company is deliberately recording false information. Whatever the explanation, you need to take corrective action. (I cover internal controls in depth in Chapter 7.)

Checking Out Computerized Journal Records

Although you don't have to close out journal pages if you keep your books using a computerized accounting system, running a spot-check (at the very least) of what you have in your paper records versus what you have on your computer is a smart move. Simply run a series of reports using your computerized accounting system and then check to be sure that those computer records match what you have in your files.

For example, in QuickBooks, go to the Report Navigator and click on Vendors & Payables. The first section of the navigator page, shown in Figure 15-2, is called A/P Aging (due and overdue bills). This section offers three possible reports: Summary, which shows how much is due for each vendor; Detail, which gives a list of bills due and overdue; and an Accounts Payable Graph that illustrates your outstanding bills.

Figure 15-2:
QuickBooks
lets you
run reports
concerning
vendors and
payables
that tell you
how much
money your
company
owes to
others.

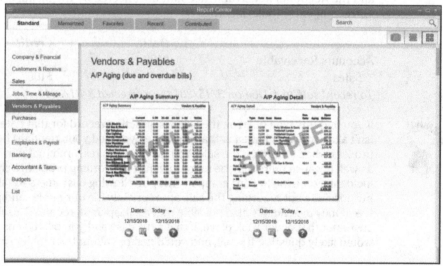

Figure 15-3 shows you the kind of detail you get when you select the Detail report. The Detail report is divided into

- Current bills

- Bills overdue by 1 to 30 days

- Bills overdue by 31 to 60 days

- Bills overdue by 61 to 90 days

- Bills overdue by more than 90 days

Obviously, anything in the last two columns — overdue by more than 60 days — is bad news. You can expect a supplier or vendor whose bills appear in these columns to soon cut you off from additional credit until your account is up-to-date.

Figure 15-3:
When you
run an
Accounts
Payable
Detail
report in
QuickBooks,
you get a
listing of all
outstand-
ing bills,
the dates
they were
received,
and the
dates
they're due.

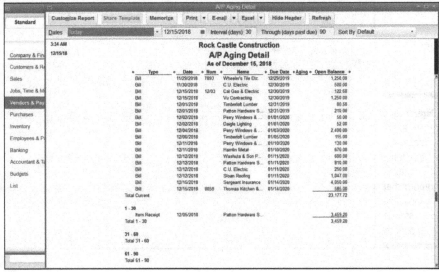

In addition to locating your bill-paying problem areas, you can also use the information in the Detail report to verify that the paper bills you have waiting to be paid in vendor files match what you have on your computer. You don't need to check each and every bill, but it's a good idea to do a spot-check of several bills. The goal is to verify the accuracy of your records as well as make sure that no one's entering and paying duplicate or nonexistent bills.

When it comes to cash flow out of the business, keep tight controls on who can actually sign checks and how the information that explains those checks is recorded. In Chapter 7, I talk more about the importance of separating duties to protect each aspect of your bookkeeping system from corruption.

You can also run reports showing the information recorded in your Accounts Receivable account. Figure 15-4 shows you a list of possible reports to run from the Customers & Receivables page. In addition to the Summary, Detail, and Accounts Receivable Graph, you can also run a report for Open Invoices, which lists outstanding customer invoices or statements, and Collections, which lists not only overdue customers but also how much they owe and their contact information.

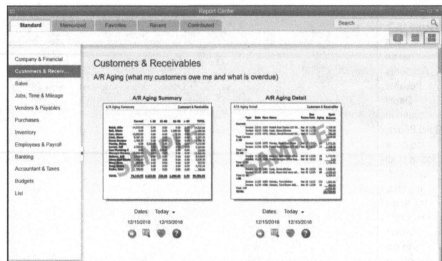

Figure 15-4:
In Quick-
Books, you
can run a
series of
reports that
summarize
customer
accounts.

Again, running spot-checks on a few customer accounts to be sure your
paper records of their accounts match the information in your computerized
system is a good idea. There's always a chance that a customer's purchase
was entered in error in the computer, and you could end up sending the bill
to the wrong person.

Some companies double-check their Accounts Receivable bookkeeping for
accuracy by sending surveys to customers periodically (usually twice a year)
to see if their accounts are correct. If you choose to do this, include with the
customer's bill a postage-paid card asking if the account is correct and giving
the customer room to indicate any account problems before mailing the
card back to your company. In most cases, a customer who has been incorrectly billed will contact you soon after getting that bill — especially if he or
she has been billed for more than anticipated.

In addition to keeping actual accounts, such as Accounts Payable or Accounts
Receivable, your computerized accounting system keeps a journal of all your
company's transactions. This journal contains details about all your transactions over a specified time period and the accounts that were impacted by
each transaction. Figure 15-5 is a sample computerized journal page.

If you need to be reminded of how you recorded a transaction into your computerized accounting system, run the Journal report by date, isolating all
transactions that took place at a particular time. Running a report by date can
be a helpful tool if you're trying to locate the source of an error in your books;
if you find a questionable transaction, you can open the detail of that transaction and see how it was entered and where you can find the original source
material.

Figure 15-5:
A computerized accounting system keeps a journal of all transactions, which you can review during the closing process.

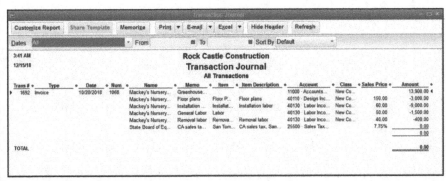

Chapter 16

Checking Your Accuracy — By Trial and Hopefully No Error

After you close out all your journals and do your darndest to catch any and all errors (flip to Chapter 15 for instructions on how to do this), the time comes to test your work. If you've entered all double-entry transactions in the books correctly, the books balance out, and your trial's a success!

Unfortunately, few bookkeepers get their books to balance on the first try. And in some cases, the books balance, but errors still exist. This chapter explains how you do a trial balance of your books and gives tips on finding any errors that may be lurking. You also find out how to take your first step to developing financial reports, which I explain in Part V, by creating a worksheet.

Working with a Trial Balance

When you first start entering transactions in a dual-entry accounting system, you may think, "This is a lot of work, and I don't know how I'm ever going to use all this information." You enter all your transactions using debits and credits without knowing whether they'll actually produce useful financial information that you can use to gauge how well your business is doing. It's not until after you close your journals and prepare your first set of financial reports that you truly see the value of double-entry accounting. Trust me.

The first step toward useable reports that help you interpret your financial results is doing a *trial balance*. Basically, a trial balance is a worksheet prepared manually or spit out by your computer accounting system that lists all the accounts in your General Ledger at the end of an accounting period (whether that's at the end of a month, the end of a quarter, or the end of a year).

Conducting your trial balance

If you've been entering transactions manually, you create a trial balance by listing all the accounts with their ending debit or credit balances. (I talk more about debits and credits in Chapter 2.) After preparing the list, you total both the debit and credit columns. If the totals at the bottom of the two columns are the same, the trial is a success, and your books are in balance.

The primary purpose of the trial balance is to prove that, at least mathematically, your debits and credits are equal. If any errors exist in your calculations or in how you summarized the journals or posted the summaries to the General Ledger, they're uncovered in the trial balance when the columns don't come out equal. Also, if you entered any transactions out of balance, you see the mistake when you add the columns of the trial balance.

The four basic steps to developing a trial balance are as follows:

1. **Prepare a worksheet with three columns: one for account titles, one for debits, and one for credits.**

2. **Fill in all the account titles and record their balances in the appropriate debit or credit columns.**

3. **Total the debit and credit columns.**

4. **Compare the column totals.**

Figure 16-1 shows a sample trial balance for a company as of May 31, 2014. Note that the debit column and the credit column both equal $57,850, making this a successful trial balance.

A successful trial balance is no guarantee that your books are totally free of errors; it just means that all your transactions have been entered in balance. You still may have errors in the books related to how you entered your transactions, including:

 ✔ You forgot to put a transaction in a journal or in the General Ledger.

 ✔ You forgot to post a journal entry to the General Ledger.

✔ You posted a journal entry twice in either the General Ledger or in the journal itself.

✔ You posted the wrong amount.

✔ You posted a transaction to the wrong account.

Trial Balance Cheesecake Shop 5/31/2014		
Account	Debit	Credit
Cash	$ 2,500.00	
Petty Cash	$ 500.00	
Accounts Receivable	$ 1,000.00	
Inventory	$ 1,200.00	
Equipment	$ 5,050.00	
Vehicle	$ 25,000.00	
Furniture	$ 5,600.00	
Accounts Payable		$ 2,200.00
Loans Payable		$ 29,150.00
Capital		$ 5,000.00
Sales		$ 20,000.00
Sales Discounts	$ 1,000.00	
Purchases	$ 8,000.00	
Purchase Discounts		$ 1,500.00
Credit Card Fees	$ 125.00	
Advertising	$ 1,500.00	
Bank Service Charges	$ 120.00	
Insurance Expenses	$ 100.00	
Interest Expense	$ 125.00	
Legal and Accounting Expense	$ 300.00	
Office Expense	$ 250.00	
Payroll Taxes Expense	$ 350.00	
Postage Expense	$ 75.00	
Rent Expense	$ 800.00	
Salaries & Wages Expense	$ 3,500.00	
Supplies	$ 300.00	
Telephone Expenses	$ 200.00	
Utilites Expenses	$ 255.00	
Totals	$ 57,850.00	$ 57,850.00

Figure 16-1:
A sample trial balance.

If, by chance, the errors listed here slip through the cracks, there's a good chance that someone will notice the discrepancy when the financial reports are prepared.

Even with these potentially lurking errors, the trial balance is a useful tool and the essential first step in developing your financial reports.

Dealing with trial balance errors

If your trial balance isn't correct, you need to work backwards in your closing process to find the source of the mathematical error. When you need to find errors after completing a trial balance that fails, follow these four basic steps to identify and fix the problem. And remember, this is why all bookkeepers and accountants work with pencils, not pens — pencils make erasing mistakes and making corrections much easier.

1. **Check your math.** Keep your fingers crossed, and add up your columns again to be sure the error isn't just one of addition. That's the simplest kind of error to find. Correct the addition mistake and re-total your columns.

2. **Compare your balances.** Double-check the balances on the trial balance worksheet by comparing them to the totals from your journals and your General Ledger. Be sure you didn't make an error when transferring the account balances to the trial balance. Correcting this type of problem isn't very difficult or time-consuming. Simply correct the incorrect balances, and add up the trial balance columns again.

3. **Check your journal summaries.** Double-check the math in all your journal summaries, making sure that all totals are correct and that any totals you posted to the General Ledger are correct. Running this kind of a check, of course, is somewhat time-consuming, but it's still better than rechecking all your transactions. If you do find errors in your journal summaries, correct them, reenter the totals correctly, change the numbers on the trial balance worksheet to match your corrected totals, and retest your trial balance.

4. **Check your journal and General Ledger entries.** Unfortunately, if Steps 1, 2, and 3 fail to fix your problem, all that's left is to go back and check your actual transaction entries. The process can be time-consuming, but the information in your books isn't useful until your debits equal your credits.

If this step is your last resort, scan through your entries looking specifically for ones that appear questionable. For example, if you see an entry for office supplies that's much larger or much smaller than you normally expect, check the original source material for that entry to be sure it's correct. If you carefully proved out the Accounts Payable and Accounts Receivable journals as I explain in Chapters 14 and 15, you can concentrate your efforts on accounts with separate journals. After you find and correct the error or errors, run another trial balance. If things still don't match up, repeat the steps listed here until your debits and credits equal out.

You can always go back and correct the books and do another trial balance before you prepare the financial reports. Don't close the books for the accounting period until the financial reports are completed and accepted. I talk more about the closing process in Chapter 22.

Testing Your Balance Using Computerized Accounting Systems

If you use a computerized accounting system, your trial balance is automatically generated for you. Because the system allows you to enter only transactions that are in balance, the likelihood that your trial balance won't be successful is pretty slim. But that doesn't mean your accounts are guaranteed error-free.

Remember the saying, "Garbage in, garbage out"? If you make a mistake when you enter transaction data into the system, even if the data's in balance, the information that comes out will also be in error. Although you don't have to go through the correction steps covered in the earlier section "Dealing with trial balance errors" to reach a successful trial balance, you still may have errors lurking in your data.

In QuickBooks, the trial balance report is the first report on the Report Navigator's Accountant & Taxes page, which appears in Figure 16-2. In addition to the trial balance, you can request a report showing the General Ledger, transaction detail by account, journal detail, voided transactions, and transactions by date.

Your business's accountant is likely to use many of the report options on the Accountant & Taxes page to double-check that your transactions were entered correctly and that no one is playing with the numbers. In particular, the accountant may use a report option called *Audit Trail,* which reveals what changes impacted the company's books during an accounting period and who made those changes.

Although it doesn't match the trial balance done manually in Figure 16-1, the QuickBooks trial balance shown in Figure 16-3 gives you an idea of what a computerized accounting trial balance looks like.

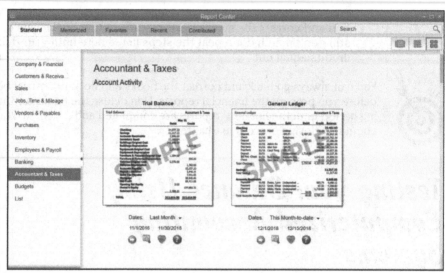

Figure 16-2: The Accountant & Taxes page of the QuickBooks Report Navigator provides the option of creating many useful reports.

Rock Castle Construction
Trial Balance
As of November 30, 2018

	Nov 30, 18 Debit	Credit
10100 · Checking	55,354.24	
10300 · Savings	43,410.19	
10400 · Petty Cash	500.00	
11000 · Accounts Receivable	83,547.91	
12000 · Undeposited Funds	0.00	
12100 · Inventory Asset	27,872.63	
12800 · Employee Advances	770.00	
13100 · Pre-paid Insurance	0.00	
13400 · Retainage Receivable	5,418.02	
15000 · Furniture and Equipment	34,326.00	
15100 · Vehicles	78,936.91	
15200 · Buildings and Improvements	325,000.00	
15300 · Construction Equipment	15,300.00	
16900 · Land	90,000.00	
17000 · Accumulated Depreciation		110,344.60
18700 · Security Deposits	1,720.00	
20000 · Accounts Payable		58,345.02
20500 · QuickBooks Credit Card		25.00
20600 · CalOil Credit Card		436.80
24000 · Payroll Liabilities:24010 · Federal Withholding		841.00
24000 · Payroll Liabilities:24020 · FICA Payable		1,293.78
24000 · Payroll Liabilities:24030 · AEIC Payable	0.00	
24000 · Payroll Liabilities:24040 · FUTA Payable	0.00	
24000 · Payroll Liabilities:24050 · State Withholding		191.21
24000 · Payroll Liabilities:24060 · SUTA Payable	0.00	
24000 · Payroll Liabilities:24070 · State Disability Payable		82.57
24000 · Payroll Liabilities:24080 · Worker's Compensation		805.83
24000 · Payroll Liabilities:24100 · Emp. Health Ins Payable		75.00

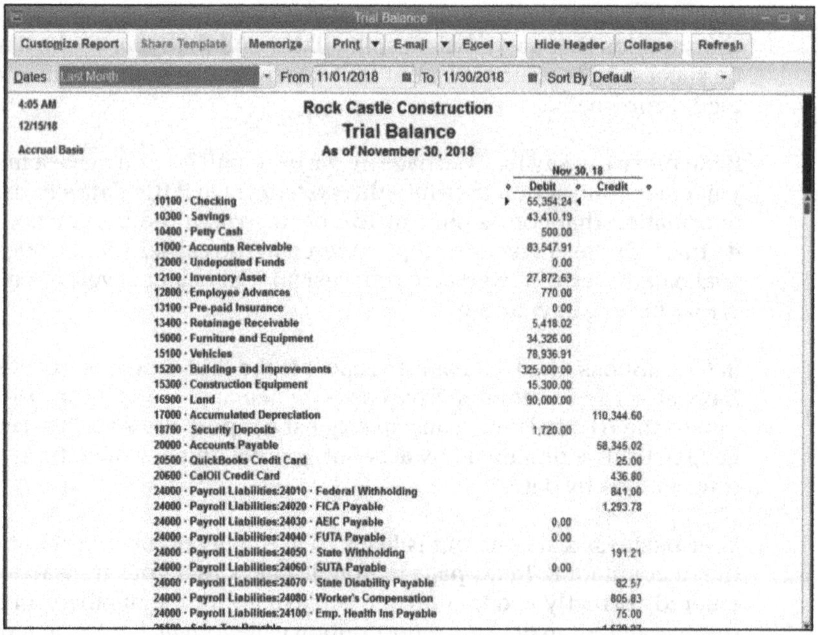

Figure 16-3: A sample trial balance report produced by QuickBooks.

Developing a Financial Statement Worksheet

After your accounts successfully pass a trial balance test (see "Conducting your trial balance" earlier in this chapter), you can then take your first stab at creating *financial statements,* including balance sheets and income statements. The first step in producing these statements is using the information from the trial balance and its corrections to develop a *worksheet* that includes the initial trial balance, the accounts that would be shown on a balance sheet, and finally the accounts that would normally be shown on an income statement.

You create the worksheet that includes these seven columns:

- ✔ **Column 1:** Account list

- ✔ **Columns 2 and 3:** Trial balance (one column for debits, one column for credits)

- ✔ **Columns 4 and 5:** Balance sheet (one column for debits, one column for credits)

- ✔ **Columns 6 and 7:** Income statement (one column for debits, one column for credits)

In Figure 16-4, you can see a sample of a worksheet developed from trial balance numbers. Note that the numbers of the trial balance are transferred to the appropriate financial statement; for example, the Cash account, which is an asset account, is shown in the debit column of the balance sheet. (I talk more about developing financial statements in Chapters 18 and 19.)

After you transfer all the accounts to their appropriate balance sheet or income statement columns, you total the worksheet columns. Don't panic when you see that the totals at the bottom of your columns aren't equal — it's because the net income hasn't been calculated yet. However, the difference between the debits and credits in both the balance sheet and the income statement totals should be the same. That amount should represent the net income that will appear on the income statement. (You'll see what I mean about net income when I develop the income statement in Chapter 19.)

In Figure 16-4, the $4,500 difference for the balance sheet is shown as a credit, representing an increase in Retained Earnings. The Retained Earnings account reflects the profits that have been reinvested into the company's assets in order to grow the company. You can find more about Retained Earnings in Chapter 18.

In some incorporated companies, part of the earnings are taken out in the form of *dividends* paid to stockholders. Dividends are a portion of the earnings divided up among stockholders. The board of directors of the corporation set a certain amount per share to be paid to stockholders.

Many other small companies that haven't incorporated pay out earnings to their owners using a *Drawing account*, which tracks any cash taken out by the owners. Each owner should have his or her own Drawing account so that you have a history of how much each owner withdraws from the company's resources.

	Trial Balance		Balance Sheet		Income Statement	
Account	Debit	Credit	Debit	Credit	Debit	Credit
Cash	2,500.00		2,500.00			
Petty Cash	500.00		500.00			
Accounts Receivable	1,000.00		1,000.00			
Inventory	1,200.00		1,200.00			
Equipment	5,050.00		5,050.00			
Vehicle	25,000.00		25,000.00			
Furniture	5,600.00		5,600.00			
Accounts Payable		2,200.00		2,200.00		
Loans Payable		29,150.00		29,150.00		
Capital		5,000.00		5,000.00		
Sales		20,000.00				20,000.00
Sales Discounts	1,000.00				1,000.00	
Purchases	8,000.00				8,000.00	
Purchase Discounts		1,500.00				1,500.00
Credit Card Fees	125.00				125.00	
Advertising	1,500.00				1,500.00	
Bank Service Charges	120.00				120.00	
Insurance Expenses	100.00				100.00	
Interest Expenses	125.00				125.00	
Legal and Accounting Expenses	300.00				300.00	
Office Expenses	250.00				250.00	
Payroll Taxes Expenses	350.00				350.00	
Postage Expenses	75.00				75.00	
Rent Expenses	800.00				800.00	
Salaries & Wages Expenses	3,500.00				3,500.00	
Supplies	300.00				300.00	
Telephone Expenses	200.00				200.00	
Utilites Expenses	255.00				255.00	
Net Income				4500.00	4,500.00	
Totals	57,850.00	57,850.00	40,850.00	40,850.00	21,500.00	21,500.00

Figure 16-4: This sample worksheet shows the first step in developing a company's financial statements.

Replacing Worksheets with Computerized Reports

If you use a computerized accounting system, you don't have to create a worksheet at all. Instead, the system gives you the option of generating many different types of reports to help you develop your income statement and balance sheet.

One of the advantages of your computerized system's reports is that you can easily look at your numbers in many different ways. For example, Figure 16-5 shows the Company & Financial Report Navigator from QuickBooks. Notice that you can generate so many different reports that the entire list doesn't even fit on one computer screen! To get the report you want, all you need to do is click on the report title.

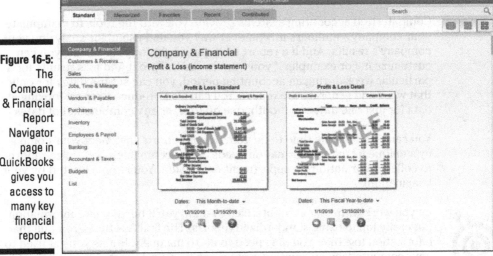

Figure 16-5: The Company & Financial Report Navigator page in QuickBooks gives you access to many key financial reports.

You can generate a number of different reports within the following categories:

✔ **Profit & Loss (income statement):** Some key reports in this section include

- A standard report that shows how much the company made or lost during a specific period of time

- A detail report that includes all the year-to-date transactions

- A report that compares year-to-date figures with the previous year (provided you kept the accounts using the computerized system in the previous year)

- ✔ **Income & Expenses:** Some key reports in this section include

  - Income by customer (both a summary and a detailed report)

  - Expenses by vendor (both a summary and a detailed report)

- ✔ **Balance Sheet & Net Worth:** Some key reports in this section include

  - A standard balance sheet showing a summary of assets, liabilities, and equity

  - A detail report of assets, liabilities, and equity

  - A report that compares the assets, liabilities, and equity levels with those of the previous year

- ✔ **Cash Flow:** Some key reports in this section include

  - A statement of cash flows for the year

  - A forecast of cash flows during the next few weeks or months based on money due in accounts receivable and money to be paid out in accounts payable

Computerized accounting systems provide you with the tools to manipulate your company's numbers in whatever way you find useful for analyzing your company's results. And if a report isn't quite right for your needs, you can customize it. For example, if you want to see the profit and loss results for a particular week during an accounting period, you can set the dates for only that week and generate the report. You can also produce a report looking at data for just one day, one month, one quarter, or any combination of dates.

You can also take the time to custom design reports that meet your company's unique financial information needs. Many companies customize reports to collect information by department or division. You're only limited by your imagination!

As you work with your computerized system, you'll be asked for information not easily found using standardized reports. The first few times you pull that information together, you may need to do so manually. But as you get used to your computerized accounting system and its report functions, you'll be able to design customized reports that pull together information in just the way you need it.

Chapter 17

Adjusting the Books

In This Chapter

▶ Making adjustments for noncash transactions

▶ Taking your adjustments for a trial (balance) run

▶ Adding to and deleting from the Chart of Accounts

*D*uring an accounting period, your bookkeeping duties focus on your business's day-to-day transactions. When it comes time to report those transactions in financial statements, you must make some adjustments to your books. Your financial reports are supposed to show your company's financial health, so your books must reflect any significant change in the value of your assets, even if that change doesn't involve the exchange of cash.

If you use cash-basis accounting, these adjustments aren't necessary because you only record transactions when cash changes hands. I talk about accrual and cash-basis accounting in Chapter 2.

This chapter reviews the types of adjustments you need to make to the books before preparing the financial statements, including calculating asset depreciation, dividing up prepaid expenses, updating inventory numbers, dealing with bad debt, and recognizing salaries and wages not yet paid. You also find out how to add and delete accounts.

Adjusting All the Right Areas

Even after testing your books using the trial balance process that I explain in Chapter 16, you still need to make some adjustments before you're able to prepare accurate financial reports with the information you have. These adjustments don't involve the exchange of cash but rather involve recognizing the use of assets, loss of assets, or future asset obligations that aren't reflected in day-to-day bookkeeping activities.

The key areas in which you likely need to adjust the books include

- ✔ **Asset depreciation:** To recognize the use of assets during the accounting period.

- ✔ **Prepaid expenses:** To match a portion of expenses that were paid at one point during the year, but benefits from that payment are used throughout the year, such as an annual insurance premium. The benefit should be apportioned out against expenses for each month.

- ✔ **Inventory:** To update inventory to reflect what you have on hand.

- ✔ **Bad debts:** To acknowledge that some customers will never pay and to write off those accounts.

- ✔ **Unpaid salaries and wages:** To recognize salary and wage expenses that have been incurred but not yet paid.

Depreciating assets

The largest noncash expense for most businesses is *depreciation*. Depreciation is an accounting exercise that's important for every business to undertake because it reflects the use and aging of assets. Older assets need more maintenance and repair and also need to be replaced eventually. As the depreciation of an asset increases and the value of the asset dwindles, the need for more maintenance or replacement becomes apparent. (For more on depreciation and why you do it, check out Chapter 12.)

The time to actually make this adjustment to the books is when you close the books for an accounting period. (Some businesses record depreciation expenses every month to more accurately match monthly expenses with monthly revenues, but most business owners only worry about depreciation adjustments on a yearly basis, when they prepare their annual financial statements.)

Depreciation doesn't involve the use of cash. By accumulating depreciation expenses on an asset, you're reducing the value of the asset as shown on the balance sheet (see Chapter 18 for the lowdown on balance sheets).

Readers of your financial statements can get a good idea of the health of your assets by reviewing your accumulated depreciation. If a financial report reader sees that assets are close to being fully depreciated, he knows that you'll probably need to spend significant funds on replacing or repairing those assets sometime soon. As he evaluates the financial health of the company, he takes that future obligation into consideration before making a decision to loan money to the company or possibly invest in it.

Usually, you calculate depreciation for accounting purposes using the *Straight-Line depreciation method*. This method is used to calculate an amount to be depreciated that will be equal each year based on the anticipated useful life of the asset. For example, suppose your company purchases a car for business purposes that costs $25,000. You anticipate that car will have a useful lifespan of five years and will be worth $5,000 after five years. Using the Straight-Line depreciation method, you subtract $5,000 from the total car cost of $25,000 to find the value of the car during its five-year useful lifespan ($20,000). Then divide $20,000 by 5 to find your depreciation expense for the car ($4,000 per year). When adjusting the assets at the end of each year in the car's five-year lifespan, your entry to the books should look like this:

	Debit	*Credit*
Depreciation Expense	$4,000	
Accumulated Depreciation: Vehicles		$4,000

To record depreciation for Vehicles.

This entry increases depreciation expenses, which appear on the income statement (see Chapter 19). The entry also increases Accumulated Depreciation, which is the use of the asset and appears on the balance sheet directly under the Vehicles asset line. The Vehicles asset line always shows the value of the asset at the time of purchase.

You can speed up depreciation if you believe that the asset will not be used evenly over its lifespan — in other words, if the asset will be used more heavily in the early years of ownership. Chapter 12 covers alternative depreciation.

If you use a computerized accounting system, you may or may not need to make this adjustment at the end of an accounting period. If your system is set up with an asset management feature, depreciation is automatically calculated, and you don't have to worry about it. Check with your accountant (he or she is the one who would set up the asset management feature) before calculating and recording depreciation expenses.

Allocating prepaid expenses

Most businesses have to pay certain expenses at the beginning of the year even though they will benefit from that expense throughout the year. Insurance is a prime example of this type of expense. Most insurance companies require you to pay the premium annually at the start of the year even though the value of that insurance protects the company throughout the year.

For example, suppose your company's annual car insurance premium is $1,200. You pay that premium in January in order to maintain insurance coverage throughout the year. Showing the full cash expense of your insurance when you prepare your January financial reports would greatly reduce any profit that month and make your financial results look worse than they actually are. That's no good.

Instead, you record a large expense such as insurance or prepaid rent as an asset called *Prepaid Expenses,* and then you adjust the value of that asset to reflect that it's being used up. Your $1,200 annual insurance premium is actually valuable to the company for 12 months, so you calculate the actual expense for insurance by dividing $1,200 by 12, giving you $100 per month. At the end of each month, you record the use of that asset by preparing an adjusting entry that looks like this:

	Debit	Credit
Insurance Expenses	$100	
Prepaid Expenses		$100

To record insurance expenses for March.

This entry increases insurance expenses on the income statement and decreases the asset Prepaid Expenses on the balance sheet. No cash changes hands in this entry because cash was laid out when the insurance bill was paid, and the asset account Prepaid Expenses was increased in value at the time the cash was paid.

Counting inventory

Inventory is a balance sheet asset that needs to be adjusted at the end of an accounting period. During the accounting period, your company buys inventory and records those purchases in a Purchases account without indicating any change to inventory. When the products are sold, you record the sales in the Sales account but don't make any adjustment to the value of the inventory. Instead, you adjust the inventory value at the end of the accounting period because adjusting with each purchase and sale would be much too time-consuming.

Here are the steps for making proper adjustments to inventory in your books:

1. **Determine the inventory remaining.** In addition to calculating ending inventory using the purchases and sales numbers in the books, you should also do a physical count of inventory to be sure that what's on the shelves matches what's in the books.

2. **Set a value for that inventory.** The value of ending inventory varies depending on your method of valuing inventory. Chapter 8 covers inventory value and how to calculate the value of ending inventory.

3. **Adjust the number of pieces remaining in inventory in the Inventory Account and adjust the value of that account based on the information collected in Steps 1 and 2.**

If you track inventory using your computerized accounting system, the system makes adjustments to inventory as you record sales. At the end of the accounting period, the value of your company's ending inventory should be adjusted in the books already. Although the work's already done for you, you should still do a physical count of the inventory to be sure that your computer records match the physical inventory at the end of the accounting period.

Allowing for bad debts

No company likes to accept the fact that it will never see the money owed by some of its customers, but, in reality, that's what happens to most companies that sell items on store credit. When your company determines that a customer who has bought products on store credit will never pay for them, you record the value of that purchase as a *bad debt*. (For an explanation of store credit, check out Chapter 9.)

At the end of an accounting period, you should list all outstanding customer accounts in an *aging report* (see Chapter 9), which shows which customers owe how much and for how long. After a certain amount of time, you have to admit that some customers simply aren't going to pay. Each company sets its own determination of how long it wants to wait before tagging an account as a bad debt. For example, your company may decide that when a customer is six months late with a payment, you're unlikely to ever see the money.

After you determine that an account is a bad debt, you should no longer include its value as part of your assets in Accounts Receivable. Including its value doesn't paint a realistic picture of your situation for the readers of your financial reports. Because the bad debt is no longer an asset, you adjust the value of your Accounts Receivable to reflect the loss of that asset.

You can record bad debts in a couple of ways:

- ✔ **By customer:** Some companies identify the specific customers whose accounts are bad debts and calculate the bad debt expense each accounting period based on specified customers' accounts.

- ✔ **By percentage:** Other companies look at their bad-debts histories and develop percentages that reflect those experiences. Instead of taking the time to identify each specific account that will be a bad debt, these companies record bad debt expenses as a percentage of their Accounts Receivable.

However you decide to record bad debts, you need to prepare an adjusting entry at the end of each accounting period to record bad debt expenses. Here's an adjusting entry to record bad debt expenses of $1,000:

	Debit	Credit
Bad Debt Expense	$1,000	
Accounts Receivable		$1,000

To write off customer accounts.

You can't have bad debt expenses if you don't sell to your customers on store credit. You only need to worry about bad debt if you offer your customers the convenience of buying your products on store credit.

If you use a computerized accounting system, check the system's instructions for how to write off bad debts. To write off a bad debt using QuickBooks:

1. **Open the screen where you normally record customer payments, and instead of entering the amount received in payment, enter "$0."**

2. **Place a check mark next to the amount being written off.**

3. **Click Discount and Credits tab on the Customer Payment screen.**

4. **On the discount tab (Figure 17-1), type the amount of the discount.**

5. **Select Bad Debt Expense from the Discount Account menu.**

6. **Click Done and verify that the discount is applied and no payment is due (see Figure 17-2).**

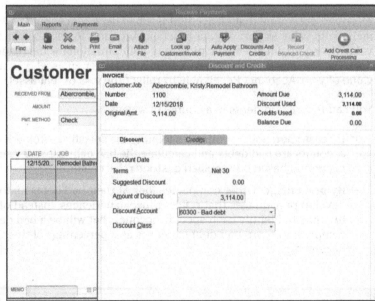

Figure 17-1: In QuickBooks, you record bad debts on the Discount and Credits page, which is part of the Customer Payment function.

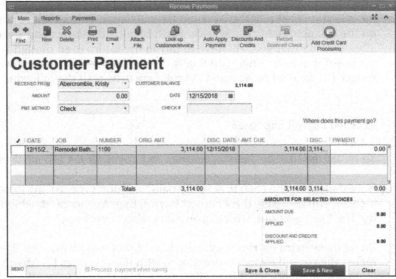

Figure 17-2:
After you
record a
bad debt in
QuickBooks,
the discount
appears,
indicating
that $0 is
due.

Recognizing unpaid salaries and wages

Not all pay periods fall at the end of a month. If you pay your employees every two weeks, you may end up closing the books in the middle of a pay period, meaning that, for example, employees aren't paid for the last week of March until the end of the first week of April.

When your pay period hits before the end of the month, you need to make an adjusting entry at month's end to record the payroll expense that has been incurred but not yet paid. You estimate the amount of the adjustment based on what you pay every two weeks. The easiest thing to do is just accrue the expense of half of your payroll (which means you enter the anticipated expense as an accrual in the appropriate account; when the cash is actually paid out, you then reverse that accrual entry, which reduces the amount in the liability account, Accrued Payroll expenses, and the Cash account, to reflect the outlay of cash). If that expense is $3,000, you make the following adjusting entry to the books to show the accrual:

	Debit	Credit
Payroll Expenses	$3,000	
Accrued Payroll Expenses		$3,000

To record payroll expenses for the last week of March.

This adjusting entry increases both the Payroll Expenses reported on the income statement and the Accrued Payroll Expenses that appear as a liability on the balance sheet. The week's worth of unpaid salaries and wages is actually a liability that you will have to pay in the future even though you haven't yet spent the cash. When you finally do pay out the salaries and wages, you reduce the amount in Accrued Payroll Expenses with the following entry:

	Debit	*Credit*
Accrued Payroll Expenses	$3,000	
Cash		$3,000

To record the cash payment of salaries and wages for the last week of March.

Note that when the cash is actually paid, you don't record any expenses; instead, you decrease the Accrued Payroll Expense account, which is a liability. The Cash account, which is an asset, also decreases.

Doing these extra entries may seem like a lot of extra work, but if you didn't match the payroll expenses for March with the revenues for March, your income statements wouldn't reflect the actual state of your affairs. Your revenues at the end of March would look very good because your salary and wage expenses weren't fully reflected in the income statement, but your April income statement would look very bad given the extra expenses that were actually incurred in March.

Testing Out an Adjusted Trial Balance

In Chapter 16, I explain why and how you run a trial balance on the accounts in your General Ledger. Adjustments to your books call for another trial balance, the *adjusted trial balance,* to ensure that your adjustments are correct and ready to be posted to the General Ledger.

You track all the adjusting entries on a worksheet similar to the one shown in Chapter 16. You only need to do this worksheet if you're doing your books manually. It's not necessary if you're using a computerized accounting system. The key difference in the worksheet for the Adjusted Trial Balance is that four additional columns must be added to the worksheet for a total of 11 columns. Columns include

- ✔ **Column 1:** Account titles.

- ✔ **Columns 2 and 3:** Unadjusted Trial Balance. The trial balance before the adjustments are made with Column 2 for debits and Column 3 for credits.

- ✔ **Columns 4 and 5:** Adjustments. All adjustments to the trial balance are listed in Column 4 for debits and Column 5 for credits.

✔ **Columns 6 and 7:** Adjusted Trial Balance. A new trial balance is calculated that includes all the adjustments. Be sure that the credits equal
the debits when you total that new Trial Balance. If they don't, find any
errors before adding entries to the balance sheet and income statement
columns.

✔ **Columns 8 and 9:** Balance sheet. Column 8 includes all the Balance
Sheet accounts that have a debit balance, and Column 9 includes all the
Balance Sheet accounts with a credit balance.

✔ **Columns 10 and 11:** Income statement. Column 10 includes all the Income
Statement accounts with a debit balance, and Column 11 includes all the
Income Statement accounts with a credit balance.

When you're confident that all the accounts are in balance, post your adjustments to the General Ledger so that all the balances in the General Ledger
include the adjusting entries. With the adjustments, the General Ledger will
match the financial statements you prepare.

Changing Your Chart of Accounts

After you finalize your General Ledger for the year, you may want to make
changes to your Chart of Accounts, which lists all the accounts in your accounting system. (For the full story on the Chart of Accounts, see Chapter 3.) You
may need to add accounts if you think you need additional ones or delete
accounts if you think they will no longer be needed.

You should only delete accounts from your chart of accounts at the end of the
year. If you delete an account in the middle of the year, your annual financial
statements will not reflect the activities in that account prior to its deletion.
So even if you decide halfway through the year to no longer use an account,
you should leave it on the books until the end of the year, and then delete
it. You can add accounts to your Chart of Accounts throughout the year, but
if you decide to add an account in the middle of the year in order to more
closely track certain assets, liabilities, revenues, or expenses, you may need to
adjust some related entries.

Suppose you start the year out tracking paper expenses in the Office Supplies
Expenses account, but paper usage and its expense keeps increasing, so you
decide to track the expense in a separate account beginning in July.

First, you add the new account, Paper Expenses, to your Chart of Accounts.
Then you prepare an adjusting entry to move all the paper expenses that
were recorded in the Office Supplies Expenses account to the Paper Expenses
account. In the interest of space and to avoid boring you, the adjusting entry

below is an abbreviated one. In your actual entry, you would probably detail the specific dates paper was bought as an office supplies expense rather than just tally one summary total.

	Debit	*Credit*
Paper Expenses	$1,000	
Office Supplies Expenses		$1,000

To move expenses for paper from the Office Supplies Expenses account to the Paper Expenses account.

Moving beyond the catch-all Miscellaneous Expenses account

When new accounts are added to the Chart of Accounts, the account most commonly adjusted is the Miscellaneous Expenses account. In many cases, you may expect to incur an expense only one or two times during the year, therefore making it unnecessary to create a new account specifically for that expense. But after a while, you find that your "rare" expense is adding up, and you'd be better off with a designated account, meaning that it's time to create some adjusting entries to move expenses out of the Miscellaneous Expenses account.

For example, suppose you think you'll only need to rent a car for the business one time before you buy a new vehicle, so you enter the rental cost in the books as a Miscellaneous Expense. However, after renting cars three times, you decide to start a Rental Expense account mid-year. When you add the Rental Expense account to your Chart of Accounts, you need to use an adjusting entry to transfer any expenses incurred and recorded in the Miscellaneous Expense account prior to the creation of the new account.

Part V

Reporting Results and Starting Over

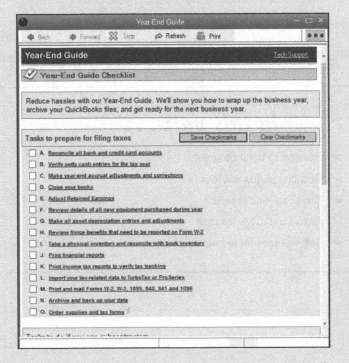

Check out an online article on the trend toward a global set of rules for financial reporting at www.dummies.com/extras/bookkeeping.

In this part . . .

- ✔ Developing balance sheets
- ✔ Detailing profits and losses
- ✔ Filing year-end reports
- ✔ Answering to the tax man
- ✔ Getting ready for the next business year

Chapter 18

Developing a Balance Sheet

*P*eriodically, you want to know where your business stands. Therefore, at the end of each accounting period, you take a snapshot of your business's condition. This snapshot, which is called a balance sheet, gives you a picture of where your business stands — how much it has in assets, how much it owes in liabilities, and how much the owners have invested in the business at a particular point in time.

This chapter explains the key ingredients of a balance sheet and tells you how to pull them all together. You also find out how to use some analytical tools called ratios to see how well your business is doing.

What Is a Balance Sheet?

Basically, creating a balance sheet is like taking a picture of the financial aspects of your business.

The company name and ending date for the accounting period being reported appear at the top of the balance sheet. The rest of the report summarizes

✔ **The company's assets,** which include everything the company owns in order to stay in operation.

✔ **The company's debts,** which include any outstanding bills and loans that must be paid.

✔ **The owner's equity,** which is basically how much the company owners have invested in the business.

Assets, liabilities, and equity probably sound familiar — they're the key elements that show whether or not your books are in balance. If your liabilities plus equity equal assets, your books are in balance. All your bookkeeping efforts are an attempt to keep the books in balance based on this formula, which I talk more about in Chapter 2.

Gathering Balance Sheet Ingredients

You can find most of the information you need to prepare a balance sheet on your trial balance worksheet, the details of which are drawn from your final adjusted trial balance. (I show you how to develop a trial balance in Chapter 16 and how to adjust that trial balance in Chapter 17.)

To keep this example somewhat simple, I assume that the fictitious company has no adjustments for the balance sheet as of May 31, 2014. In the real world, every company needs to adjust something (usually inventory levels at the very least) every month.

To prepare the example trial balances in this chapter, I use the key accounts listed in Table 18-1; these accounts and numbers come from the fictitious company's trial balance worksheet.

Table 18-1	Balance Sheet Accounts
Account Name	*Balance in Account*
Cash	$2,500
Petty Cash	$500
Accounts Receivable	$1,000
Inventory	$1,200
Equipment	$5,050
Vehicles	$25,000
Furniture	$5,600
Accounts Payable	$2,200
Loans Payable	$29,150
Capital	$5,000

Dividing and listing your assets

The first part of the balance sheet is the Assets section. The first step in developing this section is dividing your assets into two categories: current assets and long-term assets.

Current assets

Current assets are things your company owns that you can easily convert to cash and expect to use in the next 12 months to pay your bills and your employees. Current assets include cash, Accounts Receivable (money due from customers), marketable securities (including stocks, bonds, and other types of securities), and inventory. (I cover Accounts Receivable in Chapter 9 and inventory in Chapter 8.)

When you see cash as the first line item on a balance sheet, that account includes what you have on hand in the register and what you have in the bank, including checking accounts, savings accounts, money market accounts, and certificates of deposit. In most cases, you simply list all these accounts as one item, Cash, on the balance sheet.

The current assets for a fictional company are

Cash	$2,500
Petty Cash	$500
Accounts Receivable	$1,000
Inventory	$1,200

You total the Cash and Petty Cash accounts, giving you $3,000, and list that amount on the balance sheet as a line item called Cash.

Long-term assets

Long-term assets are things your company owns that you expect to have for more than 12 months. Long-term assets include land, buildings, equipment, furniture, vehicles, and anything else that you expect to have for longer than a year.

The long-term assets for a fictional company are

Equipment	$5,050
Vehicles	$25,000
Furniture	$5,600

Most companies have more items in the long-term assets section of a balance sheet than the few long-term assets I show here for the fictional company. For example, a manufacturing company that has a lot of tools, dies, or molds created specifically for its manufacturing processes would have a line item called Tools, Dies, and Molds in the long-term assets section of the balance sheet.

Similarly, if your company owns one or more buildings, you should have a line item labeled Land and Buildings. And if you lease a building with an option to purchase it at some later date, that *capitalized lease* is considered a long-term asset and is listed on the balance sheet as Capitalized Lease.

Some companies lease their business space and then spend lots of money fixing it up. For example, a restaurant may rent a large space and then furnish it according to a desired theme. Money spent on fixing up the space becomes a long-term asset called Leasehold Improvements and is listed on the balance sheet in the long-term assets section.

Everything I've mentioned so far in this section — land, buildings, capitalized leases, leasehold improvements, and so on — is a *tangible asset.* These are items that you can actually touch or hold. Another type of long-term asset is the *intangible asset.* Intangible assets aren't physical objects; Common examples of intangible assets are patents, copyrights, and trademarks (all of which are granted by the government).

- ✔ **Patents** give companies the right to dominate the markets for patented products. When a patent expires (14 to 20 years depending on the type of patent), competitors can enter the marketplace for the product that was patented, and the competition helps to lower the price to consumers. For example, pharmaceutical companies patent all their new drugs and therefore are protected as the sole providers of those drugs. When your doctor prescribes a brand-name drug, you're getting a patented product. Generic drugs are products whose patents have run out, meaning that any pharmaceutical company can produce and sell its own version of the same product.

- ✔ **Copyrights** protect original works, including books, magazines, articles, newspapers, television shows, movies, music, poetry, and plays, from being copied by anyone other than their creators. For example, this book is copyrighted, so no one can make a copy of any of its contents without the permission of the publisher, Wiley Publishing, Inc.

- ✔ **Trademarks** give companies ownership of distinguishing words, phrases, symbols, or designs. For example, check out this book's cover to see the registered trademark, *For Dummies,* for this brand. Trademarks can last forever as long as a company continues to use the trademark and file the proper paperwork periodically.

In order to show in financial statements that their values are being used up, all long-term assets are either depreciated or amortized. Tangible assets are depreciated; see Chapter 12 for details on how to depreciate. Intangible assets such as patents and copyrights are amortized (amortization is very similar to depreciation). Each intangible asset has a life span based on the number of years the government grants the rights for it. After setting an initial value for the intangible asset, a company then divides that value by the number of years it has government protection, and the resulting amount is then written off each year as an amortization expense, which is shown on the income statement. You can find the total amortization or depreciation expenses that have been written off during the life of the asset on the Balance Sheet in a line item called Accumulated Depreciation or Accumulated Amortization, whichever is appropriate for the type of asset.

Acknowledging your debts

The Liabilities section of the balance sheet comes after the Assets section (see the earlier section "Dividing and listing your assets") and shows all the money that your business owes to others, including banks, vendors, contractors, financial institutions, or individuals. Like assets, you divide your liabilities into two categories on the balance sheet:

✔ **Current liabilities:** All bills and debts you plan to pay within the next 12 months. Accounts appearing in this section include Accounts Payable (bills due to vendors, contractors, and others), Credit Card Payable, and the current portion of a long-term debt (for example, if you have a mortgage on your store, the payments due in the next 12 months appear in the Current Liabilities section).

✔ **Long-term liabilities:** All debts you owe to lenders that will be paid over a period longer than 12 months. Mortgages Payable, Loans Payable, and Bonds Payable are common accounts in the long-term liabilities section of the balance sheet.

Most businesses try to minimize their current liabilities because the interest rates on short-term loans, such as credit cards, are usually much higher than those on loans with longer terms. As you manage your company's liabilities, you should always look for ways to minimize your interest payments by seeking longer term loans with lower interest rates than you can get on a credit card or short-term loan.

The fictional company used for the example balance sheets in this chapter has only one account in each liabilities section:

Current liabilities:
Accounts Payable $2,200
Long-term liabilities:
Loans Payable $29,150

Sorting out stock investments

You're probably most familiar with the sale of stock on the open market through the various stock market exchanges, such as the New York Stock Exchange (NYSE) and NASDAQ. However, not all companies sell their stock through public exchanges; in fact, most corporations aren't public companies but rather remain private operations.

Whether public or private, ownership in a company is obtained by buying shares of stock. If the company isn't publicly traded, shares are bought and sold privately. In most small companies, these exchanges are made among family members, close friends, and occasionally outside investors who have been approached individually as a means to raise additional money to build the company.

The value of each share is set at the time the share is sold. Many companies set the initial share value at $1 to $10.

Naming your investments

Every business has investors. Even a small mom and pop grocery store requires money upfront to get the business on its feet. Investments are reflected on the balance sheet as *equity.* The line items that appear in a balance sheet's Equity section vary depending upon whether or not the company is incorporated. (Companies incorporate primarily to minimize their personal legal liabilities; I talk more about incorporation in Chapter 21.)

If you're preparing the books for a company that isn't incorporated, the Equity section of your balance sheet should contain these accounts:

- ✔ **Capital:** All money invested by the owners to start up the company as well as any additional contributions made after the start-up phase. If the company has more than one owner, the balance sheet usually has a Capital account for each owner so that their individual stakes in the company can be tracked.

- ✔ **Drawing:** All money taken out of the company by the company's owners. Balance sheets usually have a Drawing account for each owner in order to track individual withdrawal amounts.

- ✔ **Retained Earnings:** All profits that have been reinvested into the company.

For a company that's incorporated, the Equity section of the balance sheet should contain the following accounts:

- ✔ **Stock:** Portions of ownership in the company, purchased as investments by company owners.

- ✔ **Retained Earnings:** All profits that have been reinvested in the company.

Because the fictional company isn't an incorporated company, the accounts appearing in the Equity Section of its balance sheet are

Capital	$5,000
Retained Earnings	$4,500

Ta Da! Pulling Together the Final Balance Sheet

After you group together all your accounts (see the earlier section "Gathering Balance Sheet Ingredients"), you're ready to produce a balance sheet. Companies in the United States usually choose between two common formats for their balance sheets: the Account format or the Report format. The actual line items appearing in both formats are the same; the only difference is the way in which you lay out the information on the page. A third option, the Financial Position format, is more commonly used in Europe, but I explain it in this section in case you ever come across it.

Account format

The Account format is a two-column layout with Assets on one side and Liabilities and Equity on the other side.

Using the Account format, here's a sample balance sheet.

Company X
Balance Sheet
As of May 31, 2014

Current Assets		Current Liabilities	
Cash	$3,000	Accounts Payable	$2,200
Accounts Receivable	$1,000	Total Current Liabilities	$2,200
Inventory	$1,200	Long-term Liabilities:	
Total Current Assets	$5,200	Loans Payable	$29,150
Long-Term Assets:		Total L-T Liabilities	$29,150
Equipment	$5,050	Equity:	
Furniture	$5,600	Capital	$5,000
Vehicles	$25,000	Retained Earnings	$4,500
Total Long-term Assets	$35,650	Total Equity	$9,500
Total Assets	$40,850	Total L&E	$40,850

Report format

The Report format is a one-column layout showing assets first, then liabilities, and then equity.

Using the Report Format, here's the balance sheet for Company X.

Company X
Balance Sheet
As of May 31, 2014

Current Assets:		
Cash	$3,000	
Accounts Receivable	$1,000	
Inventory	$1,200	
Total Current Assets		$5,200
Long-term Assets:		
Equipment	$5,050	
Furniture	$5,600	
Vehicles	$25,000	
Total Long-Term Assets		$35,650
Total Assets		$40,850
Current Liabilities:		
Accounts Payable	$2,200	
Total Current Liabilities		$2,200
Long-term Liabilities:		
Loans Payable	$29,150	
Total Long-Term Liabilities		$29,150
Equity:		
Capital	$5,000	
Retained Earnings	$4,500	
Total Equity		$9,500
Total Liabilities and Equity		$40,850

Financial Position format

The third type of balance sheet format, the Financial Position format, is rarely seen in the United States but is used commonly in the international markets, especially in Europe. This format doesn't have an Equity section but includes two line items that don't appear on the Account or Report formats:

> ✔ **Working Capital:** Calculated by subtracting current assets from current liabilities. It's a quick test to see whether or not a company has the money on hand to pay bills.
>
> ✔ **Net Assets:** What's left over for a company's owners after all liabilities have been subtracted from total assets. (Note that Net Assets is the same number as Total Equity in the other two formats.)

Using the Financial Position format, here's the balance sheet for Company X.

Company X
Balance Sheet
As of May 31, 2014

Current Assets:

Cash	$3,000	
Accounts Receivable	$1,000	
Inventory	$1,200	
Total Current Assets		$5,200

Current Liabilities:

Accounts Payable	$2,200	
Total Current Liabilities		$2,200
Working Capital		$3,000

Noncurrent Assets:

Equipment	$5,050	
Furniture	$5,600	
Vehicles	$25,000	
Plus Noncurrent Assets:		$35,650
Total Assets less Current Liabilities	$38,650	

Long-term Liabilities:

Loans Payable	$29,150	
Less Long-term Liabilities		$29,150
Net Assets		$9,500

Putting Your Balance Sheet to Work

With a complete balance sheet in your hands, you can analyze the numbers through a series of ratio tests to check your cash status and track your debt. Because these are the types of tests financial institutions and potential investors use to determine whether or not to loan money to or invest in your company, it's a good idea to run these tests yourself before seeking loans or investors. Ultimately, the ratio tests I cover in this section can help you determine whether or not your company is in a strong cash position.

Testing your cash

When you approach a bank or other financial institution for a loan, you can expect the lender to use one of two ratios to test your cash flow: the *current ratio* and the *acid test ratio* (also known as the *quick ratio*).

Current ratio

This ratio compares your current assets to your current liabilities. It provides a quick glimpse of your company's ability to pay its bills.

The formula for calculating the current ratio is:

Current assets ÷ Current liabilities = Current ratio

The following is an example of a current ratio calculation:

$5,200 ÷ $2,200 = 2.36 (current ratio)

Lenders usually look for current ratios of 1.2 to 2, so any financial institution would consider a current ratio of 2.36 a good sign. A current ratio under 1 is considered a danger sign because it indicates that the company doesn't have enough cash to pay its current bills.

A current ratio over 2.0 may indicate that your company isn't investing its assets well and may be able to make better use of its current assets. For example, if your company is holding a lot of cash, you may want to invest that money in some long-term assets, such as additional equipment, that you need to help grow the business.

Acid test (quick) ratio

The acid test ratio only uses the financial figures in your company's Cash account, Accounts Receivable, and Marketable Securities. Although it's similar to the current ratio in that it examines current assets and liabilities, the acid test ratio is a stricter test of your company's ability to pay bills. The assets part of this calculation doesn't take inventory into account because it can't always be converted to cash as quickly as other current assets and because, in a slow market, selling your inventory may take a while.

Many lenders prefer the acid test ratio when determining whether or not to give you a loan because of its strictness.

Calculating the acid test ratio is a two-step process:

1. **Determine your quick assets.**

   Cash + Accounts Receivable + Marketable Securities = Quick assets

2. **Calculate your quick ratio.**

   Quick assets ÷ Current liabilities = Quick ratio

The following is an example of an acid test ratio calculation:

$2,000 + $1,000 + $1,000 = $4,000 (quick assets)

$4,000 ÷ $2,200 = 1.8 (acid test ratio)

Lenders consider a company with an acid test ratio around 1 to be in good condition. An acid test ratio less than 1 indicates that the company may have to sell some of its marketable securities or take on additional debt until it's able to sell more of its inventory.

Assessing your debt

Before you even consider whether or not to take on additional debt, you should always check out your debt condition. One common ratio that you can use to assess your company's debt position is the *debt to equity ratio*. This ratio compares what your business owes to what your business owns.

Calculating your debt to equity ratio is a two-step process:

1. **Calculate your total debt.**

   Current liabilities + Long-term liabilities = Total debt

2. **Calculate your debt to equity ratio.**

   Total debt ÷ Equity = Debt to equity ratio

The following is an example of a debt to equity ratio calculation:

$2,200 + $29,150 = $31,350 (total debt)

$31,350 ÷ $9,500 = 3.3 (debt to equity ratio)

Lenders like to see a debt to equity ratio close to 1 because it indicates that the amount of debt is equal to the amount of equity. With a debt to equity ratio of 3.3, most banks probably would not loan the company in this example any more money until either its debt levels were lowered or the owners put more money into the company.

Generating Balance Sheets Electronically

If you use a computerized accounting system, you can take advantage of its report function to automatically generate your balance sheets. These balance sheets give you quick snapshots of the company's financial position but may require adjustments before you prepare your financial reports for external use.

One key adjustment you're likely to make involves the value of your inventory. Most computerized accounting systems use the averaging method to value inventory. This method totals all the inventory purchased and then calculates an average price for the inventory (see Chapter 8 for more information on inventory valuation). However, your accountant may recommend a different valuation method that works better for your business. I discuss the options in Chapter 8. Therefore, if you use a method other than the default averaging method to value your inventory, you need to adjust the inventory value that appears on the balance sheet generated from your computerized accounting system.

Chapter 19

Producing an Income Statement

- -

In This Chapter

▶ Sorting out the elements of an income statement

▶ Preparing the statement

▶ Analyzing statement data

▶ Zeroing in on profitability

- -

*W*ithout one very important financial report tool, you'd never know for sure whether or not your business made a profit. This tool is called the *income statement,* and most businesses prepare them on a monthly basis as well as quarterly and annually in order to get periodic pictures of how well the business is doing financially.

Analyzing the income statement and the details behind it can reveal lots of useful information to help you make decisions for improving your profits and business overall. This chapter covers the parts of an income statement, how you develop one, and examples of how you can use it to make business decisions.

What Is an Income Statement?

Did your business make any money? You can find the answer in your *income statement,* the financial report that summarizes all the sales activities, costs of producing or buying the products or services sold, and expenses incurred in order to run the business.

Income statements summarize the financial activities of a business during a particular accounting period (which can be a month, quarter, year, or some other period of time that makes sense for a business's needs).

Normal practice is to include three accounting periods on an income statement: the current period plus two prior periods. So a monthly statement shows the current month plus the two previous months; a quarterly statement shows the current quarter plus the two previous quarters; and an annual statement shows the current year plus the two previous years. Providing this much information gives income statement readers a view of the business's earning trends.

The five key lines that make up an income statement are

- ✔ **Sales or Revenue:** The total amount of money taken in from selling the business's products or services. You calculate this amount by totaling all the sales or revenue accounts. The top line of the income statement will be either sales or revenues; either is okay.

- ✔ **Cost of Goods Sold:** How much was spent in order to buy or make the goods or services that were sold during the accounting period in review. I show you how to calculate cost of goods sold in the section "Finding Cost of Goods Sold."

- ✔ **Gross Profit:** How much a business made before taking into account operations expenses; calculated by subtracting the Cost of Goods Sold from the Sales or Revenue.

- ✔ **Operating Expenses:** How much was spent on operating the business; qualifying expenses include administrative fees, salaries, advertising, utilities, and other operations expenses. You add all your expense accounts on your income statement to get this total.

- ✔ **Net Income or Loss:** Whether or not the business made a profit or loss during the accounting period in review; calculated by subtracting total expenses from Gross Profit.

Formatting the Income Statement

Before you actually create your business's income statement, you have to pick a format in which to organize your financial information. You have two options to choose from: the *single-step format* or the *multi-step format*. They contain the same information but present it in slightly different ways.

The single-step format groups all data into two categories: revenue and expenses. The multi-step format divides the income statement into several sections and gives the reader some key subtotals to make analyzing the data easier.

The single-step format allows readers to calculate the same subtotals as appear in the multi-step format, but those calculations mean more work for the reader. Therefore, most businesses choose the multi-step format to simplify income statement analysis for their external financial report readers.

The following is an example of a basic income statement prepared in the single-step format.

Here is how the single-step format would look:

Revenues

Net Sales	$1,000
Interest Income	100
Total Revenue	$1,100

Expenses

Costs of Goods Sold	$500
Depreciation	50
Advertising	50
Salaries	100
Supplies	100
Interest Expenses	50
Total Expenses	$850
Net Income	$250

Using the same numbers, the following is an example of a basic income statement prepared in the multi-step format.

Revenues

Sales	$1,000
Cost of Goods Sold	$500
Gross Profit	$500

Operating Expenses

Depreciation	$50
Advertising	50
Salaries	100
Supplies	100
Interest Expenses	50
Total Operating Expenses	$350
Operating Income	$150

Other Income

Interest Income	$100
Total Income	$250

Preparing the Income Statement

Before you can prepare your income statement, you have to calculate Net Sales and Cost of Goods Sold using information that appears on your worksheet, which I explain in Chapter 16.

Finding Net Sales

Net Sales is a total of all your sales minus any discounts. In order to calculate Net Sales, you look at the line items regarding sales, discounts, and any sales fees on your worksheet. For example, suppose that your worksheet lists Total Sales at $20,000 and $1,000 in discounts given to customers. Also, according to your worksheet, your business paid $125 in Credit Card Fees on sales. To find your Net Sales, you subtract the discounts and credit-card fees from your Total Sales amount, leaving you with $18,875.

Finding Cost of Goods Sold

Cost of Goods Sold is the total amount your company spent to buy or make the goods or services that you sold. To calculate this amount for a company that buys its finished products from another company in order to sell them to customers, you start with the value of the company's opening inventory (that's the amount in the inventory account at the beginning of the accounting period), add all purchases of new inventory, and then subtract any ending inventory (that's inventory that's still on the store shelves or in the warehouse; it appears on the balance sheet, which I explain in Chapter 18).

The following is a basic Cost of Goods Sold calculation:

Opening Inventory + Purchases = Goods Available for Sale

$100 + $1,000 = $1,100

Goods Available for Sale – Ending Inventory = Cost of Goods Sold

$1,100 – $200 = $900

To simplify the example for calculating Cost of Goods Sold, I've assumed the Opening (the value of the inventory at the beginning of the accounting period) and Ending Inventory (the value of the inventory at the end of the accounting period) values are the same. See Chapter 8 for details about calculating inventory value. So to calculate Cost of Goods Sold using the detail on Figure 16-4 (see Chapter 16), I need only two key lines of that worksheet: the purchases made and the discounts received to lower the purchase cost.

Purchases – Purchases Discounts = Cost of Goods Sold

$8,000 – $1,500 = $6,500

Drawing remaining amounts from your worksheet

After you calculate Net Sales and Cost of Goods Sold (see the preceding sections), you can use the rest of the numbers from your worksheet to prepare your business's income statement.

It's standard practice to show three accounting periods on an income statement (see the section "What Is an Income Statement?"), so the following example lists three months' worth of figures (but shows actual numbers only for one month).

Income Statement Company X May 2014			
Months Ended	*May*	*April*	*March*
Revenues:			
Net Sales	$18,875		
Cost of Goods Sold	(6,500)		
Gross Profit	$12,375		
Operating Expenses:			
Advertising	$1,500		
Bank Service Charges	120		
Insurance Expenses	100		
Interest Expense	125		
Legal & Accounting Fees	300		
Office Expenses	250		
Payroll Taxes Expenses	350		
Postage Expenses	75		
Rent Expenses	800		
Salaries	3,500		
Supplies	300		
Telephone Expenses	200		
Utilities	255		
Total Operating Expenses	$7,875		
Net Income	$4,500		

You and anyone else in-house are likely to want to see the type of detail shown in this example, but most business owners prefer not to show all their operating detail to outsiders. They prefer to keep the detail private. Remember, the more information you give to outsiders, the more they know about how your company operates, and the easier it is for them to come up with strategies to compete with your business. Therefore, you should consider summarizing the Expense section in income statements that are distributed externally. For external statements, many businesses group all advertising and promotions expenses into one line item and all administrative expenses into another line item.

Gauging your Cost of Goods Sold

Businesses that make their own products rather than buy them for future sale must track inventory at three different levels:

- **Raw materials:** This line item includes purchases of all items used to make your company's products. For example, a fudge shop buys all the ingredients to make the fudge it sells, so the value of any inventory on hand that hasn't been used to make fudge yet should appear in the raw materials line item.

- **Work-in-process inventory:** This line item shows the value of any products that are being made but aren't yet ready for sale. It's unlikely that a fudge shop would have anything in this line item considering that fudge doesn't take more than a few hours to make. However, many manufacturing companies take weeks or months to produce products and therefore usually have some portion of the inventory value in this line item.

- **Finished-goods inventory:** This line item lists the value of inventory that's ready for sale. (For a company that doesn't make its own products, finished-goods inventory is the same as the inventory line item.)

If you keep the books for a company that manufactures its own products, you can use a computerized accounting system to track the various inventory accounts described here. However, your basic accounting system software won't cut it — you need a more advanced package in order to track multiple inventory types. One such system is the Premiere edition from QuickBooks, which sells for around $500.

Deciphering Gross Profit

Business owners must carefully watch their gross profit trends on monthly income statements. Gross profit trends that appear lower from one month to the next can mean one of two things: Sales revenue is down, or Cost of Goods Sold is up.

If revenue is down month-to-month, you may need to quickly figure out why and fix the problem in order to meet your sales goals for the year. Or, by examining sales figures for the same month in previous years, you may determine that the drop is just a normal sales slowdown given the time of year and isn't cause to hit the panic button.

If the downward trend isn't normal, it may be a sign that a competitor's successfully drawing customers away from your business, or it may indicate that customers are dissatisfied with some aspect of the products or services you supply. Whatever the reason, preparing a monthly income statement gives you the ammunition you need to quickly find and fix a problem, thereby minimizing any negative hit to your yearly profits.

The other key element of Gross Profit, Costs of Goods Sold, can also be a big factor in a downward profit trend. For example, if the amount you spend to purchase products that you then sell goes up, your Gross Profit goes down. As a business owner, you need to do one of five things if the costs of goods sold are reducing your Gross Profit:

✔ Find a new supplier who can provide the goods cheaper.

✔ Increase your prices as long as you won't lose sales because of the increase.

✔ Find a way to increase your volume of sales so that you can sell more products and meet your annual profit goals.

✔ Find a way to reduce other expenses to offset the additional product costs.

✔ Accept the fact that your annual profit will be lower than expected.

The sooner you find out that you have a problem with costs, the faster you can find a solution and minimize any reduction in your annual profit goals.

Monitoring Expenses

The Expenses section of your income statement gives you a good summary of all the money you spent to keep your business operating that wasn't directly related to the sale of an individual product or service. For example, businesses usually use advertising both to bring customers in and with the hopes of selling many different types of products. That's why you should list advertising as an Expense rather than a Cost of Goods Sold. After all, rarely can you link an advertisement to the sale of an individual product. The same is true of all the administrative expenses that go into running a business, such as rent, wages and salaries, office costs, and so on.

Business owners watch their expense trends closely to be sure they don't creep upwards and lower the companies' bottom line. Any cost-cutting you can do on the expense side is guaranteed to increase your bottom-line profit.

Using the Income Statement to Make Business Decisions

Many business owners find it easier to compare their income statement trends using percentages rather than the actual numbers. Calculating these percentages is easy enough — you simply divide each line item by Net Sales. The following shows a company's percentage breakdown for one month.

Income Statement Company X May 2014		
Months Ended	**May**	
Net Sales	$18,875	100.0%
Cost of Goods Sold	(6,500)	34.4%
Gross Profit	$12,375	65.6%
Operating Expenses		
Advertising	$1,500	7.9%
Bank Service Charges	120	0.6%
Insurance Expenses	100	0.5%
Interest Expense	125	0.7%
Legal & Accounting Fees	300	1.6%
Office Expenses	250	1.3%
Payroll Taxes Expenses	350	1.9%
Postage Expenses	75	0.4%
Rent Expenses	800	4.2%
Salaries	3,500	18.5%
Supplies	300	1.6%
Telephone Expenses	200	1.1%
Utilities	255	1.4%
Total Operating Expenses	$7,875	41.7%
Net Income	$4,500	23.8%

Looking at this percentage breakdown, you can see that the company had a gross profit of 65.6 percent, and its Cost of Goods Sold, at 34.4 percent, accounted for just over one-third of the revenue. If the prior month's Cost of Goods Sold was only 32 percent, the business owner would need to find out why the cost of the goods used to make his product likely went up. If this trend of increased Cost of Goods Sold continues through the year without some kind of fix, the company would make at least 2.2 percent less net profit.

You may find it helpful to see how your income statement results compare to industry trends for similar businesses with similar revenues; this process is called *benchmarking*. By comparing results, you can find out if your costs and expenses are reasonable for the type of business you operate, and you can identify areas with room to improve your profitability. You also may spot some red flags for line items on which you spend much more than the national average.

To find industry trends for businesses similar to yours with similar revenues, visit www.bizstats.com. To use the statistics tool on this website, you select a company structure (either corporation or sole proprietorship), enter the annual sales and hit "submit" to select the industry that best matches the one your business operates in, such as Retailing – Motor Vehicles & Parts or Manufacturing – Food Products. Once you pick the industry, you will get a report that shows the average profitability and expense percentages for similar businesses.

Here are the statistics I got for the category Retailing – Restaurants and Drinking Places with total revenue of $18,875. I'm assuming Company X is a restaurant.

Average Profitability & Expense Percentages for Retailing – Restaurants and Drinking Places

Income Statement Line Item	$	%
Total Revenue (Sales)	$18,875	100.0%
Total Costs and Expenses as % of Revenue	$16,821	89.1%
Net Income to Owner as % of Revenue	$2,054	10.9%
Detail of Costs and Expenses as % of Revenues:		
Cost of Goods Sold	$8,020	42.5%
Salaries and Wages	$2,912	15.4%
Advertising	$306	1.6%
Auto & Truck Expenses	$217	1.2%
Depreciation	$428	0.6%
Employee Benefits	$26	0.1%
Home Office Business Expenses	$15	0.1%
Insurance	$250	1.3%
Legal & Professional Services	$110	0.6%
Meals & Entertainment	$14	0.1%
Retirement Plans	$4	0.0%
Rent – Equipment	$151	0.8%

(continued)

Average Profitability & Expense Percentages for Retailing – Restaurants and Drinking Places *(continued)*

Income Statement Line Item	$	%
Rent – Business Property	$1,064	5.6%
Repairs	$234	1.2%
Supplies	$301	1.6%
Taxes – Business & Payroll	$695	3.7%
Travel	$34	0.2%
Utilities	$797	4.1%
Other Expenses	$996	5.3%
Total Costs and Expenses as % of Revenue	$16,821	89.1%

Comparing these numbers to the percentages in Company X's income statement shown in the income statement above, you can see that Mr. X's Cost of Goods Sold was only 34.4 percent compared to the industry average of 42.5 percent. His rent was a bit lower and his salaries higher, but overall, Company X's costs and expenses were 76.1 percent compared to the industry average of 89.1 percent. As a result, Mr. X made a higher net income (23.8 percent) than the industry standard (10.9 percent). Not bad at all — if your business were doing this well, you'd have good reason to be very happy.

Testing Profits

With a completed income statement, you can do a number of quick ratio tests of your business's profitability. You certainly want to know how well your business did compared to other similar businesses. You also want to be able to gauge your *return* (which means what percentage you made) on your business.

Three common tests are Return on Sales, Return on Assets, and Return on Equity. These ratios have much more meaning if you can find industry averages for your particular type of business, so you can compare your results. Check with your local Chamber of Commerce to see whether it has figures for local businesses, or order a report for your industry online www.bizminer.com.

Return on Sales

The Return on Sales (ROS) ratio tells you how efficiently your company runs its operations. Using the information on your income statement, you can measure how much profit your company produced per dollar of sales and how much extra cash you brought in per sale.

You calculate ROS by dividing net income before taxes by sales. For example, suppose your company had a net income of $4,500 and sales of $18,875. (If your business isn't a corporation but rather is run by a sole proprietor, you don't have to factor in any business taxes because only corporations pay income taxes. I talk more about business taxes in Chapter 21.) The following shows your calculation of ROS.

Net income before taxes ÷ Sales = Return on Sales

$4,500 ÷ $18,875 = 23.8%

As you can see, your company made 23.8 percent on each dollar of sales. To determine whether that amount calls for celebration, you need to find the ROS ratios for similar businesses. You may be able to get such information from your local chamber of commerce, or you can order an industry report online from BizMiner (www.bizminer.com).

Return on Assets

The Return on Assets (ROA) ratio tests how well you're using your company's assets to generate profits. If your company's ROA is the same or higher than other similar companies, you're doing a good job of managing your assets.

To calculate ROA, you divide net income by total assets. You find total assets on your balance sheet, which you can read more about in Chapter 18. Suppose that your company's net income was $4,500 and total assets were $40,050. The following shows your calculation of ROA:

Net income ÷ Total assets = Return on Assets

$4,500 ÷ $40,050 = 11.2%

You calculation shows that your company made 11.2 percent on each dollar of assets it held.

ROA can vary significantly depending on the type of industry in which you operate. For example, if your business requires you to maintain lots of expensive equipment, such as a manufacturing firm, your ROA will be much lower than a service business that doesn't need as many assets. ROA can range from below 5 percent for manufacturing companies that require a large investment in machinery and factories to as high as 20 percent or even higher for service companies with few assets.

Return on Equity

To measure how successful your company was in earning money for the owners or investors, calculate the Return on Equity (ROE) ratio. This ratio often looks better than Return on Assets (see the preceding section) because ROE doesn't take debt into consideration.

You calculate ROE by dividing net income by shareholders' or owners' equity. (You find equity amounts on your balance sheet; see Chapter 18.) Suppose your company's net income was $4,500 and the owners' equity was $9,500. Here is the formula:

Net income ÷ Shareholders' or owners' equity = Return on Equity

$4,500 ÷ $9,500 = 47.3%

Most business owners put in a lot of cash upfront to get a business started, so it's fairly common to see a business whose liabilities and equities are split close to 50 percent each.

Branching Out with Income Statement Data

The income statement you produce for external use — financial institutions and investors — may be very different from the one you produce for in-house use by your managers. Most business owners prefer to provide the minimum amount of detail necessary to satisfy external users of their financial statements, such as summaries of expenses instead of line-by-line expense details, a net sales figure without reporting all the detail about discounts and fees, and a cost of goods number without reporting all the detail about how that was calculated.

Internally, the contents of the income statement are a very different story. With more detail, your managers are better able to make accurate business decisions. Most businesses develop detailed reports based on the data collected to develop the income statement. Items such as discounts, returns, and allowances are commonly pulled out of income statements and broken down into further detail.

✓ **Discounts** are reductions on the retail price as part of a special sale. They may also be in the form of volume discounts provided to customers who buy large amounts of the company's products. For example, a store may offer a 10 percent discount to customers who buy 20 or more of the same item at one time. In order to put their Net Sales numbers in perspective, business owners and managers must track how much they reduce their revenues to attract sales.

✔ **Returns** are transactions in which items are returned by the buyer for any reason — not the right size, damaged, defective, and so on. If a company's number of returns increases dramatically, a larger problem may be the cause; therefore business owners need to track these numbers carefully in order to identify and resolve any problems with the items they sell.

✔ **Allowances** cover gifts cards and other accounts that customers pay for upfront without taking any merchandise. Allowances are actually a liability for a business because the customer (or the person who was given the gift card) eventually comes back to get merchandise and doesn't have to pay any cash in return.

Another section of the income statement that you're likely to break down into more detail for internal use is the Cost of Goods Sold. Basically, you take the detail collected to calculate that line item, including beginning inventory, ending inventory, purchases, and purchase discounts, and present it in a separate report. (I explain how to calculate Cost of Goods Sold in the section "Finding Cost of Goods Sold" earlier in this chapter.)

There's really no limit to the number of internal reports you can generate from the detail that goes into your income statement and other financial statements. For example, many businesses design a report that looks at month-to-month trends in revenue, cost of goods sold, and income. In fact, you can set up your computerized accounting system (if you use one) to automatically generate this report and other custom-designed reports. Using your computerized system, you can produce these reports at any time during the month if you want to see how close you are to meeting your month-end, quarter-end, or year-end goal.

Many companies will also design a report that compares actual spending to the budget. On this report, the income statement line items appear with their accompanying planned budget figures and the actual figures. If you were reviewing this report, you'd flag any line item that's considerably higher or lower than expected and then research it to find a reason for the difference.

Chapter 20

Completing Year-End Payroll and Reports

- -

In This Chapter

▶ Mastering employee reporting

▶ Preparing forms for vendors and contractors

▶ Taking care of annual tax summaries

- -

*E*ven though you've diligently filed all your quarterly employee reports with the federal government, you still have a lot of paperwork to complete at the end of the year. You need to file forms for each of your employees as well as any independent contractors you've paid over the course of the year.

Yes, you guessed it. End-of-the-year government paperwork takes lots of time. To help make it as painless as possible, though, this chapter reviews the forms you must complete, the information you need for each form, and the process for filing your company's payroll information with the federal government.

Year-End Employee Reporting

You may think that you've had to do a lot of government paperwork related to your payroll throughout the year, but you haven't seen anything yet. End-of-year payroll reporting requires lots of forms and lots of time.

Although the federal government doesn't require that you prepare a separate wage and tax statement for each employee during the year, it's something you have to do at the end of the year for each employee you paid $600 or more. The employee form is called the W-2, Wage and Tax Statement. If you worked for anyone prior to setting up your own company, you surely got at least one of these. The W-2 is the form people use to report any earnings from employers when they file their personal taxes each year.

Filing W-2s

When you were an employee, you probably noticed that every company you ever worked for waited until the last possible day to provide you with your W-2s. Now that you're preparing these documents for your employees, you have a better understanding of your employers' delay — it takes time to put W-2s together. Preparing these forms can be a very time-consuming task, especially if you want to make sure they're correct.

If you use a computerized accounting system's payroll software package to prepare your W-2s, there's no doubt that the task is much easier, but it still takes time to run the reports and review them to be sure everything is accurate before printing the final forms. Although you can send out corrected W-2s if necessary, filing the additional forms is just a lot of extra work, so you want to avoid correcting a W-2 whenever possible. The best way to eliminate the need for corrections is to be very careful in checking all information on the forms before distributing them to your employees.

Your company may be required to pay penalties if your W-2 forms are prepared incorrectly or aren't filed on time with your employees or with the government. The three levels of penalties for incorrectly filed W-2s or W-2s not prepared on time are as follows:

1. $30 for each W-2 that you file late or need to correct, provided that late filing is done within 30 days of the due date. The maximum penalty at this level for a company is $250,000. Small companies with average annual gross revenues under $5 million face only a $75,000 penalty maximum.

2. $60 for each W-2 that you file late or need to correct more than 30 days after the due date and before August 1. The maximum penalty at this level for large companies is $500,000, and smaller companies face a $200,000 maximum penalty.

3. $100 for each W-2 that you file after August 1 or fail to prepare altogether. The maximum penalties at this level are $1,500,000 for large companies and $500,000 for small businesses.

You can avoid these penalties if you can prove to the federal government that your failure to file W-2s on time was the result of an event beyond your control, such as a fire that destroyed all your records, and not the product of neglect. You must also indicate the steps you took to avoid filing late. You can also avoid penalties if incorrect information on a W-2 wasn't significant or didn't hinder the work of the IRS or the Social Security Administration in processing the W-2 information.

You can also be hit with a suit for civil damages if you fraudulently file a W-2 claiming you paid someone wages you didn't actually pay. The person may sue you for any damages incurred because of this fraudulent W-2.

Most of the information required to put together an employee's W-2 should be kept as part of your payroll records and therefore be easy to pull together. When filling out the W-2, which you can see in Figure 20-1, you must supply information for the following boxes:

- ✓ **Box 1: Wages, tips, other compensation.** The total in this box should also include the value of any employee bonuses, prizes, awards, or non-cash payments that aren't exempt or excluded from taxes.

- ✓ **Box 2: Federal income tax withheld.**

- ✓ **Box 3: Social Security wages.** Some benefits are exempt from wages for the purposes of federal income tax but aren't exempt from Social Security (see Chapter 10 for details).

- ✓ **Box 4: Social Security tax withheld.**

- ✓ **Box 5: Medicare wages and tips.** This amount is likely to be the same as the amount in Box 3, Social Security wages.

- ✓ **Box 6: Medicare tax withheld.**

- ✓ **Box 7: Social Security tips.** Any tips your employees reported to you should be reported here.

- ✓ **Box 8: Allocated tips.** Some businesses choose to allocate tips rather than collect and report tips for each employee separately. If you do that, report the tips in this box rather than in Box 7.

- ✓ **Box 9: Advance EIC payment.** If you paid employees advances on their Earned Income Credit, record the value of those advances in this box.

- ✓ **Box 10: Dependent care benefits.** If you provide dependent care benefits to an employee, report the provided amount in this box.

- ✓ **Box 11: Nonqualified plans.** In this box, you report any distribution to your employees of assets from nonqualified retirement plans, which are retirement plans that don't meet the requirements of the federal government. (Qualified plans such as 401(k)s, IRAs, pensions, and others are reported on 1099-R.)

- ✓ **Box 12:** The box contains numbers coded between A to Z. Each letter is for reporting a different type of income. For example, Code A is for uncollected Social Security tax on tips, and Code J is for nontaxable sick pay. You can get a complete list of these codes in the IRS publication *Instructions for Forms W-2 and W-3*, available by mail or by visiting www.irs.gov/pub/irs-pdf/fw2.pdf.

✔ **Box 13:** This box contains three boxes that you check according to what applies to the employee in question:

- Check the first box, labeled **Statutory employee,** if the employee can report income and expenses as a business, such as an agent or traveling salesperson.

- Check the second box, labeled **Retirement plan,** if you provide a qualified retirement plan for your employees.

- Check the third box, labeled **Third-party sick pay,** if you provide payment for an employee as a third-party for sick pay. This box is usually used if a third-party is paying an employee's workers' compensation. I talk more about workers' compensation in Chapter 11.

✔ **Box 14: Other.** This is the place for information you want to share with the employee, such as details about fringe benefits that were included in the total for Box 1.

✔ **Boxes 15–20:** In these boxes, you report payroll details for state and local tax information.

a Employee's social security number		OMB No. 1545-0008	Safe, accurate, FAST! Use	IRS e-file	Visit the IRS website at www.irs.gov/efile
b Employer identification number (EIN)			1 Wages, tips, other compensation		2 Federal income tax withheld
c Employer's name, address, and ZIP code			3 Social security wages		4 Social security tax withheld
			5 Medicare wages and tips		6 Medicare tax withheld
			7 Social security tips		8 Allocated tips
d Control number			9		10 Dependent care benefits
e Employee's first name and initial Last name Suff.			11 Nonqualified plans		12a See instructions for box 12
			13 Statutory employee Retirement plan Third-party sick pay		12b
			14 Other		12c
					12d
f Employee's address and ZIP code					
15 State Employer's state ID number	16 State wages, tips, etc.	17 State income tax	18 Local wages, tips, etc.	19 Local income tax	20 Locality name

Form **W-2** Wage and Tax Statement **2014** Department of the Treasury—Internal Revenue Service
Copy B—To Be Filed With Employee's FEDERAL Tax Return.
This information is being furnished to the Internal Revenue Service.

Figure 20-1: Sample W-2 Wage and Tax Statement for the 2014 tax year.

You must furnish your employees with W-2s by January 31. Usually, you give employees four copies of the form:

✔ One for the employee's file

✔ One to be filed with federal tax forms

✔ One to be filed with state tax forms

✔ One to be filed with local tax forms (which aren't always necessary)

You also need to make one copy for your company files and one copy to send along with Form W-3, the summary report of your W-2s that I discuss in the section "Sending in wage reports" later in this chapter.

W-2s for the previous year must be delivered to employees by January 31. However, if you're mailing W-2s to employees, they can be mailed on or before January 31. If January 31 falls on a weekend, you can mail the forms on the first business day after January 31. If for some reason you can't meet the January 31 deadline, you must file for an extension with the IRS by sending a letter to:

> Internal Revenue Service
>
> Information Returns Branch
>
> Attn: Extension of Time Coordinator
>
> 240 Murall Drive, Mail Stop 4360
>
> Kearneysville, WV 25430

Your letter must include

✔ Your business name and address

✔ Your employer identification number

✔ A statement indicating that you're requesting an extension to furnish W-2 forms to employees

✔ The reason for the delay

✔ Your signature or the signature of your authorized agent

If you don't get an extension and can't show reasonable cause, you'll be penalized $30 to $100 (depending how late you are) per W-2 (up to $1,500,000 for large companies and $500,000 for small businesses). The penalty from the IRS can be even stiffer if it determines that your failure to provide W-2 forms on time was an "intentional disregard of payee statement requirements" (that's straight from the IRS's mouth). If your failure's judged as intentional, the fine is $100 per W-2 with no maximum penalty.

Sending in wage reports

After you complete your W-2s and distribute them to employees, you still haven't seen the last of government paperwork. At this point, you total the numbers and fill out another form that looks very much like the W-2 — the W-3, Transmittal of Wage and Tax Statements. Figure 20-2 is a sample W-3.

DO NOT STAPLE

33333	a Control number	For Official Use Only ▶ OMB No. 1545-0008

b Kind of Payer (Check one)	941 ☐ Military ☐ 943 ☐ 944 ☐ CT-1 ☐ Hshld. emp. ☐ Medicare govt. emp. ☐	Kind of Employer (Check one)	None apply ☐ 501c non-govt. ☐ State/local non-501c ☐ State/local 501c ☐ Federal govt. ☐	Third-party sick pay ☐ (Check if applicable)

c Total number of Forms W-2	d Establishment number	1 Wages, tips, other compensation	2 Federal income tax withheld
e Employer identification number (EIN)		3 Social security wages	4 Social security tax withheld
f Employer's name		5 Medicare wages and tips	6 Medicare tax withheld
		7 Social security tips	8 Allocated tips
		9	10 Dependent care benefits
		11 Nonqualified plans	12a Deferred compensation
g Employer's address and ZIP code			
h Other EIN used this year		13 For third-party sick pay use only	12b
15 State Employer's state ID number		14 Income tax withheld by payer of third-party sick pay	
16 State wages, tips, etc.	17 State income tax	18 Local wages, tips, etc.	19 Local income tax
Employer's contact person		Employer's telephone number	For Official Use Only
Employer's fax number		Employer's email address	

Under penalties of perjury, I declare that I have examined this return and accompanying documents and, to the best of my knowledge and belief, they are true, correct, and complete.

Signature ▶   Title ▶   Date ▶

Form **W-3** Transmittal of Wage and Tax Statements   **2014**   Department of the Treasury Internal Revenue Service

Send this entire page with the entire Copy A page of Form(s) W-2 to the Social Security Administration (SSA). Photocopies are not acceptable. Do not send Form W-3 if you filed electronically with the SSA. Do not send any payment (cash, checks, money orders, etc.) with Forms W-2 and W-3.

Reminder

Separate instructions. See the 2014 General Instructions for Forms W-2 and W-3 for information on completing this form. Do not file Form W-3 for Form(s) W-2 that were submitted electronically to the SSA.

Purpose of Form

A Form W-3 Transmittal is completed only when paper Copy A of Form(s) W-2, Wage and Tax Statement, is being filed. Do not file Form W-3 alone. All paper forms **must** comply with IRS standards and be machine readable. Photocopies are **not** acceptable. Use a Form W-3 even if only one paper Form W-2 is being filed. Make sure both the Form W-3 and Form(s) W-2 show the correct tax year and Employer Identification Number (EIN). Make a copy of this form and keep it with Copy D (For Employer) of Form(s) W-2 for your records. The IRS recommends retaining copies of these forms for four years.

E-Filing

The SSA strongly suggests employers report Form W-3 and Forms W-2 Copy A electronically instead of on paper. The SSA provides two free e-filing options on its Business Services Online (BSO) website:

- **W-2 Online.** Use fill-in forms to create, save, print, and submit up to 50 Forms W-2 at a time to the SSA.
- **File Upload.** Upload wage files to the SSA you have created using payroll or tax software that formats the files according to the SSA's *Specifications for Filing Forms W-2 Electronically (EFW2)*.

W-2 Online fill-in forms or file uploads will be on time if submitted by March 31, 2015. For more information, go to *www.socialsecurity.gov/employer* and select "First Time Filers" or "Returning Filers" under "BEFORE YOU FILE."

When To File

Mail Form W-3 with Copy A of Form(s) W-2 by March 2, 2015.

Where To File Paper Forms

Send this entire page with the entire Copy A page of Form(s) W-2 to:

Social Security Administration Data Operations Center Wilkes-Barre, PA 18769-0001

Note. If you use "Certified Mail" to file, change the ZIP code to "18769-0002." If you use an IRS-approved private delivery service, add "ATTN: W-2 Process, 1150 E. Mountain Dr." to the address and change the ZIP code to "18702-7997." See Publication 15 (Circular E), Employer's Tax Guide, for a list of IRS-approved private delivery services.

For Privacy Act and Paperwork Reduction Act Notice, see the separate instructions.

Cat. No. 10159Y

Figure 20-2: Sample 2014 W-3 for Transmittal of Wage and Tax Statements.

The W-3 is essentially the cover sheet for the information you send to the Social Security Administration. This form is your last chance to reconcile your numbers before actually filing them with the government. The W-3 numbers should match the totals shown on the Form 941 reports that you submitted to the federal government quarterly throughout the year. (I discuss these reports in Chapter 11.)

The W-3 must be filed by February 28 with the Social Security Administration. As a small business owner, you can mail the W-3 and the copies of the W-2s to the Social Security Administration at:

Social Security Administration

Data Operations Center

Wilkes-Barre, PA 18769-0001

You can also file the forms online through the Social Security Administration website at www.ssa.gov/bso/bsowelcome.htm, or file them electronically. Large companies with more than 250 employees must file their W-3s and W-2s by magnetic media or electronically. Any business filing electronically can wait until March 31 to file.

If your company reports tips, you need to complete an additional form called Form 8027, Employer's Annual Information Return of Tip Income and Allocated Tips (Figure 20-3). The deadlines for filing Form 8027 are the same as for the W-3 — February 28 for regular filing and March 31 for magnetic media or electronic filings.

Producing 1099s for Vendors and Contractors

For each contractor and vendor you pay over the course of the year, instead of preparing a W-2, you must complete Form 1099, Miscellaneous Income. The 1099 is an information form used to report income, interest payments, and dividend payments. To transmit the 1099 to the federal government, you use Form 1096, Annual Summary and Transmittal of U.S. Information Returns, which I explain in the section "Filing Year-End Government Reports" later in this chapter.

Your computerized accounting program can automatically generate 1099s and 1096s. If you're using QuickBooks, you can find the 1099 Wizard in the Vendor drop-down menu under the item Print/E-file 1099s. The 1099 and 1096 Wizard then pops up to guide you through the rest of the process (see Figure 20-3).

If you can't generate these forms automatically from your computerized accounting system, or if you do your books manually, you can expect to work closely with your accountant on 1099s and 1096s. He or she can usually minimize the time it takes to prepare this paperwork by using professional tax preparation software programs.

There are actually 16 different types of 1099s. You use one form if you provide a medical savings account for your employees, and you use another if you distributed any money from an employee's retirement account. You can access full instructions for the various 1099 forms at `www.irs.gov/pub/irs-pdf/i1099gi.pdf`. As a small business owner, the one you'll use the most is Form 1099-MISC, which is shown in Figure 20-4. It's the one used to report independent contractor and vendor compensation.

The 1099-MISC contains 18 boxes, but depending on the type of payment you're reporting, you may only need to fill out a few of them. The boxes are as follows:

✔ **Box 1: Rents.** This box should contain the total of any rental payments made to the contractor or vendor for whom you're filing the form.

✔ **Box 2: Royalties.** This box should contain the total of any royalty payments made to a contractor.

✔ **Box 3: Other income.** In this box, list any miscellaneous income that doesn't fit in a designated box on the form.

✔ **Box 4: Federal income tax withheld.** Most times, you don't withhold federal income tax from a contractor or vendor, so this box remains empty. But sometimes a business does withhold federal income taxes for a contractor or a contractor.

✔ **Box 5: Fishing boat proceeds.** Total any money paid to a fishing boat contractor and list it here.

✔ **Box 6: Medical and healthcare payments.** It's unlikely that you pay medical or healthcare benefits for a contractor or vendor, so this box will probably be left blank.

✔ **Box 7: Nonemployee compensation.** In this box, record any nonemployee compensation that doesn't fit in one of the other boxes.

✔ **Box 8: Substitute payments in lieu of dividends or interest.**

✔ **Box 9:** Check this box if you made direct sales of $5,000 or more of consumer products to a buyer for resale.

✔ **Box 10: Crop insurance proceeds.** Indicate payments to farmers from crop insurance coverage by the insurance company.

✔ **Boxes 11 and 12:** Blank.

✔ **Box 13: Excess golden parachute payments.** This box should contain the total amount paid to an employee who has left the company.

✔ **Box 14: Gross proceeds paid to an attorney.**

✔ **Boxes 15a: Section 409A deferrals,** and **15b: Section 409A income.** These boxes are for payments made as part of a nonqualified deferred compensation plan.

✔ **Boxes 16–18:** These boxes are reserved for state governmental information.

You need to make three copies of your 1099s:

✔ One to be sent to the vendor or contractor by January 31

✔ One to be filed with the IRS by February 28, so that the income reported on a vendor's or contractor's individual tax return can be verified

✔ One to keep in your company files

The 1099 form is for informational purposes and not attached to individual income tax forms filed with federal and state governments, so companies only need to provide one copy of the 1099 to its vendors and contractors. A copy of the 1099 must be provided to contractors or vendors by January 31, but it does not need to be filed with the government until February 28. The IRS uses the information on this form to match income reported by these contractors and vendors on their individual tax returns. You'll need to make three copies of this form — one for the vendor or contractor, one for the IRS, and one for your own files.

When filing 1099s with the government, you need a cover sheet. That cover sheet is a summary called Form 1096, Annual Summary and Transmittal of U.S. Information Returns. This form summarizes the information filed on 1099s, including the total number of 1099s filed, total federal income tax withheld, and total income reported. Other forms that are included on this summary report, which you can see in Figure 20-5, aren't likely to be filed by a small business, including the 1098 (student loan information), W-2G (gambling winnings), and 5498 (Coverdell ESA contribution).

If your company transmits the applicable information from Form 1096 electronically, you don't actually need to use this form.

Filing Year-End Summaries

After you complete all your tax forms for individual employees, contractors, and vendors, you're left with two annual summary reports that must be filed with the federal government:

- ✓ Form 940, Employer's Annual Federal Unemployment Tax Return contains an annual summary of your federal unemployment tax payments. Because you file this form quarterly as well as annually, I discuss it in greater detail in Chapter 11.

- ✓ Form 945, Annual Return of Withheld Income Tax is a summary of all federal income tax withheld from vendors, contractors, pensions, or annuities. In most cases, this form just serves as a summary of the payments you make throughout the year as you withhold taxes. You can see a sample of Form 945 in Figure 20-6.

Do Not Staple	6969			

Form **1096**

Department of the Treasury
Internal Revenue Service

**Annual Summary and Transmittal of
U.S. Information Returns**

OMB No. 1545-0108

20**14**

FILER'S name

Street address (including room or suite number)

City or town, state or province, country, and ZIP or foreign postal code

Name of person to contact

Telephone number

Email address

Fax number

For Official Use Only

1 Employer identification number	2 Social security number	3 Total number of forms	4 Federal income tax withheld	5 Total amount reported with this Form 1096
			$	$

6 Enter an "X" in only one box below to indicate the type of form being filed.

7 If this is your **final return**, enter an "X" here . . . . . ▶ ☐

W-2G 32	1097-BTC 50	1098 81	1098-C 78	1098-E 84	1098-T 83	1099-A 80	1099-B 79	1099-C 85	1099-CAP 73	1099-DIV 91	1099-G 86	1099-H 71	1099-INT 92	1099-K 10	1099-LTC 93	1099-MISC 95	1099-OID 96
☐	☐	☐	☐	☐	☐	☐	☐	☐	☐	☐	☐	☐	☐	☐	☐	☐	☐

1099-PATR 97	1099-Q 31	1099-R 98	1099-S 75	1099-SA 94	3921 25	3922 26	5498 28	5498-ESA 72	5498-SA 27
☐	☐	☐	☐	☐	☐	☐	☐	☐	☐

Return this entire page to the Internal Revenue Service. Photocopies are not acceptable.

Under penalties of perjury, I declare that I have examined this return and accompanying documents, and, to the best of my knowledge and belief, they are true, correct, and complete.

Signature ▶

Title ▶

Date ▶

Instructions

Future developments. For the latest information about developments related to Form 1096, such as legislation enacted after it was published, go to *www.irs.gov/form1096*.

Reminder. The only acceptable method of filing information returns with Internal Revenue Service/Information Returns Branch is electronically through the FIRE system. See Pub. 1220, Specifications for Electronic Filing of Forms 1097, 1098, 1099, 3921, 3922, 5498, 8935, and W-2G.

Purpose of form. Use this form to transmit paper Forms 1097, 1098, 1099, 3921, 3922, 5498, and W-2G to the Internal Revenue Service. Do not use Form 1096 to transmit electronically. For electronic submissions, see Pub. 1220.

Caution. If you are required to file 250 or more information returns of any one type, you must file electronically. If you are required to file electronically but fail to do so, and you do not have an approved waiver, you may be subject to a penalty. For more information, see part F in the 2014 General Instructions for Certain Information Returns.

Who must file. The name, address, and TIN of the filer on this form must be the same as those you enter in the upper left area of Forms 1097, 1098, 1099, 3921, 3922, 5498, or W-2G. A filer is any person or entity who files any of the forms shown in line 6 above.

Enter the filer's name, address (including room, suite, or other unit number), and TIN in the spaces provided on the form.

When to file. File Form 1096 as follows.

• With Forms 1097, 1098, 1099, 3921, 3922, or W-2G, file by March 2, 2015.

• With Forms 5498, file by June 1, 2015.

Where To File

Send all information returns filed on paper with Form 1096 to the following:

If your principal business, office or agency, or legal residence in the case of an individual, is located in	Use the following three-line address
Alabama, Arizona, Arkansas, Connecticut, Delaware, Florida, Georgia, Kentucky, Louisiana, Maine, Massachusetts, Mississippi, New Hampshire, New Jersey, New Mexico, New York, North Carolina, Ohio, Pennsylvania, Rhode Island, Texas, Vermont, Virginia, West Virginia	Department of the Treasury Internal Revenue Service Center Austin, TX 73301

For more information and the Privacy Act and Paperwork Reduction Act Notice, see the 2014 General Instructions for Certain Information Returns.

Cat. No. 14400O

Form **1096** (2014)

Figure 20-5:
Sample of
Form 1096
for submitting 1099s
and other
forms for
reporting
nonemployee
income.

Form **945**	**Annual Return of Withheld Federal Income Tax**	OMB No. 1545-1430

► For withholding reported on Forms 1099 and W-2G.

Department of the Treasury
Internal Revenue Service
► For more information on income tax withholding, see Pub. 15 (Circ. E) and Pub. 15-A.
► Information about Form 945 and its separate instructions is at *www.irs.gov/form945.*

2013

Type or Print

Name (as distinguished from trade name) | Employer identification number (EIN)

Trade name, if any

Address (number and street)

City or town, state or province, country, and ZIP or foreign postal code

If address is different from prior return, check here. ►

A If you **do not have to file** returns in the future, check here ► ☐ and enter date final payments made. ► --------------------

1 Federal income tax withheld from pensions, annuities, IRAs, gambling winnings, etc. . . . . . . | **1**

2 Backup withholding . . . . | **2**

3 **Total taxes.** If $2,500 or more, this must equal line 7M below or Form 945-A, line M . . . . . | **3**

4 Total deposits for 2013, including overpayment applied from a prior year and overpayment applied from Form 945-X . . . . | **4**

5 **Balance due.** If line 3 is more than line 4, enter the difference and see the separate instructions . | **5**

6 **Overpayment.** If line 4 is more than line 3, enter the difference ► $ _____

Check one: ☐ Apply to next return. ☐ Send a refund.

• **All filers:** If line 3 is less than $2,500, **do not** complete line 7 or Form 945-A.
• **Semiweekly schedule depositors:** Complete Form 945-A and check here . . . . ► ☐
• **Monthly schedule depositors:** Complete line 7, entries A through M, and check here . . . . ► ☐

7 Monthly Summary of Federal Tax Liability. (Do not complete if you were a semiweekly schedule depositor.)

	Tax liability for month		Tax liability for month		Tax liability for month
A January . . .		**F** June		**K** November . .	
B February . .		**G** July		**L** December . .	
C March . . .		**H** August		**M** Total liability for	
D April		**I** September . . .		year (add lines A	
E May		**J** October		through L) . .	

Third-Party Designee Do you want to allow another person to discuss this return with the IRS (see the instructions)? ☐ **Yes.** Complete the following. ☐ No.

Designee's name ► | Phone no. ► | Personal identification number (PIN) ►

Sign Here Under penalties of perjury, I declare that I have examined this return, including accompanying schedules and statements, and to the best of my knowledge and belief, it is true, correct, and complete. Declaration of preparer (other than taxpayer) is based on all information of which preparer has any knowledge.

Signature ► | Print Your Name and Title ► | Date ►

Paid Preparer Use Only

Print/Type preparer's name	Preparer's signature	Date	Check ☐ if self-employed	PTIN
Firm's name ►			Firm's EIN ►	
Firm's address ►			Phone no.	

For Privacy Act and Paperwork Reduction Act Notice, see the separate instructions. | Cat. No. 14584B | Form **945** (2013)

Figure 20-6:
Sample of
Form 945 for
submitting
a summary
of all federal
tax withheld
from nonem-
ployees.

Chapter 21

Satisfying the Tax Man

· ·

In This Chapter

▶ Sorting out business legal structures

▶ Filing sole proprietor taxes

▶ Reporting taxes on partnerships

▶ Filing taxes for corporations

▶ Reporting and paying sales taxes

· ·

*P*aying taxes and reporting income for your company are very important jobs, and the way in which you complete these tasks properly depends on your business's legal structure. From sole proprietorships to corporations and everything in between, this chapter briefly reviews business types and explains how taxes are handled for each type. You also get some instruction on collecting and transmitting sales taxes on the products your company sells.

Finding the Right Business Type

Business type and tax preparation and reporting go hand in hand. If you work as a bookkeeper for a small business, you need to know the business's legal structure before you can proceed with reporting and paying income taxes on the business income. Not all businesses have the same legal structure, so they don't all pay income taxes on the profits they make in the same way.

Before you get into the subject of tax procedures, therefore, you need to understand the various business structures you may encounter as a bookkeeper. This section outlines each type of business. You can find out how these structures pay taxes in separate sections that follow.

Sole proprietorship

The simplest legal structure for a business is the *sole proprietorship,* a business that's owned by one individual. (If a business has only one owner, the IRS automatically considers it a sole proprietorship.)

Most new business with only one owner start out as sole proprietorships. Some never change their statuses, but others grow by adding partners and becoming partnerships. Some add lots of staff and want to protect themselves from lawsuits, so they become Limited Liability Companies (LLCs). Those seeking the greatest protection from individual lawsuits, whether they have employees or are simply single-owner companies without employees, become corporations. I cover these other structures later in this chapter.

Partnership

The IRS considers any business owned by more than one person a *partnership*. The partnership is the most flexible type of business structure involving more than one owner. Each partner in the business is equally liable for the activities of the business. This structure is slightly more complicated than a sole proprietorship (see "Sole proprietorship," earlier in this chapter), and partners should work out certain key issues before the business opens its doors. These issues include

- ✔ How the partners will divide the profits
- ✔ How each partner can sell his or her share of the business, if he or she so chooses
- ✔ What will happen to each partner's share if a partner becomes sick or dies
- ✔ How the partnership will be dissolved if one of the partners wants out

Partners in a partnership don't always have to share equal risks. A partnership may have two different types of partners: general and limited. The general partner runs the day-to-day business and is held personally responsible for all activities of the business, no matter how much he or she has personally invested in the business. Limited partners, on the other hand, are passive owners of the business and not involved in its day-to-day operations. If a claim is filed against the business, the limited partners can only be held personally liable for the amount of money that matches how much they individually invested in the business.

Limited Liability Companies (LLCs)

The *Limited Liability Company,* or LLC, is a structure that provides partnerships and sole proprietorships with some protection from being held personally liable for their businesses' activities. This business structure is somewhere between a sole proprietorship or partnership and a corporation: The business

Growth of the LLC

LLCs are relatively new to the world of business structures. They were first established in the United States about 25 years ago but didn't become popular until the mid-1990s, when most states approved the LLC as a business structure.

Many law firms and accounting firms are set up as LLCs. More and more small business owners are choosing this structure rather than a corporation because the LLC's easier and cheaper to maintain (as in a lot less government paperwork plus less legal and accounting fees), yet it still provides personal protection from legal entanglements.

ownership and IRS tax rules are similar to those of a sole proprietorship or partnership, but like a corporation, if the business is sued, the owners aren't held personally liable.

LLCs are state entities, so the level of legal protection given to a company's owners depends upon the rules of the state in which the LLC was formed. Most states give LLC owners the same protection from lawsuits as the federal government gives corporation owners. However, these LLC protections haven't been tested in court to date, so no one knows for certain whether or not they hold up in the courtroom. (For more on the LLC, see the sidebar "Growth of the LLC.")

Corporations

If your business faces a great risk of being sued, the safest business structure for you is the *corporation*. Courts in the United States have clearly determined that a corporation is a separate legal entity and that its owners' personal assets are protected from claims against the corporation. Essentially, an owner or shareholder in a corporation can't be sued or face collections because of actions taken by the corporation. This veil of protection is the reason many small business owners choose to incorporate even though it involves a lot of expense (both for lawyers and accountants) and government paperwork.

In a corporation, each share of stock represents a portion of ownership, and profits must be split based on stock ownership. You don't have to sell stock on the public stock markets in order to be a corporation, though. In fact, most corporations are private entities that sell their stock privately among friends and investors.

Roles and responsibilities of the corporate board

Corporations provide a veil of protection for company owners, but in order to maintain that protection, the owners must comply with many rules unique to corporations. The *board of directors* takes on the key role of complying with these rules, and it must maintain a record of meeting minutes that prove the board is following key operating procedures, such as:

✔ Establishment of records of banking associations and any changes to those arrangements

✔ Tracking of loans from stockholders or third parties

✔ Selling or redeeming shares of stock

✔ Payment of dividends

✔ Authorization of salaries or bonuses for officers and key executives

✔ Undertaking of any purchases, sales, or leases of corporate assets

✔ Buying another company

✔ Merging with another company

✔ Making changes to the Articles of Incorporation or bylaws

✔ Election of corporate officers and directors

Corporate board minutes are considered official and must be available for review by the IRS, state taxing authorities, and the courts. If a company's owners want to invoke the veil of protection that corporate status provides, they must prove that the board has met its obligations and that the company operated as a corporation. In other words, you can't form a board and have no proof that it ever met and managed these key functions.

If you're a small business owner who wants to incorporate, first you must form a *board of directors* (see the sidebar "Roles and responsibilities of the corporate board"). Boards can be made up of owners of the company as well as nonowners. You can even have your spouse and children on the board — I bet those board meetings would be interesting.

Tax Reporting for Sole Proprietors

The federal government doesn't consider sole proprietorships to be individual legal entities, so they're not taxed as such. Instead, sole proprietors report any business earnings on their individual tax returns — that's the only financial reporting they must do.

Most sole proprietors file their business tax obligations as part of their individual 1040 tax return using the additional two-page form *Schedule C, Profit or Loss from Business.* On the first page of Schedule C, which you can see in

Figure 21-1, you report all the company's income and expenses. The second page (Figure 21-2) is where you report information about Cost of Goods Sold and any vehicles used as part of the business.

Sole proprietors must also pay both the employee and the employer sides of Social Security and Medicare — that's double what an employee would normally pay. Table 21-1 shows the drastic difference in these types of tax obligations for sole proprietors.

Table 21-1	Comparison of Tax Obligations for Sole Proprietors	
Type of Tax	*Amount Taken from Employees*	*Amount Paid by Sole Proprietors*
Social Security	6.2%	12.4%
Medicare	1.45%	2.9%

Social Security and Medicare taxes are based on the net profit of the small business, not the gross profit, which means that you calculate the tax after you've subtracted all costs and expenses from your revenue. To help you figure out the tax amounts you owe on behalf of your business, use IRS form *Schedule SE, Self-Employment Tax*. On the first page of this form, you report your income sources (see Figure 21-3), and on the second page, you calculate the tax due (see Figure 21-4).

As the bookkeeper for a sole proprietor, you're probably responsible for pulling together the income, Cost of Goods Sold, and expense information needed for this form. In most cases, you then hand off this information to the business's accountant to fill out all the required forms.

As a sole proprietor, you can choose to file as a corporation even if you aren't legally incorporated. You may want to do this because corporations have more allowable deductions and you can pay yourself a salary, but there's a lot of extra paperwork, and your accountant's fees will be much higher if you decide to file as a corporation. However, because corporations pay taxes on the separate legal entity, this option may not make sense for your business. Talk with your accountant to determine the best tax structure for your business.

If you do decide to report your business income as a separate corporate entity, you must file Form 8832, Entity Classification Election with the IRS. This form, which you can see in Figure 21-5, reclassifies the business, a step that's necessary because the IRS automatically classifies a business owned by one person as a sole proprietorship.

SCHEDULE C (Form 1040)		Profit or Loss From Business	OMB No. 1545-0074

SCHEDULE C (Form 1040)

Department of the Treasury
Internal Revenue Service (99)

Profit or Loss From Business
(Sole Proprietorship)

▶ For Information on Schedule C and its instructions, go to *www.irs.gov/schedulec.*
▶ Attach to Form 1040, 1040NR, or 1041; partnerships generally must file Form 1065.

OMB No. 1545-0074

2013

Attachment
Sequence No. **09**

Name of proprietor

Social security number (SSN)

A Principal business or profession, including product or service (see instructions)

B Enter code from instructions ▶

C Business name. If no separate business name, leave blank.

D Employer ID number (EIN), (see instr.)

E Business address (including suite or room no.) ▶
City, town or post office, state, and ZIP code

F Accounting method: (1) ☐ Cash (2) ☐ Accrual (3) ☐ Other (specify) ▶

G Did you "materially participate" in the operation of this business during 2013? If "No," see instructions for limit on losses . ☐ Yes ☐ No

H If you started or acquired this business during 2013, check here . . . . ▶ ☐

I Did you make any payments in 2013 that would require you to file Form(s) 1099? (see instructions) . . . . ☐ Yes ☐ No

J If "Yes," did you or will you file required Forms 1099? . . . . ☐ Yes ☐ No

Part I Income

1	Gross receipts or sales. See instructions for line 1 and check the box if this income was reported to you on Form W-2 and the "Statutory employee" box on that form was checked . . . . ▶ ☐	1	
2	Returns and allowances	2	
3	Subtract line 2 from line 1	3	
4	Cost of goods sold (from line 42)	4	
5	**Gross profit.** Subtract line 4 from line 3	5	
6	Other income, including federal and state gasoline or fuel tax credit or refund (see instructions) . .	6	
7	**Gross income.** Add lines 5 and 6 . . . . ▶	7	

Part II Expenses Enter expenses for business use of your home only on line 30.

8	Advertising	8		18	Office expense (see instructions)	18	
9	Car and truck expenses (see instructions)	9		19	Pension and profit-sharing plans	19	
10	Commissions and fees .	10		20	Rent or lease (see instructions):		
11	Contract labor (see instructions)	11		a	Vehicles, machinery, and equipment	20a	
12	Depletion	12		b	Other business property . . .	20b	
13	Depreciation and section 179 expense deduction (not included in Part III) (see instructions)	13		21	Repairs and maintenance . . .	21	
				22	Supplies (not included in Part III) .	22	
				23	Taxes and licenses	23	
				24	Travel, meals, and entertainment:		
14	Employee benefit programs (other than on line 19) . .	14		a	Travel	24a	
15	Insurance (other than health)	15		b	Deductible meals and entertainment (see instructions) .	24b	
16	Interest:			25	Utilities	25	
a	Mortgage (paid to banks, etc.)	16a		26	Wages (less employment credits) .	26	
b	Other	16b		27a	Other expenses (from line 48) . .	27a	
17	Legal and professional services	17		b	**Reserved for future use** . .	27b	

28	**Total expenses** before expenses for business use of home. Add lines 8 through 27a . . . . . ▶	28	
29	Tentative profit or (loss). Subtract line 28 from line 7	29	
30	Expenses for business use of your home. Do not report these expenses elsewhere. Attach Form 8829 unless using the simplified method (see instructions).
Simplified method filers only: enter the total square footage of: (a) your home: _____ and (b) the part of your home used for business: _____. Use the Simplified Method Worksheet in the instructions to figure the amount to enter on line 30	30	
31	**Net profit or (loss).** Subtract line 30 from line 29.
• If a profit, enter on both **Form 1040, line 12** (or **Form 1040NR, line 13**) and on **Schedule SE, line 2.** (If you checked the box on line 1, see instructions). Estates and trusts, enter on **Form 1041, line 3.**
• If a loss, you **must** go to line 32.	31	
32	If you have a loss, check the box that describes your investment in this activity (see instructions).
• If you checked 32a, enter the loss on both **Form 1040, line 12,** (or **Form 1040NR, line 13**) and on **Schedule SE, line 2.** (If you checked the box on line 1, see the line 31 instructions). Estates and trusts, enter on **Form 1041, line 3.**
• If you checked 32b, you **must** attach **Form 6198.** Your loss may be limited.	32a ☐ All investment is at risk.
32b ☐ Some investment is not at risk.

For Paperwork Reduction Act Notice, see the separate instructions.   Cat. No. 11334P   Schedule C (Form 1040) 2013

Figure 21-1:
Sole proprietors report business income and expenses on the first page of Schedule C.

Schedule C (Form 1040) 2013

Page 2

Part III   **Cost of Goods Sold**   (see instructions)

33   Method(s) used to
value closing inventory: **a** ☐ Cost   **b** ☐ Lower of cost or market   **c** ☐ Other (attach explanation)

34   Was there any change in determining quantities, costs, or valuations between opening and closing inventory?
If "Yes," attach explanation . . . . ☐ Yes   ☐ No

35	Inventory at beginning of year. If different from last year's closing inventory, attach explanation . . .	35		
36	Purchases less cost of items withdrawn for personal use	36		
37	Cost of labor. Do not include any amounts paid to yourself	37		
38	Materials and supplies	38		
39	Other costs	39		
40	Add lines 35 through 39	40		
41	Inventory at end of year	41		
42	**Cost of goods sold.** Subtract line 41 from line 40. Enter the result here and on line 4	42		

Part IV   **Information on Your Vehicle.**   Complete this part **only** if you are claiming car or truck expenses on line 9 and are not required to file Form 4562 for this business. See the instructions for line 13 to find out if you must file Form 4562.

43   When did you place your vehicle in service for business purposes? (month, day, year)   ▶ _____ / _____ / _____

44   Of the total number of miles you drove your vehicle during 2013, enter the number of miles you used your vehicle for:

   a   Business _____   **b** Commuting (see instructions) _____   **c** Other _____

45   Was your vehicle available for personal use during off-duty hours? . . . . ☐ Yes   ☐ No

46   Do you (or your spouse) have another vehicle available for personal use? . . . . ☐ Yes   ☐ No

47a   Do you have evidence to support your deduction? . . . . ☐ Yes   ☐ No

   b   If "Yes," is the evidence written? . . . . ☐ Yes   ☐ No

Part V   **Other Expenses.**   List below business expenses not included on lines 8–26 or line 30.

--	
--	
--	
--	
--	
--	
--	
--	
48 **Total other expenses.** Enter here and on line 27a	48	

Schedule C (Form 1040) 2013

Figure 21-2:
Sole pro-
prietors
report Cost
of Goods
Sold as well
as business
vehicle
expenses
on page 2 of
Schedule C.

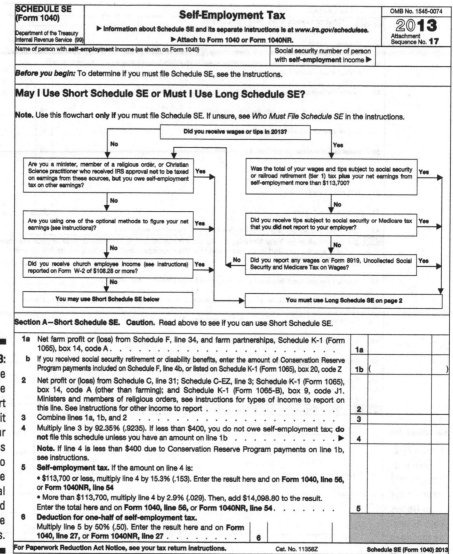

Figure 21-3:
Use
Schedule
SE to report
net profit
from your
business
in order to
calculate
Social
Security and
Medicare
taxes.

Schedule SE (Form 1040) 2013   Attachment Sequence No. **17**   Page **2**

Name of person with **self-employment** income (as shown on Form 1040)	Social security number of person with **self-employment** income ▶

Section B—Long Schedule SE

Part I   Self-Employment Tax

Note. If your only income subject to self-employment tax is **church employee income,** see instructions. Also see instructions for the definition of church employee income.

A   If you are a minister, member of a religious order, or Christian Science practitioner **and** you filed Form 4361, but you had $400 or more of **other** net earnings from self-employment, check here and continue with Part I . . . . . . ▶ ☐

1a   Net farm profit or (loss) from Schedule F, line 34, and farm partnerships, Schedule K-1 (Form 1065), box 14, code A. **Note.** Skip lines 1a and 1b if you use the farm optional method (see instructions)   **1a**

  b   If you received social security retirement or disability benefits, enter the amount of Conservation Reserve Program payments included on Schedule F, line 4b, or listed on Schedule K-1 (Form 1065), box 20, code Z   **1b** (   )

2   Net profit or (loss) from Schedule C, line 31; Schedule C-EZ, line 3; Schedule K-1 (Form 1065), box 14, code A (other than farming); and Schedule K-1 (Form 1065-B), box 9, code J1. Ministers and members of religious orders, see instructions for types of income to report on this line. See instructions for other income to report. **Note.** Skip this line if you use the nonfarm optional method (see instructions) **2**

3   Combine lines 1a, 1b, and 2 . . . . **3**

4a   If line 3 is more than zero, multiply line 3 by 92.35% (.9235). Otherwise, enter amount from line 3   **4a**
    Note. If line 4a is less than $400 due to Conservation Reserve Program payments on line 1b, see instructions.

  b   If you elect one or both of the optional methods, enter the total of lines 15 and 17 here . .   **4b**

  c   Combine lines 4a and 4b. If less than $400, **stop;** you do not owe self-employment tax. **Exception.** If less than $400 and you had **church employee income,** enter -0- and continue ▶   **4c**

5a   Enter your **church employee income** from Form W-2. See instructions for definition of church employee income . . .   **5a**

  b   Multiply line 5a by 92.35% (.9235). If less than $100, enter -0- **5b**

6   Add lines 4c and 5b **6**

7   Maximum amount of combined wages and self-employment earnings subject to social security tax or the 6.2% portion of the 7.65% railroad retirement (tier 1) tax for 2013 . . . . . .   **7**   113,700   00

8a   Total social security wages and tips (total of boxes 3 and 7 on Form(s) W-2) and railroad retirement (tier 1) compensation. If $113,700 or more, skip lines 8b through 10, and go to line 11   **8a**

  b   Unreported tips subject to social security tax (from Form 4137, line 10)   **8b**

  c   Wages subject to social security tax (from Form 8919, line 10)   **8c**

  d   Add lines 8a, 8b, and 8c **8d**

9   Subtract line 8d from line 7. If zero or less, enter -0- here and on line 10 and go to line 11 ▶   **9**

10   Multiply the **smaller** of line 6 or line 9 by 12.4% (.124) **10**

11   Multiply line 6 by 2.9% (.029) **11**

12   **Self-employment tax.** Add lines 10 and 11. Enter here and on Form 1040, line 56, or **Form 1040NR, line 54**   **12**

13   **Deduction for one-half of self-employment tax.** Multiply line 12 by 50% (.50). Enter the result here and on **Form 1040, line 27,** or Form 1040NR, line 27 . . . . .   **13**

Part II   Optional Methods To Figure Net Earnings   (see instructions)

Farm Optional Method. You may use this method **only** if **(a)** your gross farm income[1] was not more than $6,960, **or (b)** your net farm profits[2] were less than $5,024.

14   Maximum income for optional methods **14**   4,640   00

15   Enter the **smaller** of: two-thirds (⅔) of gross farm income[1] (not less than zero) **or** $4,640. Also include this amount on line 4b above **15**

Nonfarm Optional Method. You may use this method **only** if **(a)** your net nonfarm profits[3] were less than $5,024 and also less than 72.189% of your gross nonfarm income,[4] **and (b)** you had net earnings from self-employment of at least $400 in 2 of the prior 3 years. **Caution.** You may use this method no more than five times.

16   Subtract line 15 from line 14 . . . .   **16**

17   Enter the **smaller** of: two-thirds (⅔) of gross nonfarm income[4] (not less than zero) **or** the amount on line 16. Also include this amount on line 4b above **17**

[1] From Sch. F, line 9, and Sch. K-1 (Form 1065), box 14, code B.   [3] From Sch. C, line 31; Sch. C-EZ, line 3; Sch. K-1 (Form 1065), box 14, code A; and Sch. K-1 (Form 1065-B), box 9, code J1.
[2] From Sch. F, line 34, and Sch. K-1 (Form 1065), box 14, code A—minus the amount you would have entered on line 1b had you not used the optional method.   [4] From Sch. C, line 7; Sch. C-EZ, line 1; Sch. K-1 (Form 1065), box 14, code C; and Sch. K-1 (Form 1065-B), box 9, code J2.

Schedule SE (Form 1040) 2013

Figure 21-4: Calculate self-employment tax for Social Security and Medicare on page 2 of Schedule SE.

Form **8832**		**Entity Classification Election**		OMB No. 1545-1516
(Rev. December 2013) Department of the Treasury Internal Revenue Service		▶ Information about Form 8832 and its instructions is at *www.irs.gov/form8832.*		

	Name of eligible entity making election	Employer identification number
Type or Print	Number, street, and room or suite no. If a P.O. box, see instructions.	
	City or town, state, and ZIP code. If a foreign address, enter city, province or state, postal code and country. Follow the country's practice for entering the postal code.	

▶ Check if: ☐ Address change   ☐ Late classification relief sought under Revenue Procedure 2009-41
☐ Relief for a late change of entity classification election sought under Revenue Procedure 2010-32

Part I   Election Information

1   Type of election (see instructions):

a ☐ Initial classification by a newly-formed entity. Skip lines 2a and 2b and go to line 3.
b ☐ Change in current classification. Go to line 2a.

2a Has the eligible entity previously filed an entity election that had an effective date within the last 60 months?

☐ **Yes.** Go to line 2b.
☐ **No.** Skip line 2b and go to line 3.

2b Was the eligible entity's prior election an initial classification election by a newly formed entity that was effective on the date of formation?

☐ **Yes.** Go to line 3.
☐ **No.** Stop here. You generally are not currently eligible to make the election (see instructions).

3 Does the eligible entity have more than one owner?

☐ **Yes.** You can elect to be classified as a partnership or an association taxable as a corporation. Skip line 4 and go to line 5.
☐ **No.** You can elect to be classified as an association taxable as a corporation or to be disregarded as a separate entity. Go to line 4.

4 If the eligible entity has only one owner, provide the following information:

a Name of owner ▶ ....
b Identifying number of owner ▶ ....

5 If the eligible entity is owned by one or more affiliated corporations that file a consolidated return, provide the name and employer identification number of the parent corporation:

a Name of parent corporation ▶ ....
b Employer identification number ▶ ....

For Paperwork Reduction Act Notice, see instructions.	Cat. No. 22598R	Form **8832** (Rev. 12-2013)

Figure 21-5:
Use Form 8832 to change the IRS classifications of your small business.

Filing Tax Forms for Partnerships

If your business is structured as a partnership (meaning it has more than one owner), your business doesn't pay taxes. Instead, all money earned by the business is split up among the partners.

As a bookkeeper for a partnership, you need to collect the data necessary to file an information schedule called Schedule K-1 (Form 1065), Partner's Share of Income, Deductions, Credits, etc. for each partner. The company's accountant will most likely complete the Schedule K-1 forms. Your partnership must file an informational form called Schedule K-1 (Figure 21-6) for each partner to report his or her income and expenses. The entire information filing for the company is called Form 1065.

	651113

	OMB No. 1545-0099
☐ Final K-1 ☐ Amended K-1	

Schedule K-1
(Form 1065)

Department of the Treasury
Internal Revenue Service

For calendar year 2013, or tax
year beginning _____, 2013
ending _____, 20 ___

2013

Partner's Share of Income, Deductions, Credits, etc.   ▶ See back of form and separate instructions.

Part I   Information About the Partnership

A   Partnership's employer identification number

B   Partnership's name, address, city, state, and ZIP code

C   IRS Center where partnership filed return

D   ☐ Check if this is a publicly traded partnership (PTP)

Part II   Information About the Partner

E   Partner's identifying number

F   Partner's name, address, city, state, and ZIP code

G   ☐ General partner or LLC member-manager   ☐ Limited partner or other LLC member

H   ☐ Domestic partner   ☐ Foreign partner

I1   What type of entity is this partner? _____

I2   If this partner is a retirement plan (IRA/SEP/Keogh/etc.), check here (see instructions) . . . . ☐

J   Partner's share of profit, loss, and capital (see instructions):

	Beginning	Ending
Profit	%	%
Loss	%	%
Capital	%	%

K   Partner's share of liabilities at year end:

Nonrecourse . . . . . $ _____
Qualified nonrecourse financing . $ _____
Recourse . . . . $ _____

L   Partner's capital account analysis:

Beginning capital account . . . $ _____
Capital contributed during the year $ _____
Current year increase (decrease) . $ _____
Withdrawals & distributions . . $ (_____)
Ending capital account . . . . $ _____

☐ Tax basis   ☐ GAAP   ☐ Section 704(b) book
☐ Other (explain)

M   Did the partner contribute property with a built-in gain or loss?
☐ Yes   ☐ No
If "Yes," attach statement (see instructions)

Part III   Partner's Share of Current Year Income, Deductions, Credits, and Other Items

1	Ordinary business income (loss)	15	Credits
2	Net rental real estate income (loss)		
3	Other net rental income (loss)	16	Foreign transactions
4	Guaranteed payments		
5	Interest income		
6a	Ordinary dividends		
6b	Qualified dividends		
7	Royalties		
8	Net short-term capital gain (loss)		
9a	Net long-term capital gain (loss)	17	Alternative minimum tax (AMT) items
9b	Collectibles (28%) gain (loss)		
9c	Unrecaptured section 1250 gain		
10	Net section 1231 gain (loss)	18	Tax-exempt income and nondeductible expenses
11	Other income (loss)		
12	Section 179 deduction	19	Distributions
13	Other deductions	20	Other information
14	Self-employment earnings (loss)		

*See attached statement for additional information.

For IRS Use Only

For Paperwork Reduction Act Notice, see Instructions for Form 1065.   IRS.gov/form1065   Cat. No. 11394R   Schedule K-1 (Form 1065) 2013

Figure 21-6: A copy of Schedule K-1 is given to each partner, and another copy of each Schedule K-1 form is filed with the IRS.

Any partner receiving a Schedule K-1 must report the recorded income on his or her personal tax return — Form 1040 — by adding an additional form called Schedule E, Supplemental Income and Loss (see Figures 21-7 and 21-8). (Schedule E is used to report income from more than just partnership arrangements; it also has sections for real estate rental and royalties, estates and trusts, and mortgage investments.)

TIP

Unless you're involved in a real estate rental business, you most likely only need to fill out page 2 of Schedule E.

Figure 21-7:
On the first page of Schedule E, you report income from rental real estate or royalties from businesses in which you're a partner but aren't personally active.

SCHEDULE E (Form 1040)	Supplemental Income and Loss	OMB No. 1545-0074
Department of the Treasury Internal Revenue Service (99)	(From rental real estate, royalties, partnerships, S corporations, estates, trusts, REMICs, etc.) ► Attach to Form 1040, 1040NR, or Form 1041. ► Information about Schedule E and its separate instructions is at *www.irs.gov/schedulee*.	**2013** Attachment Sequence No. **13**

Name(s) shown on return   Your social security number

Part I **Income or Loss From Rental Real Estate and Royalties** **Note.** If you are in the business of renting personal property, use **Schedule C or C-EZ** (see instructions). If you are an individual, report farm rental income or loss from **Form 4835** on page 2, line 40.

A Did you make any payments in 2013 that would require you to file Form(s) 1099? (see instructions) ☐ Yes ☐ No
B If "Yes," did you or will you file required Forms 1099? ☐ Yes ☐ No

1a Physical address of each property (street, city, state, ZIP code)
A
B
C

1b	Type of Property (from list below)	**2** For each rental real estate property listed above, report the number of fair rental and personal use days. Check the **QJV** box only if you meet the requirements to file as a qualified joint venture. See instructions.		Fair Rental Days	Personal Use Days	QJV
A			A			☐
B			B			☐
C			C			☐

Type of Property:
1 Single Family Residence 3 Vacation/Short-Term Rental 5 Land 7 Self-Rental
2 Multi-Family Residence 4 Commercial 6 Royalties 8 Other (describe)

Income:	Properties:		A	B	C
3 Rents received	3				
4 Royalties received	4				
Expenses:					
5 Advertising	5				
6 Auto and travel (see instructions)	6				
7 Cleaning and maintenance	7				
8 Commissions.	8				
9 Insurance	9				
10 Legal and other professional fees	10				
11 Management fees	11				
12 Mortgage interest paid to banks, etc. (see instructions)	12				
13 Other interest.	13				
14 Repairs.	14				
15 Supplies	15				
16 Taxes	16				
17 Utilities	17				
18 Depreciation expense or depletion	18				
19 Other (list) ► _____	19				
20 Total expenses. Add lines 5 through 19	20				
21 Subtract line 20 from line 3 (rents) and/or 4 (royalties). If result is a (loss), see instructions to find out if you must file **Form 6198**	21				
22 Deductible rental real estate loss after limitation, if any, on **Form 8582** (see instructions)	22 (	)(	)(	)
23a Total of all amounts reported on line 3 for all rental properties	23a			
b Total of all amounts reported on line 4 for all royalty properties	23b			
c Total of all amounts reported on line 12 for all properties	23c			
d Total of all amounts reported on line 18 for all properties	23d			
e Total of all amounts reported on line 20 for all properties	23e			
24 **Income.** Add positive amounts shown on line 21. **Do not include any losses**	24			
25 **Losses.** Add royalty losses from line 21 and rental real estate losses from line 22. Enter total losses here	25 (	)		
26 **Total rental real estate and royalty income or (loss).** Combine lines 24 and 25. Enter the result here. If Parts II, III, IV, and line 40 on page 2 do not apply to you, also enter this amount on Form 1040, line 17, or Form 1040NR, line 18. Otherwise, include this amount in the total on line 41 on page 2	26			

For Paperwork Reduction Act Notice, see the separate instructions. Cat. No. 11344L Schedule E (Form 1040) 2013

Schedule E (Form 1040) 2013   Attachment Sequence No. **13**   Page **2**

Name(s) shown on return. Do not enter name and social security number if shown on other side.   Your social security number

Caution. The IRS compares amounts reported on your tax return with amounts shown on Schedule(s) K-1.

Part II   **Income or Loss From Partnerships and S Corporations**   **Note.** If you report a loss from an at-risk activity for which **any amount is not at risk,** you **must** check the box in column **(e)** on line 28 and attach **Form 6198.** See instructions.

27   Are you reporting any loss not allowed in a prior year due to the at-risk, excess farm loss, or basis limitations, a prior year unallowed loss from a passive activity (if that loss was not reported on Form 8582), or unreimbursed partnership expenses? If you answered "Yes," see instructions before completing this section.   ☐ **Yes**   ☐ **No**

28

(a) Name	(b) Enter P for partnership; S for S corporation	(c) Check if foreign partnership	(d) Employer identification number	(e) Check if any amount is not at risk
A		☐		☐
B		☐		☐
C		☐		☐
D		☐		☐

	Passive Income and Loss		Nonpassive Income and Loss		
	(f) Passive loss allowed (attach **Form 8582** if required)	(g) Passive income from **Schedule K-1**	(h) Nonpassive loss from **Schedule K-1**	(i) Section 179 expense deduction from **Form 4562**	(j) Nonpassive income from **Schedule K-1**
A					
B					
C					
D					

29a	Totals		
b	Totals		
30	Add columns (g) and (j) of line 29a	**30**	
31	Add columns (f), (h), and (i) of line 29b	**31** (	)
32	**Total partnership and S corporation income or (loss).** Combine lines 30 and 31. Enter the result here and include in the total on line 41 below	**32**	

Part III   **Income or Loss From Estates and Trusts**

33

(a) Name	(b) Employer identification number
A	
B	

	Passive Income and Loss		Nonpassive Income and Loss	
	(c) Passive deduction or loss allowed (attach **Form 8582** if required)	(d) Passive income from **Schedule K-1**	(e) Deduction or loss from **Schedule K-1**	(f) Other income from **Schedule K-1**
A				
B				

34a	Totals		
b	Totals		
35	Add columns (d) and (f) of line 34a	**35**	
36	Add columns (c) and (e) of line 34b	**36** (	)
37	**Total estate and trust income or (loss).** Combine lines 35 and 36. Enter the result here and include in the total on line 41 below	**37**	

Part IV   **Income or Loss From Real Estate Mortgage Investment Conduits (REMICs)—Residual Holder**

38

(a) Name	(b) Employer identification number	(c) Excess inclusion from Schedules Q, line 2c (see instructions)	(d) Taxable income (net loss) from Schedules Q, line 1b	(e) Income from Schedules Q, line 3b

39	Combine columns (d) and (e) only. Enter the result here and include in the total on line 41 below	**39**	

Part V   **Summary**

40	Net farm rental income or (loss) from **Form 4835.** Also, complete line 42 below	**40**	
41	**Total income or (loss).** Combine lines 26, 32, 37, 39, and 40. Enter the result here and on Form 1040, line 17, or Form 1040NR, line 18 ▶	**41**	
42	**Reconciliation of farming and fishing income.** Enter your **gross** farming and fishing income reported on Form 4835, line 7; Schedule K-1 (Form 1065), box 14, code B; Schedule K-1 (Form 1120S), box 17, code V; and Schedule K-1 (Form 1041), box 14, code F (see instructions) .	**42**	
43	**Reconciliation for real estate professionals.** If you were a real estate professional (see instructions), enter the net income or (loss) you reported anywhere on Form 1040 or Form 1040NR from all rental real estate activities in which you materially participated under the passive activity loss rules . .	**43**	

Schedule E (Form 1040) 2013

Figure 21-8: On the second page of Schedule E, you report income and expenses from a partnership that doesn't involve the rental of real estate properties.

In Figure 21-8, pay particular attention to Part II, Income or Loss From Partnerships and S Corporations. In this section, you report your income or loss as passive or nonpassive income, a distinction that your accountant can help you sort out.

Paying Corporate Taxes

Corporations come in two varieties, S corporations and C corporations; as you may expect, each has unique tax requirements and practices. In fact, not even all corporations pay taxes. Some smaller corporations are designated as S Corporations and pass their earnings on to their stockholders. Both C and S corporations have the same legal requirements and protections; they only vary in tax treatment.

Check with your accountant to determine whether incorporating your business makes sense for you. Tax savings isn't the only issue you have to think about; operating a corporation also increases administrative, legal, and accounting costs. Be sure that you understand all the costs before incorporating.

Reporting for an S corporation

An *S corporation* must have fewer than 100 stockholders, have only one class of stock, and only have shareholders who are individuals, certain trusts, and estates. (See a professional for other, less common eligibility requirements.) An S corporation functions like a partnership but gives owners more legal protection from lawsuits than traditional partnerships do. S corporations still file a corporate tax return, on Form 1120S. However, the tax return is for informational purposes only, with the income on each shareholder's Form K-1 passing through to the individual's tax return on Schedule E of Form 1040, just as in the previous partnership example.

Reporting for a C corporation

The type of corporation that's considered a separate legal entity for tax purposes is the *C corporation*. A C corporation is a legal entity that has been formed specifically for the purpose of running a business.

The biggest disadvantage of structuring your company as a C corporation is that your profits are taxed twice — as a corporate entity and based on dividends paid to stockholders. If you're the owner of a C corporation, you can be taxed twice, but you can also pay yourself a salary and therefore reduce the earnings of the corporation. Corporate taxation is very complicated, with lots of forms to be filled out, so I don't go into great detail here about how to file corporate taxes. However, Table 21-2 shows you the tax rates C corporations are subject to.

Table 21-2	C Corporation Tax Rates
Taxable Income	*C Corporation Tax Rate*
$0–$50,000	15%
$50,001–$75,000	25%
$75,001–$100,000	34%
$100,001–$335,000	39%
$335,001–$10,000,000	34%
$10,000,001–$15,000,000	35%
$15,000,001–$18,333,333	38%
Over $18,333,333	35%

You may think that C corporation tax rates look a lot higher than personal tax rates, but in reality, many corporations don't pay tax at all or pay taxes at much lower rates than you do. As a corporation, you have plenty of deductions and tax loopholes to use to reduce your tax bites. So even though you, the business owner, may be taxed twice on the small part of your income that's paid in dividends, you're more likely to pay less taxes overall.

Taking Care of Sales Taxes Obligations

Even more complicated than paying income taxes is keeping up-to-date on local and state tax rates and paying your business's share of those taxes to the government entities. Because tax rates vary from county to county, and even city to city in some states, managing sales taxes can be very time-consuming.

Things get messy when you sell products in multiple locations. For each location, you must collect from customers the appropriate tax for that area, keep track of all taxes collected, and pay those taxes to the appropriate government entities when due. In many states, you have to collect and pay local (for the city or county governments) and state taxes.

An excellent website for data about state and local tax requirements is the Federation of Tax Administrators (www.taxadmin.org/fta/link/default.php?lnk=2). This site has links for state and local tax information for every state.

States require you to file an application to collect and report taxes even before you start doing business in that state. Be sure that you contact the departments of revenue in the states you plan to operate stores before you start selling and collecting sales tax.

To get an idea of what you face in the way of state tax forms, check out Figures 21-9 and 21-10, which show the two-page Sales and Use Tax Return from the state of Florida. In Florida, you have to file this form monthly, between the first and 19th days of the following month — it's considered late on the 20th day of the month.

FLORIDA DEPARTMENT OF REVENUE

Sales and Use Tax Return

DR-15
R. 07/12

Rule 12A-1.097
Florida Administrative Code
Effective 01/13

You may file and pay tax online or you may complete this return and pay tax by check or money order and mail to:

Florida Department of Revenue
5050 W Tennessee Street
Tallahassee, FL 32399-0120

Please read the *Instructions for DR-15 Sales and Use Tax Returns* (Form DR-15N) before you complete this return. Instructions are posted on our website at **www.myflorida.com/dor.**

Certificate Number: **SALES AND USE TAX RETURN** HD/PM Date: / / DR-15 R. 07/12

Florida	1. Gross Sales	2. Exempt Sales	3. Taxable Amount	4. Tax Collected
A. Sales/Services	.	.	.	.
B. Taxable Purchases	Include use tax on Internet / out-of-state untaxed purchases →		.	.
C. Commercial Rentals	.	.	.	.
D. Transient Rentals	.	.	.	.
E. Food & Beverage Vending	.	.	.	.

Transient Rental Rate: Surtax Rate: Collection Period

Name
Address
City/St/ZIP

Taxpayer Copy
Verify Correct Collection Period

5. Total Amount of Tax Collected	.
6. Less Lawful Deductions	.
7. Total Tax Due	.
8. Less Est Tax Pd / DOR Cr Memo	.
9. Plus Est Tax Due Current Month	.
10. Amount Due	.
~~11. Less Collection Allowance~~	E-file/E-pay Only
12. Plus Penalty	.
13. Plus Interest	.
14. Amount Due with Return	.

Due:
Late After:
Check here if payment was made electronically.

Do not write in the space below.

9100 0 20149999 0001003031 9 4999999999 0000 5

Certificate Number: **SALES AND USE TAX RETURN** HD/PM Date: / / DR-15 R. 07/12

Florida	1. Gross Sales	2. Exempt Sales	3. Taxable Amount	4. Tax Collected
A. Sales/Services	.	.	.	.
B. Taxable Purchases	Include use tax on Internet / out-of-state untaxed purchases →		.	.
C. Commercial Rentals	.	.	.	.
D. Transient Rentals	.	.	.	.
E. Food & Beverage Vending	.	.	.	.

Transient Rental Rate: Surtax Rate: Collection Period

Name
Address
City/St/ZIP

5. Total Amount of Tax Collected	.
6. Less Lawful Deductions	.
7. Total Tax Due	.
8. Less Est Tax Pd / DOR Cr Memo	.
9. Plus Est Tax Due Current Month	.
10. Amount Due	.
~~11. Less Collection Allowance~~	E-file/E-pay Only
12. Plus Penalty	.
13. Plus Interest	.
14. Amount Due with Return	.

Due:
Late After:
Check here if payment was made electronically.

Do not write in the space below.

9100 0 20149999 0001003031 9 4999999999 0000 5

Figure 21-9: Florida requires you to file a monthly Sales and Use Tax Return to report gross sales, tax-exempt sales, and the taxes you collected.

Proper Collection of Tax: Florida's state sales tax rate is 6%; however, there is an established "bracket system" for collecting sales tax on any part of each total taxable sale that is less than a whole dollar amount. The *Sales Tax Rate Table* (Form DR-2X) provides tax rates for most counties that charge a discretionary sales surtax and it is posted on our Internet site at **www.myflorida.com/dor**.

Discretionary Sales Surtax: Most counties impose a local option discretionary sales surtax that must be collected on taxable transactions. You must collect discretionary sales surtax along with the 6% state sales tax on taxable sales when delivery or use occurs in a county that imposes a surtax. Current discretionary sales surtax rates for all counties are listed on Form DR-15DSS, *Discretionary Sales Surtax Information*, posted on our Internet site.

Under penalties of perjury, I declare that I have read this return and the facts stated in it are true.

Signature of Taxpayer	Date	Signature of Preparer	Date

( )   Telephone Number   ( )   Telephone Number

Discretionary Sales Surtax (Lines 15(a) through 15(d))

15(a). Exempt Amount of Items Over $5,000 (included in Column 3)	15(a).
15(b). Other Taxable Amounts NOT Subject to Surtax (included in Column 3)	15(b).
15(c). Amounts Subject to Surtax at a Rate Different Than Your County Surtax Rate (included in Column 3)	15(c).
15(d). Total Amount of Discretionary Sales Surtax Collected (included in Column 4)	15(d).
16. Total Enterprise Zone Jobs Credits (included in Line 6)	16.
17. Taxable Sales/Untaxed Purchases of Electric Power or Energy (included in Line A)	17.
18. Taxable Sales/Untaxed Purchases of Dyed Diesel Fuel (included in Line A)	18.
19. Taxable Sales from Amusement Machines (included in Line A)	19.
20. Rural and/or Urban High Crime Area Job Tax Credits	20.
21. Other Authorized Credits	21.

Under penalties of perjury, I declare that I have read this return and the facts stated in it are true.

Signature of Taxpayer	Date	Signature of Preparer	Date

( )   Telephone Number   ( )   Telephone Number

Figure 21-10: Page 2 of the Florida Sales and Use Tax Return lists special sales surtaxes.

Discretionary Sales Surtax (Lines 15(a) through 15(d))

15(a). Exempt Amount of Items Over $5,000 (included in Column 3)	15(a).
15(b). Other Taxable Amounts NOT Subject to Surtax (included in Column 3)	15(b).
15(c). Amounts Subject to Surtax at a Rate Different Than Your County Surtax Rate (included in Column 3)	15(c).
15(d). Total Amount of Discretionary Sales Surtax Collected (included in Column 4)	15(d).
16. Total Enterprise Zone Jobs Credits (included in Line 6)	16.
17. Taxable Sales/Untaxed Purchases of Electric Power or Energy (included in Line A)	17.
18. Taxable Sales/Untaxed Purchases of Dyed Diesel Fuel (included in Line A)	18.
19. Taxable Sales from Amusement Machines (included in Line A)	19.
20. Rural and/or Urban High Crime Area Job Tax Credits	20.
21. Other Authorized Credits	21.

All sales taxes collected from your customers are paid when you send in the Sales and Use Tax Return for your state — you must have the cash available to pay this tax when the forms are due. Any money you collected from customers during the month should be kept in an account called Accrued Sales Taxes, which is actually a Liability account on your balance sheet because it's money owed to a governmental entity. (For more on the balance sheet, see Chapter 18.)

Chapter 22

Prepping the Books for a New Accounting Cycle

....

In This Chapter

▶ Wrapping up General Ledger accounts

▶ Looking back through customer accounts

▶ Checking for unpaid vendor bills

▶ Clearing out unnecessary accounts

▶ Transitioning into a new accounting cycle

....

*I*n bookkeeping, an accounting period, or cycle, can be one month, a quarter, or a year (or another division of time if it makes business sense). At the end of every accounting period, certain accounts need to be closed while others remain open.

Just as it's best to add accounts to your bookkeeping system at the beginning of a year (so you don't have to move information from one account to another), it's best to wait until the end of the year to delete any accounts you no longer need. With this approach, you start each year fresh with only the accounts you need to best manage your business's financial activities.

In this chapter, I explain the accounts that must be closed and started with a zero balance in the next accounting cycle (see Chapter 2 for more detail about the accounting cycle), such as revenues and costs of goods sold. I also review the accounts that continue from one accounting cycle to the next, such as assets and liabilities. In addition, I discuss the process of closing the books at year-end and how you begin a new accounting cycle for the next year.

Finalizing the General Ledger

After you complete your accounting work for the accounting cycle in which your business operates, it's time to reexamine your General Ledger. Some accounts in the General Ledger need to be zeroed out so that they start the new accounting cycle with no detail from the previous cycle, while other accounts continue to accumulate detail from one cycle to the next. When you break down the General Ledger, the balance sheet accounts carry forward into the next accounting cycle, and the income statement accounts start with a zero balance.

Zeroing out income statement accounts

When you're sure that you've made all needed corrections and adjustments to your accounts and you have your cycle-end numbers, you can zero out all General Ledger accounts listed on the income statement — that's revenues, Cost of Goods Sold, and expense accounts. Because the income statement reflects the activities of an accounting period, these accounts always start with a zero balance at the beginning of an accounting cycle.

If you use a computerized accounting system, you may not actually have to zero out the income statement accounts. For example, QuickBooks adjusts your income and expenses accounts at cycle-end to zero them out so you start with a zero net income, but it maintains the data in an archive so you're always able to access it. You can set your closing date on the Company Preferences tab of the Preferences box (see Figure 22-1). To control who can make changes to prior year accounts, you should also click Set Password (see Figure 22-2) to set a special password for editing closed accounts.

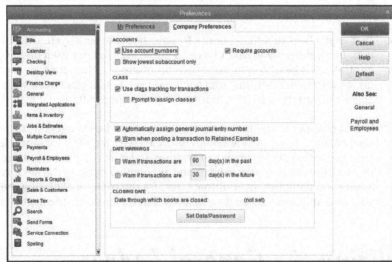

Figure 22-1:
Set the closing date for your accounts in QuickBooks.

Set Closing Date and Password   ×

To keep your financial data secure, QuickBooks recommends assigning all other users their own
username and password, in Company > Set Up Users.

DATE
QuickBooks will display a warning, or require a password, when saving a transaction dated on
or before the closing date.   More details...

☐ Exclude estimates, sales orders and purchase orders from closing date restrictions

Closing Date   [   ] 🛗

PASSWORD
QuickBooks strongly recommends setting a password to protect transactions dated on or
before the closing date.

Closing Date Password   [   ]

Confirm Password   [   ]

[OK]   [Cancel]

Figure 22-2:
Set a
password
for control-
ling data
in closed
accounts.

Carrying over balance sheet accounts

Unlike income statement accounts, you never zero out the accounts listed
on a balance sheet — that's assets, liabilities, and equity. Instead, you note
your ending balances for each of these accounts so you can prepare a balance sheet (see Chapter 18), and you carry forward the data in the accounts
into the next accounting period. The balance sheet just gives you a snapshot
of the financial state of your company as of a particular date in time. From
one accounting cycle to the next, your assets and (unfortunately) liabilities
remain, and you also need to maintain the information about how much
equity your investors have put into the company.

Conducting Special Year-End
Bookkeeping Tasks

Before you start the process of closing the books for the year, print a summary of your account information from your computerized accounting system.
If you make an error while closing the books, you can always use this printout
to backtrack and fix any problems.

QuickBooks provides a Year-End Guide Checklist (see Figure 22-3) to help you
keep track of all the year-end activities you need to do. The checklist also
includes links to help screens that explain how to do all the year-end closing

tasks. You can check off each task as you complete it and save the check marks to keep track of your progress during the closing process. You can find this checklist on the Help drop-down menu.

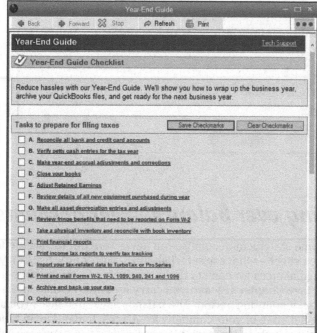

Figure 22-3: The Quick-Books Year-End Guide Checklist walks you through year-end tasks with convenient check boxes and links to help screens.

After you complete all your year-end tasks, you can condense and back up all your accounting data for the year being closed. Most computerized accounting systems have a process for condensing and archiving data. For example, the QuickBooks Condense Data wizard guides you through the process (see Figure 22-4). You can find this wizard under Utilities on the File drop-down tab.

If you're not sure what to keep and what to condense, be sure to ask your accountant before using this wizard. You can't reverse the condense data process once you click the Begin Condense button.

Checking customer accounts

As you prepare your books for the end of an accounting cycle, review your customer accounts. You never close the Accounts Receivable account. When you start a new accounting cycle, you certainly want to carry over any balance still due from customers.

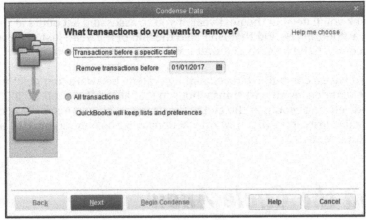

What transactions do you want to remove?　　　Help me choose

◉ Transactions before a specific date

　Remove transactions before　　01/01/2017

◎ All transactions

　QuickBooks will keep lists and preferences

Back　　Next　　Begin Condense　　Help　　Cancel

Figure 22-4:
The QuickBooks Condense Data wizard makes condensing and backing up your data at year-end easy.

Before closing your books at the end of the accounting cycle, it's a good idea to review customer accounts for possible bad debt expenses. (I talk about bad debt in greater detail in Chapter 9.) Now's the time to be more critical of past due accounts. You can use any bad debt to reduce your tax bite, so if you believe that a customer isn't likely to make good on a past due account, write off the loss.

Assessing vendor accounts

The end of an accounting period is the perfect time to review your vendor accounts to be sure they're all paid in full and ready for the new cycle. Also, make sure that you've entered into your vendor accounts any bills that reflect business activity in the period being closed; otherwise, expenses from the period may not show up in the appropriate year-end financial statements.

Review any outstanding purchase orders to be sure that your vendor accounts aren't missing orders that have been completed but not yet billed by the vendor. For example, if you received inventory on December 23 but the vendor won't bill for that inventory until January, you should record the bill in December to reflect the receipt of that inventory during that tax year.

Deleting accounts

The closing process at the end of an accounting year is a good time to assess all your open accounts and verify that you still need them. If an account has no transactions in it, you're free to delete it at any time. However, you should wait until the end of the year to delete any accounts that you don't think you'll need in the next year. If you're assessing accounts at the end of an accounting period that isn't also the end of the year, just make a list of the accounts to be deleted and wait for the year-end.

If you use a computerized accounting system, be aware that deleting an account deletes all past transactions in that account as well. So if you want to delete an account at the end of the year, you should mark the account as inactive instead so that new transactions can't be entered into the account inadvertently.

Starting the Cycle Anew

You certainly don't want to close the doors of your business as you prepare all your year-end reports, such as the financial statements and governmental reports — after all, that can be a two- to three-month process. So you need to continue making entries for the new year as you close the books for the previous year.

If you do the books manually, you probably need easy access to two sets of books: the current year and the previous year. In a manual bookkeeping system, you just start new journal pages for each of the active accounts. If you have some accounts that aren't very active, rather than start a new page, you can leave some space for adjustments or corrections, draw a line, and start the transactions for the new year on the same page.

If you keep your books using a computerized accounting system, you can zero out the necessary accounts to start the new year while leaving the data for the previous year in the password-protected, closed accounts. You can still make changes to those closed accounts, but access is limited to people who know the password — most likely you, your accountant, and your book-keeping manager.

Part of closing out your books is starting new files for each of your accounts. Most businesses keep two years of data, the current year and the previous year, in the on-site office files and put older files into storage. Some companies keep all the records electronically; others scan the older records into electronic files at the end of two years and keep them on backup hard drives, eliminating the need for costly file storage. If your company does this, be sure to check with your attorney and accountant to find out which types of paper documents are critical to keep on hand.

As you start a new year, box up your two-year-old files for storage and use the newly empty drawers for the new year's new files. For example, suppose you're creating files for 2015. Keep the 2014 files easily accessible in file cabinet drawers in your office, but box up the 2013 files for storage. Then keep your 2015 files in the drawers where the 2013 files had been.

There's no hard-and-fast rule about file storage. You may find that you need to access some files regularly and therefore don't want to put them in storage. No problem. Pull out any files related to ongoing activity and keep them in the office so you don't have to run to the storage area every time you need the files. For example, if you have an ongoing legal case, you should keep any files related to that matter out of storage and easily accessible.

Part VI
The Part of Tens

the
part of
tens

web extras

Get an extra Part of Tens chapter on the top ten mobile apps for bookkeepers at www.dummies.com/extras/bookkeeping.

In this part . . .

- ✔ Explore ways to manage your business cash
- ✔ Discover the most important account for bookkeepers

Chapter 23

Top Ten Ways to Manage Your Business Cash with Your Books

In This Chapter
▶ Keeping a handle on internal bookkeeping tools
▶ Monitoring profits and expenses
▶ Dealing smartly with vendors, contractors, and customers

Many business owners think of bookkeeping as a necessary evil, but in reality, if you make effective use of the data you collect, bookkeeping can be your best buddy when it comes to managing your cash. The key to taking advantage of what bookkeeping has to offer is understanding the value of basic bookkeeping principles and using information collected. This chapter reviews the top ten ways to use your books to help you manage your business cash.

Charting the Way

You may not think that a list of accounts, called the Chart of Accounts, is worth much attention, but this chart dictates how you collect your financial data and where in the books you put your company's transactions. In order for you to be able to use the information effectively, it's crucial that your Chart of Accounts defines each account precisely and determines exactly what types of transactions go where. (I talk more about the Chart of Accounts and how to set one up in Chapter 3.)

Balancing Your Entries

Balanced books are the only way to know how your business is doing. Without them, you can never know whether your profit numbers are accurate. In bookkeeping, you use a process called *double-entry bookkeeping* to keep the books balanced. I talk more about this basic principle and how to keep the books balanced in Chapter 2.

Posting Your Transactions

In order to be able to use the information you collect regarding your business transactions, the transactions must be posted accurately to your accounts. If you forget to post a transaction to your books, your reports won't reflect that financial activity, and that's a serious problem. Or, if you post an incorrect transaction to your books, any reports that draw on information will be wrong — again, a problem. I talk more about the posting process in Chapters 4 and 5.

Tracking Customer Collections

If your business sells to customers on store credit, you certainly want to be sure your customers pay for their purchases in the future. (Customer account information is gathered in the Accounts Receivable account as well as in individual records for each customer.) You should review reports based on customer payment history, called *aging reports,* on a monthly basis to be sure customers pay on time. Remember that you set the rules for store credit, so you may want to cut off customers from future purchases if their accounts are past due for 90 days or more. I talk more about how to manage customer accounts in Chapter 9.

Paying Bills Accurately and On Time

If you want to continue getting supplies, products, and services from your vendors and contractors, you must pay them accurately and on time. Managing your payments through the Accounts Payable account ensures accuracy and timeliness, and it also saves you from mistakenly paying bills twice. To be safe, you should review aging reports on your payment history to see that your bookkeeper is making timely and accurate payments. I talk more about managing your payments in Chapter 8.

Planning Profits

Nothing is more important to a business owner than the profits he will ultimately make. Yet many business owners don't take time to plan their profit expectations at the beginning of each year, so they have no way to gauge how well their businesses do throughout the year. Avoid this problem by taking time before the year starts to develop profit expectations and a budget that will help you meet those expectations. Then develop a series of internal financial reports from the numbers in your bookkeeping system to help determine whether or not you're meeting your sales targets and maintaining control over your product costs and operating expenses. I talk more about sales tracking in Chapter 9, costs and expense tracking in Chapter 8, and how to determine your net profit in Chapter 19.

Comparing Budget to Actual Expenses

Keeping a careful watch on how well your budget planning reflects what's actually happening in your business can help you meet your profit goals. As with profits (see the preceding section), take time to develop a budget that sets your expectations for the year, and then develop internal reports that give you the ability to track how closely your actual expenses match that budget. If you see any major problems, correct them as soon as possible to be sure you meet your target profit at the end of the year. I talk more about internal financial reporting in Chapter 19.

Comparing Sales Goals to Actual Sales

In addition to watching your expenses, you also need to monitor your actual sales so that they match the sales goals you set at the beginning of the year. Designing an internal report that tracks sales goals versus actual sales allows you to monitor how well your business is doing. If you find your actual sales are below expectations, correct the problem as early in the year as possible in order to improve your chances of meeting those year-end goals. To find out how to use internal financial reports to track your sales activity, check out Chapters 9 and 19.

Tracking Cost Trends

Awareness of the costs involved in purchasing the products you sell or the raw materials you use to manufacture your products is very important because these cost trends can have a major impact on whether or not your company earns the net income you expect. If you find that the costs are trending upward, you may need to adjust the prices of the products you sell in order to meet your profit goals. I talk more about tracking cost trends in Chapters 8 and 19.

Making Pricing Decisions

Properly pricing your product can be a critical factor in determining whether or not your product sells. If the price is too high, you may not find any customers willing to buy the product; if it's too low, you lose money.

When determining what price to charge your customers, you must consider a number of different factors, including how much you pay to buy or manufacture the products you sell, market research about what customers will pay for a product, what you pay your employees, and advertising and administrative expenses you incur in order to set a price. All these items are factors in what you'll spend to sell that product. I talk more about tracking costs and expenses in Chapters 8 and 19.

Chapter 24

Top Ten Most Important Accounts for Any Bookkeeper

In This Chapter

▶ Thinking about key asset accounts

▶ Understanding critical liability accounts

▶ Taking in money

▶ Monitoring costs and expenses

▶ Tracking the owner's share

*E*ach and every account has its purpose in bookkeeping, but all accounts certainly aren't created equal. For most companies, some accounts are more essential than others, so in case you're having trouble knowing where to start your account setup and what's necessary, this chapter looks at the top must-have accounts for bookkeepers.

Cash

All your business transactions pass through the Cash account, which is so important that you actually need two journals, Cash Receipts and Cash Disbursements to track the activity. (I discuss these journals at length in Chapter 5.) As the bookkeeper, it's your responsibility to be sure that all cash — whether it's coming into the business or being sent out — is handled and recorded properly in the Cash account.

Accounts Receivable

If your company sells its products or services to customers on store credit, you definitely need an Accounts Receivable account. This is the account where you track all money due from customers. As the bookkeeper, keeping

Accounts Receivable up-to-date is critical to be sure that you send timely and accurate bills to customers. I talk more about Accounts Receivable processes in Chapter 9.

Inventory

Every company must have products to sell. Those money-making products must be carefully accounted for and tracked because it's the only way a business knows what it has on hand to sell. As the bookkeeper, you contribute to this process by keeping accurate inventory records in an Inventory account. The numbers you have in your books are periodically tested by doing physical counts of the inventory on hand. I talk more about how to manage inventory and Inventory accounts in Chapter 8.

Accounts Payable

No one likes to send money out of the business, but you can ease the pain and strain by tracking and paying bills in your Accounts Payable account. You certainly don't want to pay anyone twice, but you also want to be sure you pay bills on time or else your company may no longer get the supplies, inventory, or other things needed to operate the business. Suppliers often penalize late-paying companies by cutting them off or putting them on cash-only accounts. On the flip side, if you pay your bills early, you may be able to get discounts and save money with suppliers, so the early bird definitely gets the worm. For more on the Accounts Payable account, check out Chapter 8.

Loans Payable

There's bound to come a time when your company needs to purchase major items such as equipment, vehicles, and furniture. Unfortunately, you may find that you don't have the money to pay for such purchases. The solution is to take on long-term loans to be paid over more than a 12-month period. The Loans Payable account allows you to monitor the activity on these loans, in order to get and keep the best rates, and to make all loan payments on time and accurately. I talk more about the Loans Payable account in Chapter 13.

Sales

No business can operate without taking in cash, mostly through sales of the company's products or services. The Sales account is where you track all incoming revenue collected from these sales. Recording sales in a timely and accurate manner is a critical job of yours because otherwise you can't know how much revenue has been collected every day. To find out more about sales and the Sales account, see Chapter 9.

Purchases

Purchases are unavoidable. In order to have a tangible product to sell, your company has to either manufacture the product, in which case you have to purchase raw materials, or purchase a finished product from a supplier. In the Purchases account, you track the purchases of any raw materials or finished goods. The Purchases account is a key component in calculating Cost of Goods Sold, which you subtract from Sales to find your company's gross profit. I talk more about the Purchases account in Chapter 8.

Payroll Expenses

It's a fact of business that you must pay employees to get them to stay around. No matter how much you beg, few people want to work for nothing. To keep up with what is for many businesses their biggest expense, you track all money paid to employees in the Payroll Expenses account. Accurate maintenance of this account is essential because it ensures that all governmental reports are filed and payroll taxes are paid. And if you don't take care of these responsibilities to the government, you'll find yourself in some serious hot water. I talk more about payroll obligations and the Payroll Expenses account in Chapters 10, 11, and 20.

Office Expenses

One key expense that can drain a company's profits is office expenses. From paper, pens, and paper clips to expenses related to office machinery, these expenses tend to creep up if not carefully monitored in the Office Expenses account. I talk more about the Office Expenses account as well as internal controls that you can put into place to keep costs down in Chapter 7.

Owner's Equity

Accounts related to owner's equity, which is the amount each owner puts into the business, vary depending upon the type of business for which you keep the books. Many small businesses are owned by one person or a group of partners; they're not incorporated, so no stock shares exist to apportion ownership. Instead, money put into the business by each of the owners is tracked in Capital accounts, and any money taken out of the business by the owners appears in Drawing accounts. In order to be fair to all owners, you must carefully track all Owner's Equity accounts. I talk more about business structures and types of ownership in Chapter 21. I discuss Owner's Equity accounts in Chapter 18.

Retained Earnings

The Retained Earnings account tracks any profits made by the company that are reinvested for growing the company and not paid out to company owners. This account is *cumulative,* which means it shows a running total of earnings that have been retained since the company opened its doors. Although managing this account doesn't take a lot of time, the ongoing accuracy of the Retained Earnings account is important to investors and lenders who want to track how well the company is doing. I talk more about retained earnings in Chapter 18.

Appendix

Glossary

Accounts Payable: An account used to record money due to vendors, contractors, and consultants for products or services purchased by the company.

Accounts Receivable: An account used to record income not yet received on products sold or services provided to customers that will be collected at a later date.

accrual accounting: The accounting method used by most businesses today. Transactions are recorded when they actually occur, even if cash has not changed hands. Income is recorded when it's earned (not when the business is actually paid for the products or services), and expenses are counted when goods or services are received, even if the business has not yet paid for the goods or services.

amortization: An accounting method used to show the using up of an intangible asset by writing off a portion of the asset's value each year.

arm's length transaction: An exchange of assets, products, or services between two unrelated or unaffiliated parties or, if the parties are related, conducted as if the parties were unrelated to avoid the appearance of conflict of interest.

assets: All things owned by the business, such as cash, buildings, vehicles, furniture, and any other item that's used to run the business.

average costing: An accounting method used to value inventory by calculating an average cost per unit sold.

bad debts expense: A categorization used to write off customer accounts that are determined to be not collectible.

cash basis accounting: An accounting method that's based on actual cash flow. Expenses are recorded only when the company actually pays out cash for the goods or services, and income is recorded only when the company collects cash from the customer.

credits: Accounting entries that increase Liability or Income accounts and decrease Asset or Expense accounts. They always appear on the right-hand side of an accounting entry.

current assets: All items owned by the company that are expected to be used in the next 12 months. This includes items like cash that can be easily liquidated. Other examples include cash equivalents, Accounts Receivable, inventory, marketable securities, and prepaid expenses.

current liabilities: All financial obligations owed by the company in less than 12 months, such as Accounts Payable (money due to vendors, contractors, and consultants) and Credit Cards Payable (payments due on credit cards).

debits: Accounting entries that increase Asset or Expense accounts and decrease Liability and Income accounts. They always appear on the left-hand side of an accounting entry.

de minimis benefits: Items that have so little value that it's unreasonable or administratively impracticable to track them. Cash, no matter how little, never qualifies as a de minimis benefit and therefore is never excludable from tax calculations.

depreciation: An accounting method used to reduce the value of an asset over a set number of years to show that an asset is being used up and its value is diminishing.

Equity accounts: Used to track the value of things owned by the company owners or shareholders after accounting for liabilities.

expenses: All costs of operating a business.

First In, First Out (FIFO): An accounting method used to value inventory that assumes the first items put on the shelf are the first items sold.

General Journal entries: Any entries made to correct or adjust balances in the General Ledger accounts.

General Ledger: A summary of all historical transactions that ever occurred since the business first opened its doors. This ledger is the granddaddy of your business's financial information.

income: All the earnings of a business.

intangible assets: Anything the company owns that has value but can't be touched, such as licenses, patents, trademarks, and brand names.

Last In, First Out (LIFO): An accounting method used to value inventory that assumes the last items put on the shelf are the first items sold.

liabilities: All debts the business owes, such as Accounts Payable, Bonds Payable, and Mortgages Payable.

long-term assets: All things a company owns that are expected to be due in more than 12 months, such as buildings, factories, vehicles, and furniture.

Lower of Cost or Market (LCM): An accounting method used to value inventory based on whichever is lower: the actual cost of the inventory or its current market value.

net profit: The bottom line after all costs, expenses, interest, taxes, depreciation, and amortization are accounted for. Net profit reflects how much money the company makes.

operating cash flow: The cash generated by a company's operations to produce and sell its products.

operating expenses: Expenses incurred by a company in order to continue its operations, such as advertising, equipment rental, store rental, insurance, legal and accounting fees, entertainment, salaries, office expenses, repairs and maintenance, travel, utilities, vehicles, and just about anything else that goes into operating a business and isn't directly involved in selling a company's products.

operating profit: A measure of a company's earning power from its ongoing operations.

periodic inventory method: Tracking inventory a company has on hand by doing a physical count of inventory on a periodic basis, whether daily, monthly, yearly, or any other time period that meets a business's needs.

perpetual inventory method: Tracking inventory a company has on hand by adjusting the inventory counts after each transaction. A computerized inventory control system is needed to manage inventory using this method.

petty cash: All cash kept on hand at business locations for incidental expenses.

point of sale: The location where customers pay for products or services they want to buy, such as a register or service counter.

retained earnings: An account used to track any net profits left in the business from accounting period to accounting period and that are reinvested in the business for future growth.

specific identification: An accounting method used to value inventory based on the actual items sold and their individual costs.

tangible assets: Any items owned by the business that can be held in one's hand or touched, such as cash, inventory, or vehicles.

workers' compensation: State-mandated protection for employees who are injured on the job or become sick because of the job. The worker's job is protected. (A worker can't be terminated just because he's injured on the job or because he has filed a workers' compensation claim.) In addition, all medical expenses incurred because of the injury are paid by the employer, and the worker's pay is continued while he recovers from the injury or sickness.

Index

Notes

Notes

Notes

Notes

About the Author

Lita Epstein, who earned her MBA from Emory University's Goizueta Business School, enjoys helping people develop good financial, investing, and tax planning skills.

While getting her MBA, Lita worked as a teaching assistant for the financial accounting department and ran the accounting lab. After completing her MBA, she managed finances for a small nonprofit organization and for the facilities management section of a large medical clinic.

She designs and teaches online courses on topics such as accounting and bookkeeping and starting your own business. She's written more than 35 books, including *Reading Financial Reports For Dummies, Trading For Dummies, The Business Owner's Guide to Reading and Understanding Financial Statements,* and *Financial Decision Making.*

Lita was the content director for a financial services website MostChoice.com and managed the website Investing for Women. As a congressional press secretary, Lita gained firsthand knowledge about how to work within and around the federal bureaucracy, which gives her great insight into how government programs work. In the past, Lita has been a daily newspaper reporter, magazine editor, and fundraiser for the international activities of former President Jimmy Carter through The Carter Center.

Dedication

To my father, Jerome Kirschbrown, who taught me the importance of accounting, bookkeeping, and watching every detail.

Author's Acknowledgments

I want to take this opportunity to thank all the people who have helped make this book a reality. In particular, I want to thank the wonderful folks at Wiley who shepherded this project to completion: Stacy Kennedy and Corbin Collins. I also want to thank my technical advisor, Shellie Moore, who is a CPA and made sure that all the bookkeeping and accounting details were accurate. Finally, I want to thank my agent Jessica Faust at BookEnds, who helps find all my book projects.

Publisher's Acknowledgments

Acquisitions Editor: Stacy Kennedy

Editor: Corbin Collins

Technical Editor: Shellie Moore

Project Coordinator: Emily Benford

Cover Image: ©iStock.com/andreync

Math & Science

Algebra I For Dummies,
2nd Edition
978-0-470-55964-2

Anatomy and Physiology
For Dummies, 2nd Edition
978-0-470-92326-9

Astronomy For Dummies,
3rd Edition
978-1-118-37697-3

Biology For Dummies,
2nd Edition
978-0-470-59875-7

Chemistry For Dummies,
2nd Edition
978-1-118-00730-3

1001 Algebra II Practice
Problems For Dummies
978-1-118-44662-1

Microsoft Office

Excel 2013 For Dummies
978-1-118-51012-4

Office 2013 All-in-One
For Dummies
978-1-118-51636-2

PowerPoint 2013
For Dummies
978-1-118-50253-2

Word 2013 For Dummies
978-1-118-49123-2

Music

Blues Harmonica
For Dummies
978-1-118-25269-7

Guitar For Dummies,
3rd Edition
978-1-118-11554-1

iPod & iTunes
For Dummies, 10th Edition
978-1-118-50864-0

Programming

Beginning Programming
with C For Dummies
978-1-118-73763-7

Excel VBA Programming
For Dummies, 3rd Edition
978-1-118-49037-2

Java For Dummies,
6th Edition
978-1-118-40780-6

Religion & Inspiration

The Bible For Dummies
978-0-7645-5296-0

Buddhism For Dummies,
2nd Edition
978-1-118-02379-2

Catholicism For Dummies,
2nd Edition
978-1-118-07778-8

Self-Help & Relationships

Beating Sugar Addiction
For Dummies
978-1-118-54645-1

Meditation For Dummies,
3rd Edition
978-1-118-29144-3

Seniors

Laptops For Seniors
For Dummies, 3rd Edition
978-1-118-71105-7

Computers For Seniors
For Dummies, 3rd Edition
978-1-118-11553-4

iPad For Seniors
For Dummies, 6th Edition
978-1-118-72826-0

Social Security
For Dummies
978-1-118-20573-0

Smartphones & Tablets

Android Phones
For Dummies, 2nd Edition
978-1-118-72030-1

Nexus Tablets
For Dummies
978-1-118-77243-0

Samsung Galaxy S 4
For Dummies
978-1-118-64222-1

Samsung Galaxy Tabs
For Dummies
978-1-118-77294-2

Test Prep

ACT For Dummies,
5th Edition
978-1-118-01259-8

ASVAB For Dummies,
3rd Edition
978-0-470-63760-9

GRE For Dummies,
7th Edition
978-0-470-88921-3

Officer Candidate Tests
For Dummies
978-0-470-59876-4

Physician's Assistant Exam
For Dummies
978-1-118-11556-5

Series 7 Exam For Dummies
978-0-470-09932-2

Windows 8

Windows 8.1 All-in-One
For Dummies
978-1-118-82087-2

Windows 8.1 For Dummies
978-1-118-82121-3

Windows 8.1 For Dummies,
Book + DVD Bundle
978-1-118-82107-7

Available in print and e-book formats.

Available wherever books are sold. **For more information or to order direct visit www.dummies.com**

Take Dummies with you everywhere you go!

Whether you are excited about e-books, want more from the web, must have your mobile apps, or are swept up in social media, Dummies makes everything easier.

For Dummies is the global leader in the reference category and one of the most trusted and highly regarded brands in the world. No longer just focused on books, customers now have access to the For Dummies content they need in the format they want. Let us help you develop a solution that will fit your brand and help you connect with your customers.

Advertising & Sponsorships

Connect with an engaged audience on a powerful multimedia site, and position your message alongside expert how-to content.

Targeted ads • Video • Email marketing • Microsites • Sweepstakes sponsorship

21 Million Monthly Page Views & 13 Million Unique Visitors

Custom Publishing

Reach a global audience in any language by creating a solution that will differentiate you from competitors, amplify your message, and encourage customers to make a buying decision.

Apps • Books • eBooks • Video • Audio • Webinars

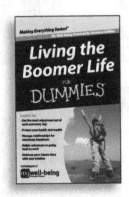   

Brand Licensing & Content

Leverage the strength of the world's most popular reference brand to reach new audiences and channels of distribution.

For more information, visit www.Dummies.com/biz

Dummies products make life easier!

- DIY
- Consumer Electronics
- Crafts
- Software
- Cookware
- Hobbies
- Videos
- Music
- Games
- and More!

For more information, go to **Dummies.com** and search the store by category.

FOR
DUMMIES
A Wiley Brand